Next Year in Cuba
A *Cubano's* Coming-of-Age in America

Books by Gustavo Pérez Firmat

Idle Fictions (criticism, 1982)

Literature and Liminality (criticism, 1986)

Carolina Cuban (poems, 1987)

The Cuban Condition (criticism, 1989)

Equivocaciones (poems, 1989)

Do the Americas Have a Common Literature?
(criticism, 1990)

Life on the Hyphen (criticism, 1994)

Bilingual Blues (poems, 1994)

Next Year in Cuba

A *Cubano's* Coming-of-Age in America

Gustavo Pérez Firmat

Arte Público Press
Houston, Texas

This volume is funded in part by grants from the City of Houston through The Cultural Arts Council of Houston / Harris County and by the Exemplar Program, a program of Americans for the Arts in Collaboration with the LarsonAllen Public Services Group, funded by the Ford Foundation.

Recovering the past, creating the future

Arte Público Press
University of Houston
452 Cullen Performance Hall
Houston, Texas 77204-2004

Cover design by Giovanni Mora
Cover art by Gustavo Pérez Firmat

Pérez Firmat, Gustavo, 1949.
    Next Year in Cuba: a Cubano's coming-of-age in America / Gustavo Pérez Firmat.
      p. cm.
    Originally published: New York: Anchor Books, 1995.
    ISBN-10: 1-55885-461-4 (pbk. : alk. paper)
    ISBN-13: 978-1-55885-461-1 (pbk. : alk. paper)
    1. Pérez Firmat, Gustavo, 1949—Childhood and youth. 2. Poets, American—Miami. 4. Miami (Fla.)—Social life and customs. 5. Cuban Americans—Florida—Miami. 6. Cuban American poets—Biography.   II. Title.
    PS3566.E69138Z47   2005
    81′.54—dc22   2005040991
    [B]   CIP

5 6 7 8 9 0 1 2 3 4   10 9 8 7 6 5 4 3 2 1

Contents

This book is for David and Miriam and Jen and Chris.

Acknowledgments

I would like to thank Roger Scholl, my editor, and Mary Anne Pérez, my wife, for their encouragement and many helpful suggestions. Explaining myself to them, I learned to explain myself to myself. I'm also grateful to my friends Isabel Alvarez Borland, Ricardo Castells, and Jorge Olivares—one-and-a-halfers all—for their comments on various drafts of the manuscript. It pleases me to think that, in some sense, *Next Year in Cuba* is also their book.

Prologue

Born in Cuba, Made in the U.S.A.

Places. Strange and common places. Places you visit and places that you can't go. Distant places and places close to home. Mine is a life in places, and a life out of place.

I'm Cuban-American, a member of what has been called the "one-and-a-half" generation, that is, Cubans who were born on the island and came to the United States as children or adolescents. I arrived in this country thirty-four years ago, when I was eleven years old, after the triumph of the Castro Revolution. As a one-and-a-halfer, I'm too old to be entirely American, but too young to be anything else—a condition that I share with many other Hispanic Americans as well as with immigrants from other cultures and lands. Born in Cuba but made in the U.S.A., I can no longer imagine living outside American culture and the English language. And yet Cuba remains my true home, the place that decisively shaped my character and my values. My life is a delicate balancing act between two countries, two cultures, two languages. Ask me where I really belong, in Cuba or in America, and I wouldn't be able to tell you, because I belong in both.

To give you a clearer picture of this duality, let me go back a few years and describe two very different places, each of which contains a part of me.

In the first place, Miami. It's July 1991 and Cuban exiles are in a frenzy. The collapse of the Soviet Union has made us hope for the long-awaited demise of Cuba's communist regime. Travel agencies are booking flights to Havana, the governor of Florida has set up a commission to plan the orderly repatriation of exiles, and any number of exile organizations are eagerly, a little too eagerly perhaps, divvying up government posts in a postrevolutionary Cuba. Many exiles who had given up on the possibility of ever returning to the island believe once again that *regreso,* or return, is not a dream, but an option. The exile dead are turning in their graves, the living are turning in their American passports. My father has taken out the deeds to his Cuban properties and sleeps with them under his pillow. For over thirty years we have been waiting for this moment, which finally seems close at hand.

I've gone to Miami on vacation, as I do every summer, and the high point of my stay is a benefit concert by Willie Chirino, a popular singer and composer who left Cuba as an adolescent and is now in his mid-forties. The concert, intended to raise money for recent arrivals from the island, takes place at the Dade County Auditorium, whose location on Flagler Street, in the heart of Little Havana, has made it a favorite venue of Cuban-exile artists. Now more than forty years old, the auditorium—or Dade County, as the Cubans simply call it—has seen better days. The royal-red carpets have dulled to a lifeless matte; the upholstered seats are pock marked with cigarette burns. But for us, this cavernous auditorium remains a magical place, a house of dreams. In the early years of exile, Cuban artists often put on shows here with titles like "Cuba Sings and Dances" and "Havana Memories." These performances, which always ended with the impassioned singing of the Cuban national anthem, a battle hymn that felt more like a prayer, transported us back to Cuba, if only in our imaginations. Now it's twenty or thirty years later, but the old fervor persists. All during the 1970s and 1980s, with Castro solidly entrenched in power, Cuban exiles continued to long for *regreso,* but without much reason to think that it would happen anytime soon. American presidents came and went, Latin American dictators rose and fell, but Fidel seemed to last forever. Now, suddenly, the Soviet Union is no more, the world has changed, and the roughly one-tenth of Cuba's population that lives outside the island thinks that our expatriation is coming to an end.

I'm at the concert with Mary Anne, my wife of five months, who is American, hardly speaks a word of Spanish, and hasn't been to Miami before. For her, Little Havana itself is a magic kingdom. The auditorium is jam-packed with Cubans of all ages. Mary Anne and I are sitting in the middle section, toward the back, and the whole row in front of us is taken up by one extended family of children, parents, grandparents, aunts and uncles. Three generations of exiles—all gathered to hear Willie Chirino, the Pied Piper of Little Havana, whose Spanish name is actually Wilfredo. *Wilfredo el mago,* he is sometimes called, Wilfred the Magician. Since the concert runs on Cuban time, the show starts forty minutes late, but nobody expects it to be otherwise. The mood is festive, celebratory, with strong perfume and glistening gold jewelry everywhere. When Chirino finally appears, wearing a white linen suit over a pastel T-shirt, a heavy-set mulatto woman with a white scarf on her head and large hoop earrings rushes up to the stage and hands him something—some sort of *santería* amulet perhaps. Chirino bends over to take it, gives the woman a kiss on the cheek, and says to the audience in Spanish, "Oh-oh, I can see that I'm in trouble tonight."

Then he launches into his upbeat, bouncy music, blending Cuban rhythms with American riffs in the way typical of the Miami sound. He invites people to dance in the aisles, and many do. On the row where we are sitting, an elderly couple gets up to do a mean *guaguancó*—the man dances like my father, with rubber-band legs and perpetual-motion hips. An hour into the second set, Chirino breaks into his current hit, the song everyone has been waiting to hear, which is met with loud applause and cheers. During the heady months of this summer, the eager anticipation of a free Cuba has inspired several compositions, the most popular of which is Chirino's "Nuestro día ya viene llegando," "Our Day Is Coming," which confidently forecasts an end to Castro's thirty-year dictatorship. For several months now, this melody has been floating in the Miami air like mist. Since everybody at the concert knows the words, we all sing along in Spanish. The song concludes with a list of the countries around the world that have recently gained their freedom— Poland, Hungary, Romania, Nicaragua, Czechoslovakia. The last country on the list is Cuba. As Chirino calls out the name of each liberated country, the audience thunders back, *"¡¡Libre!!"*—"Free!!"

By then everybody in the crammed auditorium has stood up in anticipation of hearing the last name on the list. Many people are waving little Cuban flags. When Chirino finally calls out Cuba, the country of my birth, the island that Columbus said was the most beautiful place human eyes had ever seen, the roar is deafening. Even Mary Anne, who was born in the Bronx, gets caught up in the swell of emotion and chants, "Lee-bray, lee-bray, lee-bray." Believe me, a couple of thousand Cubans and at least one American, all screaming at the top of their lungs, will make a lot of noise. But this isn't just noise—it is a cry, a plea, a lament, an ejaculation, a cathartic howl—maybe even a last gasp. Thirty years of waiting, thirty years of hopes and frustrations, thirty years of broken promises and abortive plans, are jammed into the two syllables of the Spanish word for freedom. For Americans, Cuba Libre may be no more than the name of a cocktail, but for Cuban exiles it's a dream too long deferred, the story of our lives.

When I come out of Dade County Auditorium, I'm ready to buy one-way tickets to Cuba and take Mary Anne with me. I'm in a daze, spent from so much screaming and the rush of emotion. Is it true, could it be that Cuba soon would be free? Could I, who have lived in the United States much longer than I lived in Cuba, actually go back to the Havana of my childhood? Could my father make good on his promise to return? Would my mother make good on her threat not to? Could we get our home and our business back? Could we resume lives that had been interrupted for half a lifetime? Caught up in the mood of the moment, I imagine that all these things are not only possible but likely. I believe that I'm about to find my place, about to recover the life I lost as a child. Yes, I can go home again. On the way out, Mary Anne gets a Chirino poster. I buy my kids T-shirts that say on the front, "Our Day Is Coming," and on the back, "Cuba Libre 1992."

Now let's switch to a very different place.

Several weeks earlier during that same summer, I'm at the DAP, the Durham Athletic Park, in Durham, North Carolina, and what's in the air is not Cuban music but the ever-present aroma of tobacco leaves. The smell is teasingly familiar—as a Cuban, I have been around cigar smokers all my life—yet I know that there's not enough fine tobacco in all of North Carolina to make one good Havana, not even one good Little Havana. No matter. Although I don't feel about North Carolina the way I do about Miami, this place also is home. My children and stepchildren were born here; the only houses I have ever owned are located here; this is where I have spent all of my professional life. In fact, I have lived in Chapel Hill longer than in any other place, including Havana and Miami. If all these years in North Carolina haven't quite made me a good ole boy, a *cubanazo* redneck, spit and hick in equal parts, they certainly have colored my tastes and my values. By now, American sights and sounds are so embed ded within me that I know I would find it difficult to spend the rest of my life only among Cubans.

This afternoon I've put on a pair of shorts and a tank top, rounded up my ten-year-old son and my seven-year-old daughter, and headed for the quaint old stadium to watch the Durham Bulls play a game of what Cubans call simply *pelota,* our word for baseball. At the game David and Miriam spend most of their time standing by the first-base dugout with a glove and ballpoint pen, hoping for a foul ball or an autograph, while I parcel my attention between what happens on the field and what goes on in the stands. I love this scene, in no small measure because of the number of skimpily clad, good-looking *americanas* in attendance. Women from the area who would never go without a bra in their normal daily lives lose their inhibitions when they attend Bulls games; not just the young brash ones, who quiver rather than bounce, but even more arresting, middle-aged women with children and husbands in tow. By Cuban standards, it's quite a spectacle, wholesome but seductive. Although middle-class Americans don't show off, they do display themselves with offhanded casualness. Very unlike Cubans, who can't walk for strutting. For the American women sitting around me in the bleachers, sexuality seems to be a simple fact of life. For the Cuban women I grew up with, it's a cultural achievement, as much art as instinct. I'm not sure which attitude I like better.

Before the game begins, the crowd rises for "The Star-Spangled Banner." Because this is Durham rather than New York or Miami, even the players on the field join in the spirited singing. Looking at the American flag fluttering above the center-field fence, I put my hand over my heart and belt the song out, like everyone around me. Although I didn't learn the words to the anthem until I was almost a teenager, I sing them with feeling and conviction, as if I had known them all my life. It moves me to be singing in unison with my children, who know no other nation's anthem.

During the game kids run up and down the bleachers, sweating vendors shoulder trays with popcorn or cotton candy, and a tall cop who looks like Arthur Treacher shoos the kids away from the fence. I make a couple of trips to the concession stand and wait in a long line to go to the rest room. Although I hardly say a word to anyone except the toothless old guy at the beer concession, I don't feel alone. I feel connected to the crowd, where I recognize several faces from work or our neighborhood. Every time the home team scores a run, the cardboard bull in right field lights up, smoke billows from its flaring nostrils, and the tail jerks up and down. Miriam roars, and I roar along with her. The belly of the beast bears an inscription that says, with admirable parsimony, "Hit Bull Win Steak." I think to myself how much more complicated it would be to say that in Spanish.

During the seventh-inning stretch, I shake my limbs and join the organist and the thinning crowd in a few choruses of "Take Me Out to the Ball-Game." Sitting with my children in the cheap seats of the Bulls stadium, clad in Duckheads and sneakers and sipping warm beer, I feel like I've just stepped out of an Alabama CD. Surrounded by soft drawls and rebel yells, I forget that I haven't heard or uttered a word of Spanish in several hours. This evening my history as a Cuban exile no longer seems so central to my life; more important than where I come from is the fact that I'm here with my children, who are not exiles, and who have made it possible for me to look upon North Carolina as my home. I emerge from the stadium heartened, even exhilarated, by the experience of belonging to a community of people who live in the country of their birth. Walking back to the car holding hands with David and Miriam, I feel rooted, in my place.

But how is this possible? How can I feel at home in North Carolina, given my heritage? Is my feeling the result of a part I'm playing, or a part of who I am? A pose or an identity? A few weeks later I will be at the Dade County Auditorium, screaming and dreaming in Cuban. But today I've spent my evening in Durham cheering and leering, pulling for the home team and lusting in my heart after the local lovelies. A one-way ticket to Havana? If I were to go back to the country of my birth, I'd have to leave behind my life in the States. I'd have to give up ogling at *americanas,* singing "The Star-Spangled Banner" with my kids, and speaking English. After more than three decades of living here, I don't know whether I could bring myself to relinquish my allegiance to America.

This brings me back to places, strange and common places. Where am I most me? Which of these two locales that I have described is my true place? Dade County Auditorium or Durham Athletic Park? Miami or North Carolina? Cuba or America? This book grows out of my need to find an answer to these questions, or at least to understand more completely why I cannot answer them. Even if in the end I'm one of those people who don't know their place, I want to believe that not knowing your place doesn't have to leave you placeless. Beneath or beyond the panoply of my national loyalties and cultural allegiances, something and someone persist. I write to grasp and hold that unchanging core. I write to become who I am, even if I'm more than one, even if I'm *yo* and you and *tú* and two.

Years ago Miami Cubans used to group their fellow exiles into two camps: those who would be allowed to return to a free Cuba and those who wouldn't. Of someone in the latter camp, it was said that *no tiene regreso,* literally, "he has no return." The less-than-salutary idea behind the labeling (which varied in its application according to one's political persuasion) was to weed out from a future Cuban polity either sympathizers of Fulgencio Batista, the strongman who ruled Cuba from 1952 until 1958, or former collaborators of the Revolution.

Much as I would like to think otherwise, deep down I fear that I belong with those for whom there is no going back: *no tengo regreso.* But my reasons are broadly personal rather than narrowly political. One does not need to be a political exile in order to realize that, quite often, there is no going back to the country or the culture of one's origin. For most immigrants and exiles, there also comes a moment when we must begin to define ourselves not by our place of birth, but by our destination. Paradoxically, for someone like myself, returning to Cuba would be tantamount to going into exile a *second* time. I'd have to quit my job, give up my American citizenship, completely reshape my life. I'm not sure that I could do it.

And yet the temptation of return remains strong. Even after all these years, the land of my birth beckons with the promise of a different and more complete life; and unlike countless other exiles and immigrants who have come to the United States, I may actually have the opportunity to bring this life about. As I write this, late in the summer of 1994, Cuba is in transition. The island's economy is a shambles, and public disaffection is growing. On August 5 thousands of Cubans took to the streets of Havana to voice their dissatisfaction with the Castro regime—the first time in more than thirty years that such a demonstration has occurred. Although no one can predict the exact timetable of events, it is certain that the Cuban Revolution has entered its final stages.

For U.S. Cubans like myself, the change will be both liberating and perplexing—liberating because it will mark the end of a long historical nightmare, but perplexing because we will be forced to abandon structures of thought and feeling that have sustained us for over thirty years. Exile is disconcerting, but after three decades the possibility of return may be more disconcerting still. What happens to the exile who can go back but who decides not to? What does he become then, a post-exile? An ex-exile? After the demise of the Cuban Revolution, the question of what it means to be Cuban in America will become more rather than less urgent. I write out of the need to puzzle out what it means to be a Cuban man living in the United States in a time when I no longer will be able to think of myself as an exile. I write in anticipation of the moment when I may well have to choose *not* to return to Cuba.

This decision will not be easy, nor is it the kind that one makes once and for all. Because there are many things about my American life that I would change if I could, I tantalize myself with the possibility of return. Perhaps I could go back and start over; perhaps I'm wrong to think that I'm no longer Cuban enough; perhaps Cuba is where I finally belong, the only place where a one-and-a-halfer's fractional existence can be made whole.

As an exile, my experience is different from that of immigrants in that I came to this country fully intending to return to my homeland as soon as possible. As a *Cuban* exile, I grew up in a foreign land, but was surrounded by the language and culture of my birth. Cuban culture runs deep in me. Although I have lived three-fourths of my life in this country, I have lived less than half of it outside what I would term "Greater Havana," an extended urban area that encompasses both Havana and Miami. Indeed, with a Cuban population of over half a million, Miami is second only to Havana as the largest Cuban city. For over three decades *regreso* has been this community's magical, monotonous mantra. The Cuban version of the Jewish

promise "Next year in Jerusalem" is *El año que viene en Cuba,*
"Next year in Cuba," a toast that I have heard and uttered every
Christmas Eve since 1960. But even if my Cuban self, my *yo
cubano,* resists the refusal of *regreso,* my American me suspects that
return may not be feasible. The truth may well be that once an exile,
always an exile.

Members of the one-and-a-half generation occupy a unique
intermediate position. For my parents and my children, the options
are more limited than they are for me. My father, who is now in his
seventies, has no choice but to be Cuban. The thirty years of living
and working in the United States seem to have had little impact on
his Cuban ways. His English is a little better than when he first got
here, but he still views *los americanos* with the same mixture of awe,
disdain, and incomprehension that he did upon his arrival. The fact
that my mother and all of his children and grandchildren are now
American citizens seems not to have reduced his distance from U.S.
culture. He will never be an *americano,* either legally or in spirit. No
matter how many years he has resided away from the island—and if
he survives a few more years there will come a time when he too will
have lived longer in Miami than he did in Havana—he remains as
unassimilated today as he was on the day in October 1960 when he
got off the ferry at Key West.

My children, who were born in this country of Cuban parents
and in whom I have tried to inculcate some sort of *cubanía,* are
American through and through. They can be "saved" from their
Americanness no more than my father can be "saved" from his
Cubanness. Although they belong to the so-called ABC generation
(American-born Cubans), they are Cubans in name only, in last
name. A better abbreviation for them would be the reverse, the CBA
generation (Cuban-bred Americans). Like other second-generation
Americans, my children maintain a connection to their parents'
homeland, but it's a bond forged by my experiences rather than their
own. For David and Miriam, who are twelve and nine years old,
Cuba is an endearing, hopefully an enduring fiction—as ethereal as
the smoke and as persistent as the smell of their grandfather's cigars
(which these days are not even Cuban but Miamian).

Like my father, I too smoke cigars, except that I buy them a couple at a time from a yuppie tobacconist in Chapel Hill, whereas my
father buys his by the box from the factory in Little Havana. If smok-

ing cigars is a token of Cuban maleness, then I'm an occasional Cuban, a Friday-night *cubanazo,* for I light up a couple of evenings a week after dinner. While my children watch TV sitcoms, I observe my roots go up in smoke. If for my father Cuba is a burdensome fact, and if for my children it's an endearing fiction, for one-and-a-halfers like me, the country of my birth is a blend of both fact and fiction. Since my recollections of the island are an indeterminate mix of eye-witness and hearsay, what I know is mixed in with what I have been told. My memories merge with others' dreams.

Spiritually tied to Cuba, yet firmly rooted in the United States, I belong to a rare group of exiles that could, should Castro be over-thrown in the near future, genuinely choose whether to return or stay. My father does not have this choice; in a sense, he never left. My children also do not have the choice; they cannot even speak the Spanish language. My son occasionally brags to his friends that he is Cuban—but he can only assert his Cubanness in English. Wedged between the first and second generations, the one-and-a-halfer shares the nostalgia of his parents and the forgetfulness of his chil-dren. For me, homecoming would feel like departure.

This generational conundrum obsesses me. I want to affirm that the conundrum hides a continuum, that it's possible to identify val-ues and attitudes and codes of conduct that survive uprootings and reroutings. In my life and my writing I play endless variations on three core themes: cultural continuity, family loyalty, and personal identity. My life coheres only when I find things that bind me to my Cuban parents and my American children, and things that bind us to each other. I need to believe that the generational segments can be joined into an unbroken line.

Although I will be writing mostly about my life, this isn't a memoir, for the past is not my destination. Rather than memorious, I intend to be recollective, in both senses of the word: my purpose is not simply to recall the past but also, and primarily, to weave togeth-er the different strands of my life as an exile into a design for the present and the future. I write to collect myself, to shape disparate fragments into a portrait that I can recognize and embody.

But the face inside the frame will not be mine alone, for the por-trait is also a group picture—of my family, of some of my friends, as well as of people I don't even know. Although my narrative relies on the circumstances of my life in a foreign and familiar land, I share these circumstances with countless other immigrants. I can't presume to speak for all Hispanic Americans, or even for all Cuban-Americans; yet it would be disingenuous for me to think that my words, my feelings, my experiences, are mine alone. The truth is that they emerge from a choral or communal setting and resonate with shared experiences and expectations. The essential nature of those experiences and expectations can be summarized in a treacherously simple proposition: first you lose your place, then you find your place. I write about the places I have lost and found, and about those I have not entirely lost nor entirely found.

Most of all, I write about the marriage of person and place. The exile is someone for whom this marriage has broken up; the "after-exile" is someone who has sought out a new relation between person and place, someone who's found, or founded, another home. Although it may seem that in order to move past exile one has to renounce one country for another, I prefer to think that moving past exile means staking out a place that spans more than one country, more than one culture, more than one language. A place that is two places at once. Like the Dade County Auditorium and the Durham Athletic Park—all rolled up into one. This book is my search for such a place.

ᘏ   ᘏ   ᘏ

PART ONE
Waving Good-Bye

ᘏ   ᘏ   ᘏ

ONE

The Past Is a Foreign Country

Havana, October 24, 1960

That morning Nena, my mother, woke us up earier than usual. It was a school day, but we weren't going to school. In the hallway outside my bedroom the queue of suitcases stretched all the way to the front door. For several years I had been coming to the States once or twice a year, always taking the *City of Havana*, the overnight ferry to Key West. From there we would drive or take a train to Crowley, Louisiana, the rice capital of America, where my father did business. At first I was the only one of the four children old enough to travel with my parents; later my brother Pepe also came, and on the last trip Carlos had been there too. Only Mari, the baby of the family, had not been to *el norte* before. As usual, I got up that morning looking forward to sleeping aboard the ship and waking up the next day to the sight of the sandbars ranged along the Keys like pillows.

We arrived at the pier a couple of hours before the ferry was scheduled to sail. I had been here many times before, since my father's food wholesaling business, which we always called *el almacén,* was only a few blocks away. (An *almacén,* literally, is a storehouse, but in Cuba the term referred primarily to food wholesalers and distributors; *almacén* was short for *almacén de víveres,* a storehouse of eatables.) This morning my aunt Cuca drove us to the dock, where my father joined us. After our suitcases were opened and checked, some question arose about his passport. The ferry's departure was delayed for an hour. Finally, the problem was straightened out and sometime in the early afternoon the *City of Havana* began to inch away from the pier. My aunt waved good-bye. We waved back. Pepe and I clutched the small metal safes with the money that we had saved to spend on our next trip to the States. Always the best part of these trips was getting a chance to load up on war toys of various vintages, which my brother and I bought by the dozens at the five-and-ten in Crowley.

When this scene took place, I was eleven years old, my brothers, Pepe and Carlos, were nine and seven, and my sister, Mari, had turned five three weeks earlier. Although Fidel Castro had been in power less than two years, Cuba was on the fast track to communism. The man who was going to save Cuba from years of dictatorial rule would turn out to be the worst tyrant in Cuban history. Much of the wealth of the country had already fallen into government hands with the nationalization of the public utilities, banks, and American-owned enterprises. Ten days earlier, on October 14, the regime had promulgated a law confiscating *almacenes* and other large, Cuban-owned businesses. A few days after the *almacén* was confiscated, my parents decided to leave the country. By then almost 100,000 other Cubans had fled, mostly professionals, entrepreneurs, and white-collar workers who had already lost their jobs or possessions; several hundreds of thousands more would soon follow. By 1973 nearly one-tenth of Cuba's population would be living outside the island, the largest per capita exodus in the history of Latin America, and a percentage that remains basically unchanged to this day. Years ago a joke that made the Cuban-exile rounds asked why Cuba was the largest country in the world. The answer: because it had its territory in the Caribbean, its rulers in Moscow, and its population in Miami.

Both my parents spoke English and had lived in the United States before. My mother had been born in Newport News, Virginia, where her father was Cuban consul; she was seven years old before she lived in Cuba. My father, expelled from a Catholic school in Havana, had been sent to Bowles military academy in Jacksonville, Florida. After my parents were married in 1942, they spent the next several years traveling around the States buying merchandise for the *almacén*. They did not return to Cuba until 1948, when my mother got pregnant with me.

Although the Cuban government only allowed emigrants to take sixty dollars with them, my father had a few thousand dollars in a New York bank, a sum that he thought would tide us over until Castro's government collapsed, as he thought it soon would. In the American presidential campaign that fall, both Senator John F. Kennedy and Vice President Richard Nixon had adopted militant anti-Castro stands. Indeed, Kennedy had advocated military action against Fidel. It wouldn't be the first time in the island's history that the *americanos* rode to the rescue. At the end of the SpanishAmerican War, General Rufus Shafter, the commander of the American troops in Cuba, famously remarked, "Cubans are no more fit for self-government than gun-powder is for hell." Since then the American government intervened often in Cuban affairs, with varying justification and mixed results.

My parents' intention was to wait the Revolution out. No Cuban regime, whether elected or imposed, had lasted more than a few years. Why should Castro's be any different? Soon enough either Cubans would get fed up with the Revolution and overthrow Castro, or the Marines would show up on the Malecón and wrest the government from him. Then we and the thousands of other exiles could return. My father would go back to his *almacén,* my mother would go back to the house and the rounds of baptisms and birthday parties, the children would go back to our schools and our *tatas* (nannies), and we would all pick up where we had left off.

All this happened a lifetime ago. We left off, but we never did pick up. My father, who was forty at the time, still hopes to go back to his *almacén.* My mother, who was a year older, still complains that she never had to do laundry or clean bathrooms in Havana, though she swears that she will never go back to Cuba, a crazy country. As for the four of us, Nena and Gustavo's children, we're still trying to figure out what exile has done to our hearts and our minds.

I have replayed our departure from Cuba in my mind hundreds, perhaps thousands, of times. I have dreamed about it, fantasized about it, and matched memories with my parents and with my brother Pepe, who was old enough to remember. In my night and day dreams, I visualize the departure exactly as I have described it, with one difference. As the ferry lurches away from the pier, I look back and see a small boy waving good-bye to me. He's my age, or perhaps a year or two younger, dressed as I would have been dressed-a pullover with horizontal stripes and short pants almost down to his knees. You can't see his socks because he's wearing cowboy boots. His hair is cut in *malanga* fashion, with the whole head clipped very short except for a tuft of hair in the front, kept stiffly in place by a generous helping of *gomina,* a gooey hair grease (American Vaseline is to Cuban *gomina* as Johnson's baby oil is to Slick 50). The boy is what in Spanish you'd call *un niño de su casa,* which doesn't quite translate as a homeboy, since this kid is more homebody than homeboy.

I realize that this boy on the dock is me. Somehow, in my dream, I'm in two places at once. I'm on the dock and I'm waving; I'm on the ferry and I'm waving. From the dock, I can see myself on the ferry, getting smaller and smaller, until what is left is no bigger than a swallow's flutter. From the ferry, I can see myself on the dock, getting smaller and smaller, until what is left is no bigger than a swallow's flutter. The last image in my dream is of me on the ferry, with my hands gripping the deck railing and my head barely above it, looking toward the shore and seeing the Cuban boy I was, the Cuban boy I am no longer, fade to a point and then to nothing. Finally, the only kid is the one on the ferry, which has sailed out into the open sea.

More than three decades later, the distance between the boy on the dock and the man I am today seems incalculable. I look at myself now: a man in his forties, a tenured professor at a prestigious American university, writing in English from his home in Chapel Hill, North Carolina. I'm an American citizen. I have not been back to Cuba since that day, and perhaps I never will. My wife is American and my two children understand but can barely speak Spanish. When I was a kid in Cuba, I wanted to go to Annapolis and become a sailor. But my real future was the *almacén,* as it had been my father's and his father's before him. To anybody in my Spanish-immigrant family the idea of making a living as a university professor was altogether incomprehensible. To this day Nena and Gustavo, my mother and father, aren't quite sure how I spend my time.

Do I still have anything in common with the boy who wanted to go to Annapolis? I'd like to think that I grew out of that boy, although it may be truer to say that I grew away from him. English, unlike Spanish, is a language of growing. In Spanish there's only one kind of growth, *crecer,* to grow, pure and simple; but English affords other possibilities: you grow up and you grow old, you grow fond and you grow distant. You can grow things and they can grow on you. You outgrow clothes, you ingrow toenails, and you grow back hair. Yes, in English you can actually grow back. Imagine that. The past as prologue. Yesterday as tomorrow. What was as what will be.

The paradox of growing back, of a growth that's also a recovery, best describes the connection I'd like to have to the Cuban boy I left behind. Having outgrown him, I want now to grow him back, to let him grow in and on me until we are the same person again. Refugees are amputees. Someone who goes into exile abandons not just possessions but a part of himself. This is true especially of children, who leave before achieving a durable, portable identity. Just as people who lose limbs sometimes continue to ache or tingle in the missing calf or hand, the exile suffers the absence of the self he left behind. I feel the loss of that Cuban boy inside me. He's my phantom limb, at times dogging me like a guilty thought, at other times accompanying me like a guardian angel. I need to bring him out of the shadows. I need to grow him back.

I left Cuba on the brink of adolescence, when my hormones were beginning to churn and my fantasies were swerving away from cowboys and toys. I grew up and I grew away and now I am growing old. What happened to the boy I left behind? Would his growth have been accelerated or stunted by the Revolution? Compare the imaginary adult version of him and me and perhaps it would be like those longitudinal studies of twins. A lifetime of separation, perhaps to find out that both subjects use the same brand of toothpaste and sleep on the same side of the bed. But ours would have to be a latitudinal study: what happens to twins who are cleft by geography. I wonder whether we would have a lot in common.

In a complementary fantasy I have entertained, I return to Cuba, three decades after I left, and on a street somewhere in Old Havana, perhaps near the docks, I run into that boy, who has grown into the Cuban man I never became. We should look exactly the same, but we don't. I imagine him darker, perhaps thinner (there's not much to eat in Cuba!), perhaps not boyish-looking. I look like my father, but he does so even more. He's wearing khaki pants and a short-sleeved shirt. Sporting a *guayabera* over Levi's, I'm culturally cross-dressing, like the one-and-a-halfer that I am. Perhaps he's a technician of some sort, or the manager of an *almacén*. Would I recognize this man? Would we have anything to say to each other? In which language would we speak? Mine or his? And if we communicated in my language, do I mean Spanish or English?

The Cuban boy is both my ingrown and my outgrown self. There are times when I feel that I'm more like the kid who stayed behind than like the one who, a month after we left Cuba, enrolled in a sixth-grade class at an American elementary school. At these times I can barely get a word out in English, and I look at my children and my wife and they seem like aliens from another planet. But at other times I can barely recognize myself in that boy I left behind. Then he becomes my guilty conscience, a Cuban incubus, and it's at these times that I see him on the dock, waving good-bye. Sometimes when I see him waving to me, I want to wring his neck, make him stop. Stop waving, I say to him, leave me alone. It wasn't my decision to leave. But had it been my decision, I still would have left. Is exile a choice or a fate?

In the black-and-white photo my mother took of us on the ferry to America, my brother Pepe and I are horsing around next to the railing. Pepe is doing his Jerry Lewis imitation, and I'm making monkey faces. The open sea is behind us. My brother Carlos and my sister, Mari, are hiding behind a funnel, with only a leg and two hands showing, as if their limbs had already been detached from their bodies. My father is standing off to one side, wearing tinted glasses in heavy black frames, a half-smoked cigar in one hand. Staring at the camera with an empty, affectless expression, he looks as if he doesn't know whether he's coming or going. Traveling to the States on a tourist visa, maybe he foresees or intuits that in a few weeks, when our visas expire, he'll have to request political asylum and begin a new life. As I look now at the photograph that my mother took thirty-four years ago, I wonder what phantom on the dock waved good-bye to him. I wonder whose neck he wanted to wring.

All of us remember when we first left home, whether it was to go off to college, to get married, or simply to start a life on our own. Imagine how much more vivid the images are when you're leaving not just your home but your homeland. No immigrant ever forgets the day he or she left the country of his or her birth. All the Cuban exiles I know who are old enough have a story or anecdote to tell about their departure from Cuba. Going into exile is one of those events that, paradoxically perhaps, increase in importance as time goes by. Like a new house, exile grows on you. Since most Cubans came to this country expecting to return to the island within a short time, leaving may not have seemed especially momentous at the time it happened. But after five or ten or fifteen years, it turns into the pivotal event in our lives. As you revisit that day over and over, the memory doesn't dim, it grows sharper. Just as Americans of a certain age all seem to know exactly what they were doing the afternoon when Kennedy was shot (I was in Latin class), Cuban exiles remember the day we left our island.

Some years ago, I was at a convention with a couple of professor friends, both Cuban. As we stood outside a conference room waiting for the next dull session to begin, our small talk turned to the day each of us left Cuba. I told them about the ferry and the thirty suitcases and the eerie feeling that we were going on vacation. Ricardo and Tony talked about their departures. Both had arrived in this country by plane, a few months after the Bay of Pigs invasion, with a couple of dollars in their pockets and only the clothes on their backs. Tony had come here by himself as part of Operation Peter Pan, a Church-sponsored program to get children out of Cuba. He lived in a foster home for a couple of years, until his parents were allowed to leave the island. Ricardo had come with his mother and his older brother. Both were thirteen or fourteen at the time.

Tony remembered that his flight out of Havana was full of nervous old ladies who crossed themselves and prayed as the plane was about to take off. Ricardo had also been on a plane full of *viejas* with rosaries in their hands. "That's right," said Tony. "And when the pilot announced that we had left Cuban airspace, one of the *viejas* got up from her seat, threw her arms up in the air, and screamed at the top of her lungs"—Ricardo completed the sentence—*"¡Viva Cuba Libre!"* "Long live Free Cuba!"

Twenty-five years earlier, without being aware of it, Ricardo and Tony had been on the same flight out of Cuba. Their memories matched point by point. For both of them that old lady who got up and screamed had acquired mythological proportions, for she divided their lives in halves—Cuban half and American half. They still could see and hear that old lady as if the incident had happened only a short time ago. And here they were now, three decades later, in a convention hotel somewhere in New York City, recalling that moment they unknowingly shared, which by then had become an indispensable memory.

Before 1959 there were perhaps three dozen *almacenes* in Havana. Some specialized in specific products, say rice and potatoes, while others covered the entire alimentary spectrum from veg-etables to wines. Several wholesalers also had their own brands; my father's firm packaged and sold El Sabio rice and Bola Roja beans.

Many of these *almacenes* were owned by first-generation Span-ish immigrants. My grandfather Pepe, who started the business, was born in Villaodrid, a small town in the province of Galicia, in the northwest corner of Spain. When he was thirteen, after his mother died and his father remarried, he ran away from home and reached Cuba as a deck boy on a merchant ship. This happened in 1903, one year after Cuba became a republic. The severance of the island's political ties to Spain in 1898 had done nothing to quench the transatlantic flow of immigrants like my grandfather. Paradoxically, the economic and spiritual malaise produced in Spain by the loss of Cuba, the last jewel in the Spanish imperial crown, only strength-ened the island's spiritual and cultural ties to the mother country. During the first two decades of this century, the streets of Old Havana were teeming with young gallegos like my grandfather who crossed "the puddle" (as the Atlantic Ocean was called) fleeing the poverty back home. Although my grandfather made his fortune in Cuba, he died without renouncing his Spanish citizenship.

After he arrived in Havana, Pepe worked at various odd jobs until he had saved enough money to buy a bicycle, his first *almacén,* since he used it to pedal and peddle, to ride around Old Havana selling potatoes on commission. By the time he married my grandmother Constantina in 1917, he had bought a small warehouse in Baratillo, a street in one of the oldest sections of the city, and the bicycle years were behind him. Dating back to the nineteenth century, the ware-house had been built against one of the few surviving sections of the old city walls, which had gone up to protect the population from Sir Francis Drake and other pirates. The warehouse's location turned out to be a stroke of good fortune, for some years later the government bought the property at a premium in order to turn the chunk of wall into a landmark. The sale allowed Pepe and Constantina to buy anoth-er, much larger warehouse, which had belonged to the British Rail-way Company and stood only a block away from the docks.

This was the *almacén* that I knew as a child, a huge, hangarlike structure with an attached office building that occupied a block of land at the corner of Paula and San Ignacio. Five blocks away was the house where the Cuban patriot and poet José Martí had been born; across the street was the church where the first mass in Havana had been celebrated. Engraved in cement above the front door of the *almacén* was the company's name, J. Pérez S.A. (my grandfather's name plus the abbreviation for a private corporation, Sociedad Anónima). Almost everyone in the family worked there: Pepe was president, Constantina was treasurer, my father vice president, my aunt Cuca assistant treasurer, while my great-uncle Vicente oversaw shipments and deliveries. For Abuelo Pepe the *almacén* was not just his livelihood but his life. With no family in Cuba except the one he founded, he did little else but work and listen every day at noon to his favorite radio serial, *Los Matalobos*. Unlike my father, he did not drink, dance, or smoke. What little hair he had he kept closely cropped, which made him look like a convict. I remember him as a serious man, paunchy and short, who wore loose pleated pants high above his belly and held his shirtsleeves in place with thick rubber bands. A teetotaler, he died of cirrhosis of the liver in 1954, one day after my brother Carlos was born. The news of the birth reached him just before he lost consciousness. His last words to my father were, "Good, Gustavo, another *machito* for the *almacén*."

After Pepe's death, my father took over as president of the company, which became the center of his life as it had been his father's. By the time I was old enough to start going to work with him, the *almacén* was prosperous enough to support Pepe's children and grandchildren in grand Cuban style. Grand Cuban style meant big: big houses, big cars, a big yacht, big jewelry, big furs, big cigars. A Cuban proverb says, *Caballo grande, ande o no ande;* it means roughly that a big lame horse is preferable to a small healthy one. Thus it was with my father, who loved the outward signs of wealth more than wealth itself. Although the business had its good and its lean years, our privileged standard of living—which was certainly far above that of most Cubans—never seemed to change.

On October 14, 1960, a decree handed down by the INRA (National Institute for Agrarian Reform) altered our lives forever. It provided for the nationalization of several hundred private enterprises, including sugar and rice mills, distilleries, textile factories, department stores, movie theaters, and all of the large wholesale grocers, including J. Pérez S.A. The text of the decree asserted that these companies had been "following a policy contrary to the interests of the Revolution and the economic development of the country." The government's action may have come as a shock, but it did not really catch anybody by surprise, since the October 14 decree was only the latest of many large-scale confiscations of private property. Although the loss of the *almacén* was not unexpected, for months my father had hoped that Cuban-owned enterprises like his would be spared the Revolution's collectivizing fury. The same day that the *almacén* was confiscated my father's bank account and other assets were also impounded.

Less than two years earlier, we had greeted the Revolution with apprehension. Unlike the majority of Cubans at the time, my parents were leery of Fidel. When the guerrillas entered Havana during the first week in January 1959, many thousands of people lined the streets to greet them, but we did not. My best friend at school, Sergio Fernández, lived in a high-rise a few blocks away from our house. On the front door of his apartment, his mother had taped a sign that said, "Fidel, this is your house." Many Havana residents put up signs similar to the one on Sergio's door. Not so at our house, where anything having to do with the Revolution was forbidden. From the start we knew we were *gusanos*, worms, the sobriquet given by the Castro regime to its opponents. Although not active in politics, my father sympathized with Batista and had friends in the government and the armed forces. Although Batista had been a deeply flawed ruler, my father felt that he was far better than Fidel, who was rumored to be a communist.

Some of my father's *batistiano* friends attended a New Year's party at our house on December 31, 1958, the night that Batista unexpectedly fled the country. One of them was Admiral Casanova, a high-ranking officer in the Cuban Navy, such as it was (a few hydroplanes and a couple of gunboats). Shortly after midnight, Casanova got a call that Batista and his family were at Camp Columbia, a military base in Havana, about to board a plane for the Dominican Republic. Urged to follow the dictator into exile, he did. But my brother Carlos's godfather, Abelito, who was also a desk officer in the navy, decided to stay, since he hadn't been involved in the war against Castro's guerrillas. His naiveté cost him twenty-five years in Cuban jails. When he finally got out in the mid-eighties, his wife had remarried and he had not seen his son in twenty years.

Between January 1959, when Castro took power, on October 1960, when we went into exile, my brothers, my sister, and I lived practically behind closed doors. During this period it seemed that the venetian blinds in our house were always drawn and that the front door was always locked. Our home was a tightly sealed can of *gusanos*. We couldn't watch Fidel on TV (though every once in a while we caught a glimpse), nor could we listen to his endless speeches on the radio. Unlike my friend Sergio and other kids I knew, we weren't allowed to collect stamps and other Revolution memorabilia. As late as December 1958 Castro's forces had numbered no more than a few hundred men; after Batista's departure the ragtag revolutionary army suddenly swelled to thousands, and Havana was awash with war heroes and souvenirs—gun belts, army caps, fatigues, bullets, and rosaries and holy medals that the guerrillas supposedly had worn. One night when we were coming home in my mother's Lincoln, we were stopped by a *miliciano* who demanded a ride. Sitting in the backseat between my brother Pepe and me, his olive-green fatigues smelling of sweat and gunpowder, he offered to give us some bullets from his munition belt as a souvenir. To my disappointment, Nena instantly intervened, declining on our behalf. We rode silently the rest of the way.

Soon after the triumph of the Revolution, a group of guerrillas moved in across the street from where we lived, into what had been the residence of one of Batista's ministers. Every morning, noon, and afternoon they would cross the street, knock on the door, and, Garand rifles in hand, ask to be fed. When they came over, my mother would hurry us into the back of the house, from which we could not emerge until they had left. Some days, I suppose in an act of defiance, the *milicianos* lounged on the granite stairs leading to the front door. They chatted, cleaned and showed off their weapons, and flirted with the maids, who were enthralled with these bearded young men who had just come down from the mountains. When the *milicianos* occupied our front steps and we needed to go out, we left the house through the back door. We were taught to avoid all contact with this *chusma,* my mother's all-purpose insult for people not of our social class.

After the triumph of the Revolution, we lived under siege, in a kind of residential or inner exile. Surrounded by sympathizers of the new regime, we tried to keep our distance. At school likeminded friends and I wrote political graffiti on the bathroom walls—*¡Fidel comunista!* I belonged to the JEC, a Catholic youth organization that distributed stickers with religious slogans that we pasted on the school walls. Terrified of getting caught, we believed we were engaged in significant political activity. But given that our actions took place inside a Catholic school, and given that the Church already had strained relations with the government, there wasn't much chance that we would be punished too severely for defacing the walls with anti-Castro slogans.

The ten days between the confiscation of the *almacén* and our departure to America were utter chaos. Every evening family, friends, and other *almacenistas* gathered at our house and talked late into the night. How long will Fidel hold on to power? Do we stay? Do we leave? Where do we go? Since in the fall of 1960 there was still a considerable amount of organized opposition to the Revolution, including armed resistance in the mountains, every day brought a new tale of bombings or sabotage. The situation was lent urgency by the rumors that travel to the United States was soon going to be curtailed. With the nationalization of American assets, relations between the two countries had been steadily worsening, and there was talk that the United States was going to recall its ambassador (which indeed happened a few days after we left). It was also widely rumored that the Revolution would abrogate the principle of *patria potestad,* which gave parents control over their children.

Once my parents and most of my immediate family made the decision to leave, there were accounts to settle, possessions to dispose of, logistics to work out. My mother scoured the stores in Havana looking for winter clothes and packed everything she thought we would need, including kitchen utensils, bed sheets, and pillows. (When I once asked her why she had thought it necessary to bring pillows, her sibylline reply was, "I knew what the United States was like.") Since the only jewelry one could take out of the country was a wedding ring and a watch, and then only if their total value did not exceed $400, she covered her jewelry with nail polish, hoping to sneak it out in a bag full of medicines and cosmetics. All told we took thirty-two suitcases, many more than other Cubans who left later. (Nena is still using some of the same kitchen utensils she brought on the ferry in 1960.)

Another problem was disposing of cash, cars, furniture, and other valuables. Although bank accounts had been frozen, for the last several months before the confiscation my father had been bringing home the cash receipts from the *almacén* and changing them into dollars in the black market (at the time the unofficial exchange rate was about five pesos to the dollar). His original plan had been to use this money, which came to about $50,000, to live on if we stayed in Cuba. When he decided to leave, a friend at the American embassy offered to try to smuggle the money out of Cuba. The tricky part was getting the money into the embassy, which was closely guarded. In the end Nena put the cash in a beach bag and had Manuel, my grandmother's chauffeur, drop her off in the Vedado neighborhood, which is a short bus ride from the embassy. She took my sister with her, figuring that a woman with a five-year-old child and a beach bag wouldn't arouse suspicions. She was right: getting off the bus in front of the embassy, she walked right past the *milicianos* at the gate. Once inside, their American contact took her to his office. He told her not to get her hopes up but that he would see if anything could be done. When he opened the vault behind his desk, she saw that it was crammed with beach bags, presumably all stuffed with money. Unfortunately for us, the United States and Cuba broke off diplomatic relations a couple of months later, and the money stayed behind along with the beach bag.

With her jewelry my mother had better luck. After she had covered it with nail polish (I've never quite understood how this paint job was supposed to work), the friend at the embassy offered to smuggle the most valuable pieces out of Cuba. My mother hatched a plan which she must have gotten from a Hollywood movie. She put the jewelry in a purse and went to El Carmelo restaurant, where she was met by their friend's secretary. In the ladies' room they exchanged purses. Several weeks later, in Miami, she received two packages in the mail. Although they had been stamped in the United States, they bore no return address. Inside were her nail-polished earrings and bracelets. The man who had helped them, Joe Floyd, was a naval attaché at the embassy who actually worked for the CIA. They never saw or heard from him again.

When we left, the house remained in my uncle Pedro's care, although we knew that sooner or later the government would take it over. Before he went into exile a few weeks later, my uncle spent an afternoon ripping out the toilets, the sinks, and all of the electrical wiring that he could get his hands on. He did the same thing to his own house. To the victors belong the spoiled fixtures. He was not going to make it easy for the new occupants, whoever they were.

Although my memories of Cuba may seem firm and clear, in fact I remember very little. The day we left is still vivid in my mind, but much of my life before then has become a soft blur. Soon after our arrival in the States, I stopped thinking about the details and routines of our lives in Havana. Cuba quickly became abstract, a topic of obsessive discussion and debate rather than a place I would lovingly or morbidly reconstruct in memory. Part of the reason for my amnesia may have been my age. Propelled toward the future, children are not much given to nostalgia. Their bodies tell them to grow up, to move on, to look forward. A child with a past is no less a contradiction than an old man with a future. As L.P. Hartley wrote, the past is a foreign country, and kids don't live there willingly. Shedding Cuba seemed as natural as outgrowing a pair of shoes.

But there were also other, more complicated reasons for my forgetfulness. I was eleven and a half in October 1960. This made me old enough to be aware of what was going on, but not old enough to understand it. I knew the *almacén* had been taken over by the government, the word "confiscation" was constantly on everybody's lips, and I remember hearing my father telling my mother that the *interventor,* the man appointed by the Revolution to run the business, was a former employee. Sensing that our departure was connected to the confiscation, I knew that this trip was unlike previous ones. But I also thought, because my parents were always saying so, that it was only a matter of weeks or months before we returned. What for them may have been wishful thinking for me was a promise. Why shouldn't I believe what my parents said?

As the weeks and the months and then the years went by, I came to feel that they had let me down. Of course they misled me only inasmuch as they misled themselves; and whatever the Revolution took from me, it was a pittance compared to what it took from them. But resentment responds to its own reasons. They had let me down, and I resented them for it. Part of me never stopped taking pleasure in their reminiscences about our privileged life before Castro; but the larger part of me hated every moment wasted in recollection. It was like mixing sugar and salt and rubbing the mixture into my open wounds. Why talk about what we had in Cuba when it was not what we had now? Why talk about *regreso* when they could do nothing to bring it about? As I grew up, I also grew tired—tired of hearing about our maids, our Cadillacs, the pricey restaurants and fashionable hotels. I was angry that this life had been promised me, that this life was still being promised me, but could not possibly be granted. Since Cuba wasn't where I was, I began to put it out of my mind. Cuba became someone else's memories. I sliced my life in halves and threw away the bitter half.

Now I'm struck by how much more clearly I remember people and events beginning with October 24, 1960. Sometimes it has seemed to me that I was born on that day. I should have the same sharpness of recollection about events that took place only days or weeks before, but I don't. No matter how hard I try, I cannot recall the name or the face of my sixth-grade teacher in Cuba, nor the classroom where I sat, nor the names of many of my classmates. Yet I can draw you a detailed picture of my American sixth-grade classroom, give you the names of at least half of my classmates, and tell you where everybody sat. Although I attended La Salle (a Christian Brothers school named after the founder of the order, Saint Jean-Baptiste de La Salle) in Havana for six years, my recollections of this school are hazy at best—the building itself, with its interior courtyards and cavernous corridors, always appears enveloped in shadows. Yet, my mental images of Dade Elementary in Miami, which I attended for only six months, are brightly lit, as if everything there happened in the morning. Traveling in memory from one school to the other is like bartering dusk for dawn. My Cuban childhood is a bittersweet blur; my American childhood has more sharp edges than broken glass.

Some years ago I received a phone call from someone who said he had been one of my best friends in Cuba. He had come across my name in a book and tracked me down to Duke University. I had to interrupt the class I was teaching to talk to him. Even though his name sounded familiar, I didn't recall anything about the boy to whom it belonged. Yet he told me that at La Salle we had been best friends and had been in the same classes since first grade. He ran other names by me. The ones I remembered were mostly those of kids I had also known later in Miami, where I had attended the exile reincarnation of La Salle. I was surprised and dismayed at the distinctness of his recollections. He seemed to recall everything clearly, effortlessly, while I had to struggle to disinter shreds and fragments. Cuba was available to him in a way it had not been to me for many years, perhaps since that morning on the ferry. Don't you remember Brother so-and-so, he said, or the day we did such-and-such, or the time you and I went here or there. But I didn't. Don't you remember our friend something-ito, he said, that you were the one who . . . what happened when . . . Again, I did not. And so it went, this pointless conversation between a mnemophile and an amnesiac.

For most of the last thirty years, I've done without my Cuban childhood. The Florida Straits separating Cuba from the U.S. mainland have been an unbridgeable chasm, impassable even in memory. Is it because my memory feeds on spatial continuity? Is it because I find it difficult to remember events that happened in a different language? Or is it because of the specific circumstances of my family's life in exile? Whatever the reasons, and it's probably a combination of all of them, I have placed an embargo on my Cuban memories. Much has been written about an exile's nostalgia, his fixation on the past, his longing for the lost homeland. I found it otherwise. I must speak for the exile's forgetfulness, for the pain of not being able to remember enough. Unlike my classmate Gustavo Vázquez, I grope for names and incidents, I dig for images to feed my nostalgia. I'm not haunted by memory, but by its loss, and I envy those who can actually live in the past, for this means they have enough past to live in. I have a whole childhood inside my head, yet I can't seem to get much of it out.

Over the last twenty years, many young Cuban exiles, one-and-a-halfers like me, have traveled to Cuba. They go back to the old house, the old school, the neighborhood park; they get depressed over how decrepit and faded everything is; and they return with rolls and rolls of color photographs. I think these people go looking not for roots or relatives, but for memories. They go back to recover childhood images that, when they survive at all, exist in shadowy, broken outlines. Quite often these are private images that parents and older siblings cannot authenticate: Was it in fact possible to climb onto the roof of the house from the mango tree? Did the little nook behind the shrine to Our Lady of Carmen really exist? And often these private images are the most precious, for they testify to the uniqueness of our lives. The young exiles who visit Cuba come back anguished by what they have seen, but replenished by what they have remembered.

I have refused to go back not just because I don't want to help Fidel out with my dollars, but primarily because I'd find it intolerable to visit places that belonged to us, that were taken from my parents and my family. For me, this amounts to acquiescence and even complicity in the theft. This view is not shared by all Cuban exiles, however, even within my own family. My brother Pepe, who is much more sympathetic to the Revolution than I am, has gone back to Cuba two or three times. He has visited the *almacén* and recently spent an hour in our Havana house talking to the people who live there now (a pilot and his family). I could never bring myself to follow in my brother's footsteps. My rage wouldn't let me. I would find it unbearable to set foot in the house, much less talk civilly to the people whom, whatever their specific histories and motives, I cannot help regarding as usurpers. When I put myself in my brother's place, sitting in what used to be our living room and talking to these people, I lose my composure. I know that at some point in the conversation I would say, "Tell me, Sr. Piloto, where are you and your family planning to go when we get our house back?"

No, this kind of *regreso* is not for me. It feels too much like crawling. It reminds me too much of when, as a child, I used to see some old women ascend the stairs of the San Agustín Church on their knees. Instead of going with my brother to Cuba, for the past several months I have been making lists to myself, lists of words, names, and places from my childhood. After all these years I'm intent on lifting my mental embargo, prying open the gates of memory, allowing my childhood to trickle back to me in dribs and drabs. One drib that I have recovered: the word *hollín,* which means soot. In the last thirty years I may have come across this word in a book somewhere, but I'm certain I have not heard it spoken since I left Cuba. Yet when I was a child, *hollín* was everywhere, for our patio seemed always to be covered with a fine black powder. Since we lived in the suburbs, far from any *hollín*-spouting factories, my parents think I must be mistaken. They have no recollection of it. But I know I'm not mistaken. In those days I spent a lot more time in the patio than they did, and I was closer to the ground. I remember that we had *hollín* in the cracks between the tiles, *hollín* in the nooks and crannies of the low stone wall in front of the hibiscus, *hollín* on the white blinds of the windows.

It's a word that is pleasurable to pronounce, thrilling to write. That final acute syllable wakes me up like a buzzer. Although I have the annoying scholarly habit of looking up etymologies, this is one word about which I intend to remain ignorant. This time, I am determined to rely on my own half-educated guesses. The Spanish for pot is *olla,* and *hollín* literally may be the black scum that sticks to the bottom of the pan, except that the correct spelling would then be *ollín,* without the silent *h.* Other possible roots: a hole in Spanish is *hoyo,* and perhaps *hollín,* which would then be spelled *hoyín, is* the dirt that accumulates inside an *hoyo.* Or perhaps *hollín* is a variant of *orín,* which means rust. No matter. In truth I don't care where the word *hollín* comes from, since for me it originated in our patio. *Hollín* sticks to my memories of Cuba like black fairy dust.

Another memory exercise: Do I remember enough to describe our house in Havana, the one Pepe recently visited? Do I remember enough to walk myself through the house I have not seen, and not thought about much, since the morning we got on the ferry? I'm going to do my brother one better, for I'm going to walk through our house not the way it looks now, practically a shambles, but the way it was the last time I saw it.

The house is exactly my age. Married in 1942, my parents remained childless until 1949. For most of this time, when they weren't living in the States, they stayed with my father's parents, an arrangement that didn't work out well. My mother wanted her own home, but my father, in one way or another, gave her to understand that he would build her a house when she gave him a son. She had given him to understand that she would have children only if she had a house in which to raise them. The standoff lasted until 1949, when their understandings merged: my mother had me and construction began on a lot next to my grandmother's house in the Reparto Kohly, a Havana suburb named after a former mayor. Like other Havana residences of the time, the house was a one-story masonry structure with a vaguely modernist or Art Deco look. The architect, a man named Santana, wanted to design a structure that was both homey (to fit my mother) and suitable for entertaining (to fit my father). Completed a few months after I was born, that's where I spent my first Christmas.

I begin my imaginary visit by walking up from the sidewalk onto the wide granite stairs, which taper at the top. My hand slides along the top of the low stone wall where I sit in the morning waiting for the school bus. Behind the wall lies a large patch of greenery— *arecas*. The front door has a dark iron grating and thick milky glass; I don't remember the pattern of the grating, but I imagine it similar to those I have often seen in Miami—flamingos or palm trees or some other leafy, vegetable design. When I ring the doorbell, our manservant ("butler" is too formal a word for Vargas) lets me in. On the wall next to the door is a shiny gadget, a set of golden cylinders of varying lengths shaped like a pan flute: the doorbell. A long hallway runs down the middle of the house, with the rooms opening out on either side. The terrazzo tiles, joined together by thin copper strips, are always cool, and in the summers my brother Pepe and I like to take our shirts off and lie with our bellies to the floor.

Taking a few steps to the right, I go through a wide opening into the dining room, which contains the console TV where my brothers and I watch our favorite American programs, *Wyatt Earp* and *Highway Patrol*. On this particular afternoon I'm going to help Vargas polish the silverware inside the vitrines and cabinets, and in return he's going to play catch with me. A black man in his early twenties, Vargas once played first base for a semipro team, and in my eyes he's as good as Rocky Nelson, the American first baseman on Almendares, my favorite Cuban baseball team. As we rub the pleasant-smelling gray paste into the forks and knives, the radio in the kitchen is playing the hit song of the day, a *cha-cha-chá* about a merchant who dances in his *bodega*. Tapping on a silver tray as if it were a conga drum, Vargas does a few steps of his own, which I try to imitate.

A swinging door leads from the dining room back to the kitchen. The right side is the Cuban wing, ruled over by Caridad, the mulata cook with a raised two-inch scar on her cheek, the legacy of a jealous boyfriend; the left side reminds me of the States, because it has a little fold-down table where my brothers and I have our breakfast of bacon and eggs every morning. Although Cubans tend to begin their days with *café con leche,* espresso coffee mixed with warm milk and sugar, my mother prefers the large American-style breakfasts of her Virginia childhood. Another of her Americanisms is *bistí,* a foultasting concoction made from the juice of boiled ground meat that my brothers and I are forced to drink in small orange-juice glasses before every dinner. Since numberless little slivers of meat always remain inside the broth, drinking *bistí* is like gulping wet sand. I was an adult before it dawned on me that the name of this drink was actually beef tea, or what I have heard others call blood juice. *Bistí* may be one reason I have repressed so much of my Cuban childhood.

Off the kitchen is the pantry, which we call *despensa*. I love this dank little room, our domestic *almacén*, a household cornucopia. Because of my father's business, the *despensa* is always crammed with sacks of rice and beans, cases of olive oil, and cans of every size and description. Every year the La Salle Brothers mount a drive to collect food for the poor, which they call the drive of *la lata,* since the most desirable item is canned food (*lata* is Spanish for can). Each morning during the drive, I raid the pantry in my quest to be the boy who brings in the most *latas.* My father, who isn't thrilled to see his stores depleted day after day, says to me, *"Estás dando mucha lata"*—literally, "You are giving too many cans"—but in Cuban slang what he's really saying is that I'm becoming a pain in the ass.

The kitchen leads out to a small foyer where Vargas and the maids sit and eat with their plates on their laps. That's also where, a couple of years later, my mother fed the *milicianos* who came knocking. Sometimes the servants eat the same thing we do; at other times, particularly when my mother asks Caridad to cook some bland American dish, they prepare their own food. The foyer opens into a room that serves as an informal dining room and parlor, furnished with wrought-iron furniture and cushions with flower patterns. Zoila, one of the maids, spends part of her evenings here, chatting with her bus-driver husband, Neno. Zoila's son, who is the same age as my brother Pepe, spends the summers with us, but I don't like him and keep my distance. I do like Neno, though, and enjoy hearing stories about his bus routes.

From the parlor I return to the central corridor and take a right into the *sala*, or living room, an area where I don't spend too much time because it has the most elegant furniture in the house. This is where my parents hold their parties after my brothers and I are asleep. This is also where we set up the Christmas tree every year, next to the fake brick fireplace. Shaped like a "T," the room opens out on one end to a terrace that overhangs the garage. Through the venetian blinds of the terrace I can see the broad, dense tree with the myriad shades of green and fiery orange flowers (the name of the tree is another magic word: *flamboyán*). But since in this fantasy I'm eleven years old, perhaps the tree isn't there anymore, for my grandmother Constantina, who didn't like the mess the flowers made on the sidewalk, had it cut down during one of our trips to the States. Across from the terrace the living room opens out to the bar. Built into the pale blue wall are the outlines of two enormous martini glasses set in a cross.

I'm beginning to like this memory exercise. I find it easy to see myself, in a T-shirt and short pants, roaming from one room to another, seeking out my brother Pepe or spending a few quiet hours playing in a favorite corner of my bedroom. One part of the house that I haven't revisited yet, and which figured prominently in my childhood, is the area that contained the patio and the servants' quarters. Bordered all around by a cement wall and a tall hedge of hibiscus bushes, the patio was a safe, secluded haven. Since my brothers and I were not allowed to play in the street, I probably spent more time in the patio than anywhere else. Frequently, my cousins Maggie and Alina would come over from their house next door, and we would pass away the long summer afternoons in endless games of hide-and-seek and *chucho escondido*. When my sister, Mari, was born in 1955, my mother built a grotto to Our Lady of Carmen, to whom she had prayed for the little girl she had wanted ever since I was born. Mari's arrival was a godsend for us children also, since the grotto created terrific new hiding places. The only problem was that it always smelled of urine, not all of it from stray cats. It was quicker to pee behind Our Lady of Carmen than to go inside to the bathroom.

Vargas and the two maids slept in a rectangular building behind the patio. Although these rooms had many windows and several ceiling fans, they always smelled of sweat. On weekends or when I came home from school, I would knock on Vargas's door to ask him to play catch; if he didn't answer when I first knocked, I went around the side and peeked in his window. In a good mood even when I interrupted his siesta, Vargas was the only one of our servants whom I missed when we left for the States. Like everybody else in the house, he called me junior, but on his lips the moniker didn't sound American. Although he normally wore a short-sleeved shirt and casual pants, for dinner and parties he had to dress in uniform— patent-leather shoes, black pants, and a white Nehru jacket called a *filipina.* On these formal occasions his easy, friendly manner vanished. My mother would shake the little silver bell at the dinner table, the door would swing open, and a poker-faced Vargas would come in to serve our food, pour water from the pitcher I helped him polish, or clear the table. He addressed my parents as Señor Gustavo and Señora Nena; when he talked to me, he used the formal *usted* rather than the familiar *tú*. But sometimes on the way out he would give me a wink, as if to say, you and I are buddies, Junior.

In the middle of the patio, next to Vargas's room, stood a tall mango tree girded by a small stone bench. One day when I was nine or ten, one of the maids climbed up into the tree to pick some mangoes; sitting on the bench, I sneaked a look up her dress. Vargas caught me looking and called up to Aselia, "Hey, see what Junior is doing!" Aselia laughed and said, "*Déjalo que mire que eso es bueno*"—"Let him look, it's good for him"—and kept right on picking mangoes. I cannot say now exactly what, if anything, I saw. I suspect that my recollection of Aselia's white panties, with strands of curly black hair peeking out from under the elastic, has been embroidered with subsequent fantasies. A few years later, in Miami, many were the adolescent daydreams I sun around the general theme of "maid in the mango tree." Proust had his madeleines; I have my mangoes. To this day I cannot bite into the pulp of this juicy fruit without thinking of Aselia's undies. This is one memory I did not repress.

I'm surprised by how much I can recollect of our life in Cuba, once I put my mind to it. Perhaps, unlike my brother Pepe, I don't need to travel to Havana to visit our house. The floor plan I drew for myself contains renderings of the furnishings in nearly every room, including the wine cellar that was tucked away in the garage. If I can do this for our Cuban home, perhaps I could also reconstruct other segments of my childhood—Constantina's house, my other grandmother's apartment, the Casino Español beach club, the park on the corner, the Miramar hotel where we spent out summers. It may be that I can draw a similar plan of shadowy La Salle, which in turn might jog my recollections of teachers and classmates. Perhaps the Cuban boy that I was isn't lost, as I have often thought, only stowed away somewhere in my mind's attic, like useless furniture. Except that he's far from useless.

It was a mistake for me to believe that, once in the United States, that boy no longer mattered. Because for years I did not look back, my faculty for recollection atrophied. Since I did not think that my Cuban past could help me live my American present, I did little to nourish those memories. Growing up in Miami, I didn't often stop to reflect about our life in Cuba—even though that life was only a few years away, and even though my parents talked about it all the time. Growing up among Cubans, growing up Cuban, I was quickly losing touch with that part of my biography that unfolded in Cuba. To me it seemed as if my real life began on the ferry. The Florida Channel was my birth canal; debarking in Key West was a birth, delivery as well as deliverance. Had I ever really lived in Cuba? Had my parents really owned a house in the Reparto Kohly? Were my brothers and I really being groomed to take over the *almacén?* Cuba was the premise, the promise, not the reality.

Although I continued to lave my native land and never stopped thinking of myself as an exile, my patriotism did not entail the survival of memory, as if I could be loyal to my homeland without remaining loyal to my past. Like an atheist who prays, I participated in exile rituals without truly believing in them. More than an exiled Cuban, I considered myself a Cuban exile. Exile was my essence, what I was most deeply and truly; the Cuban part was aleatory, a topographical accident. Somehow it seemed to me that my national origin derived from my exile status, and not the other way around. I didn't sufficiently acknowledge the obvious fact that I was Cuban long before I became an exile.

It has taken me too many years to learn that there are continuities that transcend time and place and language. Exile explains but does not define me. The Cuban child is the father of the American man. I cannot understand most things about myself unless I honor that child. I cannot live without me. It's not a question of eliminating ambiguities, but of grasping them; not a question of dropping fractions, but of integrating them into a whole. A strong and stable sense of identity does not come easy for people who are forced to leave their country and straddle cultures. On his fifty-fifth birthday, an uncle of mine wrote a note to my mother asking her who he was; I wasn't that much different. Although I understand the reasons why I put away my past, I was wrong to think that, absent the material trappings, I no longer needed who I had been. Take away the house and the Cadillacs, and you still have the kid who lived and rode in them. Take away nimble Vargas, and I still wanted to do the *cha-cha.*

Take away naughty Aselia, and I still yearned to grow up into a Cuban man. That boy on the dock is not a phantom. In truth, he is perhaps *mi yo más mío*, the part of me that is most me.

Two
A Crash Course in Americana

Miami, 1960-61

When we got off the ferry on the morning of October 25, we were met by my parents' friends Arturo and Orquídea. Arturo was a *comisionista*, a sales rep for American food companies. In January 1959, when Castro took over, he and his wife had been in the United States on business, and they had decided to stay in Miami rather than go back to Cuba. While we drove over the mile-long bridges that connect the Florida Keys to the mainland, my father and his friend took stock of the situation. Arturo talked about the rumors that a U.S.-sponsored invasion was imminent. My father wanted to find a place to stay for a few weeks until the situation in Cuba became clearer. Sitting between the two men in the front seat of the car, I listened quietly to their conversation and wondered whether my father would be part of the invasion.

The Leamington in Downtown Miami was a modest, four-story hotel that had been built in the 1920s. The sand-colored building with the maroon trimmings stood on Northeast First Street across from the Greyhound bus station, only a short walk from Gesu Catholic Church, Bayfront Park, and the soon-to-be-famous Tower of Liberty, which housed the immigration and naturalization offices. My parents rented two connecting rooms on the second floor, one for my brothers, my sister, and me, and the other one for them. In a few days we would be joined at the hotel by other family members—my two grandmothers, various cousins and aunts and uncles, and several sets of godparents and their children. Although there must also

27

have been Americans staying at the Leamington, for a while most of the guests seemed to be Cubans I knew from Havana.

Once at the Leamington, we fell into a routine. Every morning my mother and my aunt Mary would take a group of us children to the corner drugstore for breakfast; then we would walk to Gesu Church for mass, return to the hotel and play in the lobby for a while, have sandwiches or a hamburger for lunch (in those days you could buy a hamburger at the Royal Castle on Flagler Street for a dime), and spend the afternoon at Bayfront Park, which we called *el parque de las palomas,* Pigeon Park. In the evenings, while the grown-ups gathered in the lobby to talk about the invasion, the children played canasta or bingo in our rooms. Sometimes my uncle Mike would take some of the older children aside, sit down with us in a corner of the lobby, and pass the time away by explaining evolution. His favorite prehistoric ancestor, or at least the one I remember most vividly, was *Australopithecus Prometheus,* which he pronounced as if it were a Spanish word.

For my brothers, my sister, and me, our first couple of weeks of exile were a mix of boredom and bewilderment. Since the Leamington wasn't a resort hotel like the ones we were used to, there wasn't much to distract us from our parents' constant conversations about our uncertain future. Only a few days before, we had been rich Cubans; now we were homeless exiles. My father said that we couldn't stay at the Leamington indefinitely, since the little money he had in the bank would soon run out, but he wasn't sure what else to do. For a while he talked about going on to Crowley, Louisiana, where his rice-grower friends could get him a job. But what was the point of moving so far away when Castro's overthrow might be only days or weeks away? Old enough to realize that this trip wasn't just another vacation, I didn't know what it was. I remember that my sister, Mari, sometimes would start whimpering, "I want to go back to Kohly, I want to go back to Kohly"—the neighborhood in Havana where we lived.

After nearly a month at the Leamington, my father put a $1,900 down payment on a house near Coral Gables, in the area that Cubans later called *la sagüesera* (a hispanicization of "Southwest"), and which Americans came to know eventually as Little Havana. The house, previously owned by an elderly American couple, stood in the middle of a grid of identical two-story duplexes that had been erected after World War II. Although soon this whole area would be teeming with exiles, at the time, the only Cubans in the neighborhood lived down the block from us; our other neighbors were all working-class Americans who didn't seem to notice that their neighborhood was about to change complexion.

We moved into our new house on a Thursday; Monday morning, my brothers and I went off to the public school a few blocks away. We were about to enter a new world.

With a gymnasium and cafeteria, basketball and volleyball courts, and several wings of bright cinder-block classrooms, Dade Elementary was the picture-perfect suburban school from the 1950s. Unlike the austere, high-ceilinged rooms of the Cuban school I had just left behind, my sixth-grade classroom had several bulletin boards, a full-color world map, and pictures of famous Americans. In the front of the class, an American flag hung at an angle from the upper left-hand corner of the blackboard. On one side, large windows looked out on a little patio with a couple of picnic tables where we did our art projects; beyond the picnic tables was Douglas Road Park. Because the desks weren't nailed to the floor as they had been in Cuba, we moved them around according to the activity. I did not miss the dark corridors and shadowy courtyards of La Salle.

Mrs. Myers, my sixth-grade teacher, was fiftyish, tall and wiry, with short reddish hair and very thin lips that she tried to disguise by smearing them with lipstick. She wore pale short-sleeved blouses and circle skirts with flowered prints. A devout Presbyterian, she would come in every Monday and begin the week by summarizing the sermon she had heard in church the previous day. Because she was the first woman teacher I'd ever had, at first I didn't know what to make of her. She once stopped in the middle of one of her warmed-over sermons to ask if anyone in the class would prefer not to listen to it. Understanding her question as an honest inquiry rather than a veiled threat, I was the only kid to raise his hand, and as a result spent the rest of the morning in the cafeteria. Unlike the La Salle Brothers in Cuba, Mrs. Myers knew nothing about my family and seemed uninterested in finding anything out. Her job was to teach me and the other students, which she did conscientiously. At the time, I thought her crotchety and cold, but now I realize that, like many Americans, she lived in compartments, and teaching was just one of them. All I knew of her life outside school was that she went to church on Sundays; all she knew about mine is that we had just arrived from Cuba fleeing communism. Maybe that's all she needed to know.

Although in a few years most children at Dade Elementary would be exiles, in November 1960 I was the only Cuban in my class. When I wasn't trying to act interested in Mrs. Myers's Monday-morning sermonizing, I absorbed American culture. In civics I read the U.S. Constitution; in history I found out about the Boston Tea Party and Paul Revere; in English I learned to diagram sentences; in music I memorized the words to "The Twelve Days of Christmas" and "Far Away Places" (some of my classmates must have thought I came from a faraway place, but this didn't occur to me). The one subject I actively disliked was current events, which required a group of us to put on a newscast every two weeks. Every other Friday we set up a row of chairs at the front of the class and took turns acting as newscasters. Someone did news, someone else did sports, someone else did the weather; it was my bad luck to have to report on the Teamsters. Since I hadn't the slightest idea who or what the Teamsters were, come Thursday evening I would pore over whatever story I had found in the *Miami News* that week. On Friday morning I was a nervous wreck, my bowels boiled and my hands trembled, but when my turn came I regurgitated the story back to the class word for word, sentence for sentence, all the while not understanding a thing. After my first time, Mrs. Myers went out of her way to be complimentary. "Listen, class," she said, "I want you to notice how much effort Gustavo put into his presentation." She didn't know what a superhuman effort it was. I must have given a half dozen reports on the Teamsters, and throughout those months I never realized that the Teamsters were a trade union; whatever it was they did in those days, to me it seemed shady, and I thought they were gangsters.

For the most part, however, classes went smoothly for me in sixth grade, especially since I never had the painful experience, common to so many immigrant children, of being thrown into a classroom full of people who speak a strange, unintelligible language. For me and my brothers, as for other Cuban exiles, English may have been foreign, but it wasn't strange. As Havana's unofficial second language, English permeated my childhood. We watched American movies, drove American cars, consumed American products, and listened to rock-

and-roll music. In school we had studied English since the first grade; at home my aunt Mary gave Pepe and me weekly lessons, which I loathed but which improved my fluency. Since my grandfather Firmat had been a consul in the United States, my mother fancied that she spoke English like a native, which she didn't really, but she spared no opportunity to flaunt her considerable fluency. She spoke English in the car, at the beach, over the dinner table. When she wanted to speak to my father without being understood by the servants, she resorted to English (he always replied in Spanish). Already in Cuba my brothers and I were being trained to become American; without knowing it, our parents were grooming us for exile.

As a result, my English was good enough for me to get by in school without much difficulty. Although my pronunciation was atrocious (it's not that good even today), I understood everything that was said, knew the names of most things, and was able to put words together into simple sentences. My language problems at Dade Elementary were of another sort, not cognitive but auditory. I understood Mrs. Myers well enough; the problem was I couldn't hear her. Used to loud, excitable Cuban voices, I experienced exile initially as hearing loss. Making things worse, since I had started the year late, my desk was in the back row. Even though I craned my neck and concentrated as hard as I could, I missed much of what she said. Straining to read Mrs. Myers's brightly painted lips, I found myself in a world where things went without saying or were uttered *sotto voce*, a world of understatement, of polite whispers and diffident silences. When I spoke up in class, which I didn't do often, my nervous rat-a-tat-tat delivery shattered the quiet like a drumroll. I could hear myself loud and clear (or rather, too loud and not clear enough), but Mrs. Myers hardly at all.

Because of her barely audible monotone, English first took hold of me through the eyes, not the ears. The compound-complex sentences I learned to diagram made a much deeper impression than the muffled sounds I heard around me. Words on a printed page stayed with me longer than fragments of conversations. Although I didn't like to read, I read better than I heard. Even now I tend to think of English as a speechless language, a Sanskrit, an arabesque of silent signs. Spanish is for the voice, it resonates in my eardrum; English speaks to the inner ear, its rhythms and cadences are the noiseless rustle of unheard melodies. Although I now make a living teaching Latin

American literature, on the written page the English language moves me in a way that Spanish never has. I find English prose smooth, elastic, capable of shades of expression that the Spanish does not allow. If my life depended on a sentence, I would write it in English. But switch from the page to the podium, and I become Spanish-dominant, a Cuban conquistador. When it comes to giving voice to my silent thoughts, I'm far more at home in my mother tongue. Even when I'm relaxed and rested, American words often stick to my mouth like mounds of molasses. Yet in Spanish my diction is flawless; there's no *r* I can't trill, no consonant cluster I can't conquer. If my life depended on a spoken sentence, I'd die if I couldn't speak it in Spanish.

Learning to live in English, I also had to get used to the new sound of my name. Some names translate, others don't, and Gustavo is one of those that don't. "Goose-tai-vough," Mrs. Myers would say, replacing the short, flat Spanish syllables with voluptuous American vowels. In her soft but unwarm voice my name became elongated, languorous, not a kid's name like Tommy or Pete, but the name of some Latin lover like Ricardo or Fernando. Taking it slow, laboring over every syllable, Mrs. Myers needed forever to get the whole word out: "Goose . . . tai . . . vough." Wishing desperately that I had a commonplace American name, I soon started going by "Gus," which I used for several years but eventually came to hate, because it struck me as one-third of a name. The omitted syllables ached like missing limbs. Render Gustavo as Gus, and most of who I am gets lost in translation.

Who doesn't want to have a comfortable relation with his name? I know that one reason I'll never be entirely American is that my name doesn't have an adequate equivalent in English. Having to choose in my daily life between a gloomy Gus and an unctuous Gustavo, I opt for the latter, which means that I'm always having to explain my name. To the day I die, I'll be the bugbear of bank tellers and telephone operators. Add to the mix my compound last name (patronym Pérez plus matronym Firmat), season it with an accent, and I become alphabet soup. Gustavo Pérez Firmat—can you say it? Do you know where the stresses go? How would you index me? A few days ago I received an unsolicited credit card in the mail that bore the name "Gus P. Fi." Talk about chopping off syllables as if they were limbs! Semper Fi, that's me.

Aside from occasional tongue twistings, I actually thrived in Mrs. Myers's cold hands. Exile had brought me a special kind of freedom. At Dade Elementary, for the first and only time in our lives, my brother Pepe and I walked ourselves to school. After school, he went back home and I headed for the park or the Boys Club, where I stayed until nightfall. In Cuba no kid in my family was allowed to walk to school, much less roam the streets. In fact, most things public were off limits to us in Havana. We didn't ride public transportation, didn't bathe at public beaches, didn't play in public parks, and certainly didn't go to public schools, which were for poor people. Although my life in Havana was crowded with cousins and friends, it had transpired exclusively in that middle realm between the public and the private that we call domestic. Kids who played in the streets and kids who walked to school were *chusmas,* while we were *personas decentes,* and decent people did not use public facilities, get mixed up in politics, or make friends with *chusmas,* even if they lived down the block.

Once in the United States, these proscriptions necessarily eased, partly because my mother no longer had the leisure to supervise us closely, and partly because she believed that *chusmería* was less prevalent in America. Within certain limits, we were on our own and we made the most of it. Although I sometimes felt isolated wandering the streets all by myself, I was happy to trade solitude for latitude. I especially enjoyed sneaking past the houses of the two girls I had a crush on, whom I had secretly followed home from school one day. As I hurried by their homes, they would be sitting on the steps or playing in the yard, looking exceedingly beautiful in their shorts and sleeveless blouses.

Jocelyn, with straight brown hair held in a ponytail that went down to her waist, was a preteen *femme fatale:* haughty, inaccessible, disdainful toward all suitors, or at least toward me. She was the kind of girl that a few years later my Cuban buddies would dub *una yegua americana,* an American mare, a term of reverence that probably originated in the fact that some of these girls were taller than we were. No matter what you did to get her attention, a *yegua americana* never gave you the time of day. Push her, and she would kick. That was Jocelyn. In my mind's eye, she's always wearing beige Capri slacks and a white sleeveless blouse. She has hazel eyes, full lips, and I probably would have sold my parents to the communists for a peck on the cheek.

Brigitte was more approachable but less seductive. With rabbit teeth and short blond hair, she always acted like somebody's cousin (which she was, Pete Apeland's). Although neither one was developed (Mrs. Myers wasn't either, for that matter), both were excruciatingly desirable. Although I never got to know Jocelyn at all, Brigitte used to call me Speedy Gonzalez. I took this to mean that she was in love with me and I became her silent suitor. The romantic high point of our muted relationship was picking her name in the Valentine's Day drawing.

Retracing my steps thirty years later, I'm struck by how close my old haunts really are. Our house—where my parents still live—is only four or five blocks from the school, and the school another four or five blocks from the Boys Club. But in those days a solo journey of only a couple of blocks turned into a dangerous, exciting adventure. Returning home at dusk, I saw myself as an explorer discovering uncharted territory. One wrong turn and I would end up hopelessly lost. In Havana I had to play hide-and-seek inside our patio; but in Miami there were open grassy spaces everywhere—at Dade Elementary, at the Boys Club, at Douglas Road Park. Although I lacked many friends, I was a good athlete and had plenty of teammates for our games of baseball, basketball, and football. For the first time my house had a lawn, one of the grand compensations of exile. I found a spot where the ground was raised a little and, pretending that the little mound was a base, I slid into it over and over until I left a patch of bald earth two yards long and a yard wide. When I wasn't at the park or the Boys Club, I spent my days running up and down our yard, tearing up the grass, imagining that I was scoring the winning run at Yankee Stadium.

But my love affair with Americana never did make me a *cubano arrenpentido*, a renegade Cuban. Even at the height of my all-American, eager *Leave It to Beaver* phase, I remained fiercely attached to my homeland, at least once arousing Mrs. Myers's wrath. Each morning in school we had to recite the pledge of allegiance. However American I may have been in other ways, this was something that my *cubanito* self wasn't about to do. I had just left Cuba a few weeks earlier; I wasn't about to pledge allegiance to another country. Since I sat at the back of the class, at the beginning my defiance went unnoticed. But when my seat was moved forward to improve my hearing, I could no longer hide. The good news was that now I could hear Mrs. Myers; the bad news was that now she could see and hear me. One morning Mrs. Myers took me aside and asked why I wasn't joining the rest of the class in the pledge. In my fairly broken English I replied that since I was Cuban I couldn't pledge allegiance to any other flag but my own. She insisted, I resisted. As a result, I spent some more time in the cafeteria. She insisted again, I kept right on resisting. Soon she realized that the punishment wasn't working and that I couldn't afford to spend all my mornings in the cafeteria.

To break the standoff, Nena and Gustavo were called in. At the time, my parents didn't pay much attention to my schooling—what did a few months spent in an American Public School matter?—but they didn't want any trouble either, because trouble was for *chusmas*. It was embarrassing to be summoned to school because of your son's misconduct, something that had never happened in Havana, where I had always been a model student. The conference took place in the little patio outside the classroom, with Mrs. Myers, my parents, and me sitting at one of the picnic tables. All business, Mrs. Myers explained the problem to my parents, and then offered me an olive branch: I didn't have to speak the words of the pledge so long as I placed my hand over my heart in order not to seem disrespectful. Relived but unbowed, I reciprocated with a palm frond: yes, I could do that without betraying my principles. Oh, the art of compromise. Oh, American women. They will bring you to your knees, but they won't make you grovel.

The next day Mrs. Myers explained to the class why I wasn't joining them in the pledge. American teachers, unlike their Cuban counterparts, believed in explanations. "Goose-tai-vough loves Cuba very much," she said in that whisper of hers, "and since he plans to go back to his country soon, he doesn't think he should pledge allegiance to our flag." She went on to explain that I would show respect for the flag by putting my hand over my heart with the rest of the class. The compromise worked like an *azabache* (an Afro-Cuban good-luck charm), and Mrs. Myers and I resumed our peaceful coexistence.

In the weeks that followed our confrontation, standing in the front row with my lips pressed tightly together, I listened to the rest of the class intone the pledge and felt vaguely heroic. I too was doing my bit for Cuba's liberation. I too was a patriot. Thinking about the incident now, what strikes me is the powerful poetry of the sentence I could not say as a child, a sentence that as an adult I'm able to utter without feeling too guilty. The naturalization oath, which I finally took in 1977, is not half as moving, for it's essentially a negative covenant. Haunted by the specter of treason, the oath is punctilious to the point of awkwardness. The neophyte citizen does not so much swear as forswear: "I hereby declare on oath that I absolutely and entirely renounce and abjure all allegiance and fidelity to any foreign prince, potentate, state, or citizen." The pledge of allegiance is far more graceful, for it doesn't burden itself with technical distinctions between renouncing and abjuring, allegiance and fidelity, prince and potentate. It consists only of one of those plain and lovely English-language sentences that sing to my inner ear. It's not legalistic prose, but lyrical poetry:

> I pledge allegiance to the flag
> of the United States of America,
> and to the country for which it stands,
> one nation, under God, indivisible,
> with liberty and justice for all.

Although reciting the pledge still makes me a little uncomfortable, I am moved by these words. I love the simple, sentimental equation of flag and country. I love their insistence on oneness—one flag, one nation, one God. Most of all, I love how the pledge concludes in those two emphatic, ringing monosyllables: for all. For all—to me that presupposes a people who occupy a common place, not an itinerant population of exiles. Someone who's lived his life wrapped in two flags and torn between two cultures and countries can't help yearning for an undivided allegiance. Give me one flag, one nation, one language, one geography. Give me a pledge of allegiance that I can recite without a guilty conscience.

When the Bay of Pigs invasion took place, in April 1961, I had been in Mrs. Myers's class for five months. Awakened before dawn by the scratchy sounds of a shortwave radio, I opened my eyes to my father and his cousin Joseíto, next to me an my brothers in the still-dark Florida room, trying to monitor broadcasts from the island. At this point the invasion was only a few hours old, but everyone in Miami already knew about it. For months rumors of a military action against Fidel had been circulating. Young men kept disappearing from the streets, and it was an open secret that they were going to Central America for military training. So when the day of the invasion arrived, exiles were ready with their shortwave radios and their Cuban passports.

I went off to school as usual. Going toward my classroom, at the end of the hall I sighted Carlitos Reyes, the other Cuban boy in my class, who had arrived in the States only a couple of months earlier. We ran toward each other and fell into a tight hug. Not doubting for a minute that the invasion would triumph, we celebrated, slapping each other on the back, shaking each other by the shoulders. I don't think I had ever felt a less unmixed happiness than I did at that moment. It was better than birthdays, better than Christmas, better than sliding home. Because Fidel's fall accorded with our sense of how the world worked, because it was the right thing to happen, because we kept hearing from our parents that it would happen any moment, we rejoiced without reserve. Of course the invasion would succeed. Of course this was our last day of school at Dade Elementary. It didn't occur to us to hedge against disappointment.

Carlitos whispered that his older brother was a member of the exile brigade. For an instant a cloud darkened our euphoria, but it quickly passed. We reassured each other that Ernesto would be all right, our good spirits came back, and then it was time to say good morning to Mrs. Myers, who must have been wondering what on earth had gotten into these usually quiet *cubanitos*. A few minutes later, as the class stood up to recite the pledge of allegiance, I thought I was listening to these words for the last time.

That afternoon I skipped the Boys Club and rushed home. When I got there, the reports from Cuba weren't good, though hopes still ran high. The Brigada 2506 seemed to be on the verge of defeat (how could this be?), but there was still the possibility, indeed the likelihood, that President Kennedy would take action—provide air cover, send reinforcements, invade the island. But within a matter of days it became clear that the expedition had failed miserably and that, regardless of what had been planned or promised, no help from the United States was forthcoming. Carlitos and I had celebrated too soon. My friend's brother Ernesto was wounded and taken prisoner.

Because my parents expected to go back to Cuba at any moment, all that year my brothers and I were pretty much left to fend for ourselves. We weren't really on vacation, but often it felt that way, for our lives had not yet settled into a routine. Inside our house, there was no escaping our uncertain situation; my father didn't have a permanent job yet, my mother strained to make ends meet, and relatives and friends kept arriving from Havana. But once I walked out the door in the morning, the worries of home and homeland dropped away. I could do what I wanted, and mostly what I wanted was to be an American kid like everybody else.

Had we been living somewhere other than Miami, my Americanization may well have continued unimpeded, and today I'd be writing a different book. But after a few months of benign neglect, and particularly after the failure of the Bay of Pigs invasion, my parents realized that we needed to make a life in Miami, however ephemeral that life might prove to be. This meant trying to recreate in exile the habits and routines of our life in Havana. As a result, my experience with public schools was short-lived. The following year Pepe, Carlos, and I were yanked from Dade Elementary and put into the sheltered and more familiar environment of St. Hugh, a parochial school where some of our classmates came from families we had known in Cuba. Instead of walking to school, we were driven by my mother, who every morning in the car made us repeat a prayer to Saint Thomas Aquinas, the patron saint of students and scholars. I never saw Jocelyn or Brigitte or Mrs. Myers again.

THREE

Mooning over Miami

Little Havana, 1960s and beyond

Our duplex in Miami was nothing like the spacious house in the Reparto Kohly. The downstairs apartment, which had a living room, a kitchen, two tiny bedrooms, and a Florida room, became our home away from our homeland. My two brothers and I slept on couches in the Florida room; Abuela Martínez, my mother's mother, occupied one of the bedrooms and my parents and my sister the other. At the beginning my other grandmother, Constantina, lived upstairs by herself, but soon the upstairs apartment had to be rented for the income it provided, and she moved in with the rest of us. Nena bought three stand-up metal closets with which she partitioned the Florida room. The boys slept on one side, Abuela Martínez slept on the other, and Constantina got Abuela Martínez's bedroom. (The reason was not favoritism: Abuela Martínez was slight and nimble, whereas Constantina was as big as her name was long; she tipped the scales at 220 pounds.)

For several years the 800-square-foot apartment provided a cramped but cozy home for my parents, two old ladies who were seldom on speaking terms, four boys between the ages of seven and sixteen (Carlos Rego, the teenage son of friends who had stayed in Cuba, also lived with us), and my sister, who spent her childhood sleeping on the floor next to my parents' bed. In Miami our can of *gusanos* became a *lata* of Spanish sardines. Meals were served in shifts on a pink dinette set (keep the two *viejas* away from each other!), and we all had to share a single bathroom, which made it difficult for me to think about Aselia too much. Although the master bedroom of our Havana house was probably as big as the entire Miami apartment, the conviction that these makeshift arrangements were transitory made the cramped conditions easier to take. In our hearts and minds, we were still a well-to-do family of *almacenistas* temporarily out of money. We weren't really poor, we were just slumming. As my mother always reminded us, we were exiles, not immigrants. Because I was the eldest of the four children, I was the one most likely to remember how things had been in Cuba, but somehow I didn't feel deprived. I noticed the contrast between Cuba and Miami, but I put my mind on other things—such as the New York Yankees and the girls in my classes. I didn't even pay much attention to the differences between our living situation and what I saw on the TV shows that we watched avidly—*Leave It to Beaver, Ozzie and Harriet, My Three Sons, The Donna Reed Show* (at some point in my early adolescence, Aselia picking mangoes was toppled in my fantasy life by Shelley Fabares singing "Johnny Angel").

Like most teenagers, I was more concerned with the state of my face than with the state of the world. I went to school, played sports, got crushes on girls, and learned about sex from Carlos Rego, a steady old hand if there ever was one. The first movie I remember seeing in the States was *Please Don't Eat the Daisies,* which my mother loved because she identified with the Doris Day character, a harried, sometimes bewildered, sometimes bemused, child-besieged housewife and mother. I liked the picture because I thought our household was like the one in the movie—chaotic but happy.

It was a point of pride with my father that he never sought or received assistance from the Cuban Refugee Center. During the sixties El Refugio, as the Cubans called it, provided food, clothing, and a modest stipend for the thousands of Cuban exiles who had arrived in this country penniless. Since we had many friends who received more food than they needed, however, my mother's cupboards were always filled with powdered milk, Spam, cement-tough blocks of American cheese, and other army-surplus delicacies. Nothing if not resourceful, Nena did wonders with these foods. A staple of the Cuban table is breaded steak, *bistec empanizado.* But meat, of course, was unaffordable (no more *bistí!*), so Nena cut the rolls of Spam into inch-thick slices, rolled them in bread crumbs, and served us the next best thing. Not that she actually told us what we were eating; when we asked, she said we were having *bistec empanizado.* Soon we knew not to expect breaded steak to taste like breaded steak. Spam became the meat for all seasonings. Since it took the place of everything from hamburger to venison, the street name for it was simply *carne del Refugio,* meat from the Refugee Center. In addition to Spam steaks, Nena prepared Spam meatballs, Spam lasagna, Spam hamburgers, and Spam *picadillo* (hash). In our school lunches she packed Spam sandwiches; for birthday parties she made Spam croquettes. Other products brought out the same creativity: with peanut butter she made cookies, shakes, and turnovers; with powdered milk and eggs, custard, cupcakes, and crème caramel.

Only years later, thinking back, did it dawn on me that ours was something other than an average middle-class household. At the time, everyone we knew lived the same way. Everyone ate Spam steaks. Everyone pinched pennies. Everyone was sardined into small houses or apartments. It was not until I was in high school that I had a friend with a room of his own, and it was not until Pepe went away to college in 1969, when I was already in college, that I had a room of my own. Those families lucky enough to have their own transportation drove old beat-up Chevys or Fords. Everyone else took the bus. I thought of ourselves as privileged, since my father, who found a job as a car salesman, bought a new Rambler station wagon that my mother drove for many years. She was the envy of the neighborhood.

During those early years of exile, Cuban Miami was a small, tightly knit community of families struggling hard to make ends meet. Since we knew we were better than our circumstances, there was no shame or embarrassment at being poor. For the grown-ups, the principal goal was to make do until the return to the beloved island. For the children, America was an adventure. Almost every week we went to the airport to meet relatives or friends arriving from Cuba. Those were the days when one could go up on the roof of the terminal and wave and call out to the people getting off the plane onto the tarmack. We were there the day my old teachers, the Christian Brothers from La Salle, arrived en masse. After greeting them at the airport, a throng of former students and their parents went to the hotel in Downtown Miami where the Brothers were going to stay. In the lobby of the hotel, surrounded by small groups of people, each of the Brothers held court in his black suit with the white ecclesiastical collar. I remember seeing Hermano Victoriano, the feared vice-principal, describing how the Catholic schools were shut down and the horrors of the Revolution. As always, the bad news was good news, for it filled us with hope and anticipation.

Oh, the good old exile days. It was exciting sleeping three or four to a room, having people come and go all the time, packing everybody into the Rambler and going to the Tropicaire drive-in on a steamy summer night. In spite of the language barrier, school in the States was easier than it had been at La Salle. And the classes were full of girls! (My Cuban school had been for boys only.) Falling in love with the *americanas*, which Rego and I did with clockwork regularity, was a thrill. Unlike many of the Cuban girls, they would actually let you hold their hand and kiss them.

Because at the time my brother Pepe was barely a teenager and Carlos and Mari were still in elementary school, I gravitated toward Carlos Rego, who became my mentor and partner in crime. Since there was already a Carlos in the family, I anglicized his name to "Reeg" or "Reego." He called me gus or Junior. Rego and I played sports together, double-dated, went to beach parties at Crandon Park, slow-danced, twisted, and frugged. He went steady with Marti, a pretty blonde, and I hung out with her best friend, Nancy, who wasn't as cute or as curvy and sometimes had bad breath but, on the other hand, was interested and available. Even when Rego and I fought bitterly and didn't talk to each other for a couple of days, which sometimes happened, we had a good time. Once, in a dispute over who would mow the beloved lawn, I went after him with the rake; he retaliated by trying to cripple me with the Sears mower. In Cuba, had we had a lawn, which we didn't, neither one of us would have been asked to mow it, because that's what the servants and the gardeners were for.

When I entered ninth grade in 1963, La Salle High School in Southwest Miami already had many Cuban students, but it was still predominantly American. American kids starred on the sports teams, ran the student council, edited the newspaper and the yearbook. But by the time I became a senior, La Salle had metamorphosed into "Lah-Sah-yeh," an exile franchise of my old Havana academy, with some American Brothers and lay teachers, but also with some of the same Brothers and students from Cuba. At La Salle I had classmates whom I had known since the first grade in Cuba. My Spanish teacher in high school, Hermano Andrés, was the same teacher who had taught third grade in Cuba; he now taught Spanish because he didn't know any English. Elio the bus driver, who drove the La Salle varsity teams to their games, had driven a bus at the Cuban school.

The chemistry teacher at La Salle, Hermano Ramón, was another transplant from Havana. Everyone called him Plátano, because his curved, elongated body and head made him look like a banana. Unlike the other Cuban Brothers, Plátano was a loner who always wore a pained, doleful expression on his face. I never saw him without his black habit. If you ran into Plátano in the hall, he would acknowledge your existence by lifting his drooping head an inch or two and curling his lips ever so slightly, but without stopping or saying a word. Inside the classroom, he was all business—I should say, all chemistry, a subject he loved but that he didn't seem to have mastered. What happened to the Spanish Armada sometimes happened to him—he was defeated by the elements. Although Plátano set up every experiment carefully and deliberately, at times the anticipated chemical reaction did not take place, or worse, an unanticipated one did. When something blew up or fizzled out, he was just as startled as the rest of us, although he quickly regained his composure. He accepted failure with a kind of resignation, as if it were a consequence of exile. The sad expression on his long face seemed to say, "In Cuba sulfur and magnesium would not have reacted this way; in Cuba the elements did what they were supposed to." If anyone made fun of the botched experiment, he would issue a reprimand in Spanish, the only time he lapsed from his heavily accented but fluent English. "*Oye, chico,*" he would say sharply to the culprit, "we didn't come to this country to fool around."

As more and more exiles arrived in Miami, La Salle became known as the "Cuban" high school in the diocese. Although many Americans still attended—kids with names such as Perantoni and Pascawicz and MacSwiggan and Koziol—the dominant culture of the school quickly changed. At the sock hops and dances in the school cafeteria, even if we began with the music of Wilson Pickett, we ended up with Beny Moré. Sooner or later, someone would start a conga line. Although many of us went by the American version of our names—Gus (Pérez), Willie (Díaz), Charlie (Castillo), Joe (Martínez), Manny (Álvarez)—we mostly spoke Spanish and considered ourselves unassailably Cuban. Even as we absorbed American culture, we tended to "Cubanize" things we came in touch with. In football a tackle was *un palo* (the same word was used to denote a drink, a home run, and sexual intercourse); in basketball a blocked shot was *un tapón*. A nerd was *un mechero,* a drunk *un curda,* and a good-looking American girl was a *yegua* (but Cuban ones were *jebitas*). The school's signature cheer was one I had learned in Cuba: *"Bon-bon-chíe-chíe-chíe./Bon-bon-chíe-chíe-chá./ Lah-Sah-yeh, Lah-Sah-yeh, ¡rrah-rrah-rrah!"* The emotional high points of each basketball game came when the cheerleaders, who were American, started into a *bon-bon-chíe.* (Although many girls in our sister school, Immaculata, were also Cuban, they considered it vaguely slutty to parade in front of a crowd in a tight sweater and short skirt.) It was wonderful to see perky Catholic girls like Marti and Nancy lead a throng of rowdy Cuban teenagers in a *bon-bon-chíe.* Here we were, Cuban exiles in a foreign country, playing a sport like football or basketball and screaming in Cuban, being led by American cheerleaders in the same cheers we would have chanted in Havana. For the duration of the cheer, it seemed that we had never left, that our lifelines had not veered to the north. Screaming *bon-bon-chíe* in the Columbus High gym, where the La Salle Royals played home games, we were defying distance, denying discontinuity.

If the other students resented the *bon-bon-chíe,* I didn't notice. They seemed to launch into it with the same gusto that we did. What I remember is the American parents and kids and teachers looking upon us with a mixture of amusement and benevolence. Since we were as smart, as Catholic, as good-looking, and often as athletic as the Americans, there didn't seem to be any reason for condescension or disdain. If anything, *we* pitied the Americans because they weren't lucky enough to have been born Cuban. The only difference between the two groups was that the American kids had more money and nicer homes. They drove Mustangs and GTOs and lived in places like Coral Gables or South Miami; we lived in Little Havana and felt fortunate if we got our hands on a 1956 Olds. I search my memory now and I cannot come up with one single example of feeling ostracized or discriminated against because I was Cuban. I recall coming back in the team bus from a football or basketball game with everybody—at least I thought it was everybody—singing Cuban songs like "Los Elefantes" and "Guantanamera." Not once did I hear any of the Americans complain about the loud Cubans or their music. One Cuban guy on the team, Carlos Ziegenhirt (we called him Ziggy), had a beautiful tenor voice. When we got tired of singing in unison, Ziggy would serenade us with *boleros*. The darkened bus seemed a perfect setting for his romantic melodies. While Ziggy sang, our imaginations roamed free. Johnny Mathis had nothing on him.

At La Salle *los americanos* and *los cubanos* went their separate ways, but without friction or hostility. Each group had its customs, its coteries, its hangouts, its language. When we partied, we partied among ourselves. When we fought, we fought among ourselves. Although the Cubans sometimes dated American girls (the converse—a *cubana* with an *americano*—was very rare, because most Cuban girls required chaperones), almost everyone I hung out with eventually settled into a same-culture *novia* (girlfriend). Sometimes Cuban teenagers did American things—went to beach parties and drive-ins. Other times we hewed to old-country mores and learned the *danzón*—a ballroom dance—so that we could perform it at the *quinces,* the traditional coming-out ball for Cuban teenage girls. The convention of sticking to our own kind was not formal or explicit, and nobody ever told me or any of my friends to socialize with Cubans or stay away from Americans. It was just how we liked it.

The Chinatowns and Little Italys of large American cities suggest that most immigrants, upon first arriving in the U.S., tend to stick together. We were no different. A clannish people, Cubans seek out other Cubans. Not surprisingly (given that we are islanders), we like to insulate ourselves. When I was at La Salle, the American girls were enticing but the *cubanitas* were more comfortable. Yes, the Cuban girls expected (and got) more attention and commitment, but in return they looked after you in ways that the American girls didn't. For every pretty blonde there was an equally pretty, dark-haired girl like Ana María, my *novia* of several years.

For most of us, the *americanas* were a lark, a hobby, a sometimes dangerous adventure in foreign relations. For a while during my senior year, my best friend was a guy called Grifolito (Cubans are big on diminutives—Grifolito was the younger of two brothers whose last name was Grifol). On Friday nights Grifolito and I would go to dances sponsored by the Police Benevolent Association. Held in an auditorium somewhere in South Miami and attended almost entirely by Americans, these dances provided happy hunting grounds for young Cuban charmers like us looking to meet and pick up *americanas,* an endeavor at which Grifolito excelled. Our word for picking up girls was *ligar,* literally to fasten or bind, and Grifolito was quite a *ligador.* In fact, he was a blonde-binding dynamo. I could never figure out Grifolito's secret—whether it was his clear complexion, his baby-blue eyes, his macho swagger, or his fearlessness—but whatever it was, it worked time after time. After the dances ended, I often had to wait in the car for half an hour while Grifolito, our Cuban goodwill-ambassador-in-exile, finished getting acquainted with his sweetheart for the night. On a good night, he didn't have to dance more than one or two songs before spending the rest of the evening outside, embracing a foreign culture.

One Friday I was milling around in the crowd, trying to hide from Grifolito the fact that I wasn't getting anywhere with any of the girls, when I brushed shoulders with some American guy. As usually happened with me, the brush led to a bump and the bump led to a face-off. Suddenly, I found myself surrounded by a horde of six-foot-tall, crew-cut, football-playing Charles Atlases. Although I was a football player myself—starting halfback on La Salle's varsity team, which won our conference my junior year—I was no match for my formidable gringo foes. Several inches short of six feet, I never could push my weight above 157 pounds, no matter how many barbells I lifted or how much food I ate (Spam isn't particularly rich in protein). Grifolito, who was heftier, came to my rescue, but the odds didn't look good for us. It would have been like the Spanish-American War all over again. I didn't mind rumbles, and the gang I belonged to (we called it a fraternity) started a few of them, but always against other Cubans, who may have been meaner or stronger than I was, but who weren't nearly as big as these action-figure types.

Just as Grifolito and I were about to get our army-surplus lunches handed back to us, I saw an apparition (remember, we were Catholic)—actually two apparitions—from my past, Pete Apeland and Buzzy Horne, who had been in Mrs. Myers's class at Dade Elementary and with whom I had played sports at the Boys Club. Although I hadn't run into them in years, I remembered Pete well, for he wasn't only the quarterback on our team but Brigitte Johnson's cousin as well. Pete and Buz had been short and skinny when we had played together in the 115-pound-and-under league, but as teenagers they had sprouted into muscle-bound behemoths. Pete was a full head taller than I and had a scar that ran from his forehead to his cheek (the result of a motorcycle accident), and Buzzy was even bigger. He looked like Ray Nietzsche with hair. When Pete spotted me, he pushed his way through the crowd, with Buzzy right behind. Getting between me and the guy I had bumped shoulders with, Pete told the guy, "Gus is a friend of mine. If you want to fight him, you're going to have to fight me first." God bless *americanos!* The Rough Riders backed off, no Cuban blood was spilled that night, and Grifolito and I gratefully went back to our pursuit of the American dream.

For better and for worse, Cubans face hardship lightly. Confronted with difficult times, we fall back on *relajo* or *choteo*, a type of humor that deals with life's adversities by mocking them. I'm sure you've heard the proverb, if life gives you lemons, learn to make lemonade. As soon as Cubans arrived in Miami, we started making lemonade in industrial quantities. A spoonful of *choteo* made the spam steaks go down. The *carne del Refugio* became the subject of endless jokes and stories, as did the *factorías* where many people had to work for subsistence wages. Just as my mother and her friends exchanged recipes for Spam and powdered milk, my father and his friends traded jokes about Fidel or life in exile. The Miami buses, notoriously untimely, became *la aspirina*—you took one every three hours. As *relajo* relaxed us, the town began to fill up with colorful characters. One man who had been a sergeant in Batista's army liked to walk the streets of Little Havana holding up a signed photograph of the ex-dictator; he became known as *el hombre del cuadro*, the man with the picture. A transvestite who hung out on Eighth Street was dubbed *La engañadora*, the deceiver, after the title of a fifties *cha-cha*. A woman nicknamed Beba de Cuba was famous for holding wild parties every May 20 to celebrate Cuba's day of independence. For the party Beba wrapped herself in a Cuban flag and tied her hands and feet. At around midnight, when Beba was good and tipsy, the partygoers would start the chant, "Beba, break the chains; Beba, break the chains." Beba would start to shake and shimmy and shudder until not only the chains but part of her clothing came off, symbolizing the liberation of Cuba.

As the sixties advanced into the seventies, Cubans began to take possession of the city, to make it our own in small but crucial ways.

Like Adam in paradise, we named. In some cases American place names were hispanicized. Not only did "Southwest" become *la sagüesera* but "Northwest" became *la norgüesera;* Miami Beach was simply *la playa.* Tony Key Biscayne became Hialeah by the Sea, after a working-class neighborhood at the western edge of Dade County, or more simply, *el cayo,* the key. In other instances Cuban names were imported, so that a popular apartment complex off Eighth Street was rebaptized Pastorita, a take-off on the name of Castro's minister of housing. The corner where Cuban men congregated to talk politics was dubbed La ONU, the U.N.; and the corner where they played dominoes became *el parque del dominó,* Domino Park. Crandon Park turned into *"palito* beach," since that's where teenagers went to make out *(palito* is Cuban slang for intercourse). The fact that the streets in Coral Gables already had Spanish names—Sevilla, Granada, Alcazar, Romano—offered a kind of confirmation that Miami had been destined all along to become a Hispanic city. By the early seventies so many neighborhoods had been taken over by Cubans that the longtime Miami residents began to display bumper stickers with the question, "Will the last American to leave please take the flag?"

It's hard to describe now, more than twenty years later, the bizarre yet comforting atmosphere of those years. We spent our days in the mode of crisis, hyped to a continuous state of alert. Like zealots on the eve of the millennium, Cuban exiles were certain that something was going to happen to Fidel at any moment. Talk of Cuba was constant, and constantly wistful, for *regreso* was always around the corner. Miami was like an Irish wake, with the same admixture of festiveness and grief, but with the difference that we expected the corpse to come back from the dead at any minute. By the end of the sixties the rest of the country was in the throes of turbulent social changes, but for us the only thing that mattered was Cuba. Even the war in Vietnam was relevant only insofar as it had an impact on U.S. policy toward Fidel. Even though most exiles supported the war, we were puzzled by it: why go halfway across the world to fight communism when you can fight it on your door-step? I wasn't anxious to get drafted and go to Vietnam, but I did sign up with Alpha 66, a paramilitary exile group that mounted raids to Cuba. (Since I had no prior military training, they never used me, but my nominal membership in this organization almost prevented me from becoming an American citizen a decade later.)

Inside our house, the radio was always tuned to one of the Cuban stations, where the political talk was relieved occasionally by an old song or two, or by a nostalgia program. Among the latter, one of the most popular was a call-in show featuring a man who had been a mailman in Havana. People would call in, give him an address, and ask him what building or landmark stood at that address. Sometimes they would give him the addresses of their own homes or places of business. The mailman usually knew the answer. I used to listen to this show with my grandmother Martínez, who herself had an impressive recall of Havana streets, and marveled at the mailman's freakish memory of the smallest details of the city's topography. The only time I remember him stumped was when a clever caller asked him what stood across from a certain building on the Malecón, the coast-side avenue that girds the city. After hesitating for a moment, the mailman named some monument, but it was not what the caller had in mind. Across from the Malecón, he informed the mailman, was the Atlantic Ocean.

Years later, when Cubans of my generation reached adulthood, this kind of program was ridiculed with the slogan "*Más música y menos bla-bla-blá*," "More music and less blab-blah-blah." But at the time, all we wanted was to hear about Cuba. Reports from the island were our life's blood. The radio on my father's night table was always set to Radio Reloj, a station that told the time every minute and in between summarized the news. As the announcer read the latest from Cuba, the seconds ticked away in the background. This went on without surcease hour after hour, day after day, month after month, year after year. Every morning my father woke to the sound of Radio Reloj droning in his ear, and every night he went to sleep the same way. It was eerie. Ticking away, Radio Reloj was like a time bomb set to explode at any moment, except that it never did. The one piece of news we all craved was never broadcast.

And yet each day brought new signs of the Revolution's deterioration. There would be rumors of an uprising outside the capital, or a recent arrival would share horror stories about food shortages or political repression, or the State Department would release a strongly worded statement about the Revolution. These rumors swept across Little Havana like hurricane gusts. Someone would call our house with a news flash and my father would in turn call his friends and relatives. Even though most likely it was a *bola,* a false alarm, the rumor bounced around unchecked. For years *bolas* of all shapes and sizes filled the Miami air, launched not only by ordinary citizens but by radio stations and the numerous exile tabloids, or *periodiquitos.* Since many *bolas* started out as practical jokes, *relajo* played a part here also. I doubt that there are any Cuban exiles who at one time or another have not received a call from a friend telling them, in an agitated voice, that Fidel is dead. And if you were the one who got the *bola* rolling, chances are that within the hour someone would phone *you* with the same rumor that you set in motion. My father got a kick out of doing this to my gullible aunt Cuca, who lived in New York and was therefore chronically starved for the latest exile gossip. When he called her with the *bola* that there had been a coup in Cuba, half an hour later someone else called my house with the news that Fidel was dead.

For years we lived like this, in booms and busts, having a ball with our *bolas* and grieving when they fell flat. Nourishment as well as narcotic, news from Cuba jolted us, made us buzz with anticipation, fed our hopes and blunted our frustrations. All this gossip helped us cope with exile, but it also diminished our need to move beyond it. Perhaps if we had been less prone to wishful thinking, we would have paid more attention to the American here and now; but instead, here and now collapsed into nowhere, and we lived dreaming about the island across the water.

Miami is a city of mirrors and mirages. Under the relentless Florida sun the ubiquitous chrome and glass splinter into myriad reflections. Barely touching the earth, the city floats in a sea of images, a swelter of illusions. In the sixties and seventies, when the return to Cuba was foremost on everyone's mind, hardly a few weeks went by without the arrival of a new savior. These monthly messiahs always promised the same thing: to lead us from the wilderness of the Everglades back to our Cuban paradise. Some of these men were honest and well-meaning, while others were crooks and opportunists. But one man, the illusionist par excellence, fits none of these labels. His may have been the greatest *bola* of all.

José Francisco Alabau Trelles was born in 1924 into a prominent family from the province of Cienfuegos. Graduating at the head of his class from the University of Havana Law School, he went back to Cienfuegos and opened a law practice. Soon he became involved in politics, appearing frequently on radio panels and contributing editorials to newspapers and magazines. He first came to national prominence in 1958, when as a magistrate in Havana, he indicted two of Batista's henchmen for the murder of four students. Always a devout Catholic, that same year he published a modern adaptation of the life of Jesus Christ, but he was destined to become another prophet without honor in his own country. When his indictments were quashed by Batista's minister of justice, Alabau went into exile. Returning to Cuba in 1959 right after the triumph of the Revolution, he was appointed by Fidel to the Cuban Supreme Court. Like many other early supporters of the Castro regime, Alabau Trelles quickly became disenchanted with Fidel's Marxist leanings and joined the thousands of Cubans already living in Miami.

In exile for a second time, Alabau Trelles remained active in Cuban politics. As a former justice on the Cuban Supreme Court, he was a figure of some prominence, and his name surfaced sporadically in newspaper columns and political gatherings. Joining the Republican Party in 1968, he campaigned for Nixon among Cuban exiles. By then he had formed a political organization called Movimiento Unitario Invasor (United Invasion Movement), and the scuttlebutt had it that he enjoyed Nixon's backing. His plan was to infiltrate Cuba and establish a provisional government in the expectation that the United States would recognize it and offer military assistance.

One morning in September 1971 Alabau Trelles showed up at a radio station in Little Havana wearing battle fatigues and a bloodied bandage around one arm. "Two nights ago," he began his broadcast, "forty soldiers of the United Invasion Movement disembarked on the southern coast of the province of Camaguey, where we occupied the town of Guayabal and killed more than thirty communist soldiers." He went on: "After completing our mission, we withdrew in perfect order and returned to the place from which we had come, whose name I cannot reveal, for obvious reasons. On our side we suffered only one casualty, José Rodríguez Zafra, who will forever remain in our memory as a martyr to our homeland. I myself was wounded in one arm by a piece of shrapnel." He concluded with an appeal to all Cuban exiles: "The end of the Cuban nightmare is at hand. With this heroic feat the Movimiento Unitario Invasor has begun the last stage of the war. Now is the time for all Cubans who love their country to join together in support of our cause!"

This stunning news was greeted with a mixture of euphoria and disbelief. If the attack occurred two days ago, on September 19, why did Alabau look like he had just gotten off the boat? And why had there been no *bolas* about the sortie beforehand? Cubans are notoriously bad at keeping secrets; we have many virtues, but discretion is not one of them. But Alabau's tale was too good to be false. After all, he came from a good family; he was educated and articulate; he had been a judge on the Supreme Court in Cuba; and he was friends with President Nixon.

To top it off, Alabau had pictures of the attack, which he distributed to the newspapers. The photographs showed a damaged building and a large cement mixer engulfed by flames. Could it be that Alabau, who was known as Frank to his friends, was indeed telling the truth? Perhaps the war for the liberation of Cuba had begun at last.

During the hours that followed Alabau's revelations, the denizens of Little Havana, my parents included, talked about nothing else. Although by then we had been in Miami for ten years, in some ways our life hadn't changed much. Pepe and I had already graduated from La Salle. After attending a local community college for two years, I was in my first semester at the University of Miami and living at home. Pepe had gotten a scholarship to New College in Sarasota, one of those progressive sixties institutions where the professors gave no grades and held class in their living rooms. Carlos was a junior at La Salle and Mari had just started at Immaculata. My mother was working as a secretary at St. Hugh and my father was still selling Datsuns at a dealership on Calle Ocho. Rego had moved with his parents to New Orleans and Constantina had gone back to the upstairs apartment. Abuela Martínez still lived with us, on the other side of the partition in the Florida room. By then she had gone almost completely blind, and we could hear her at night crashing into the metal closets looking for the way to the bathroom.

In a feat worthy of Fidel himself, Alabau stayed on the radio for nine hours straight, answering questions about the attack, making cryptic comments about future operations, and asking for support. The action became known as the Battle of Guayabal, after the town where it had taken place. I spent that evening listening to the radio with my father. Although Gustavo Sr. is not a talkative man, that night he was full of hopeful words about Cuba, about his *almacén* and the life we had left behind. There were rumors of other attacks. Alabau would not say for certain, but he hinted that more military operations were in the offing. Many people, my parents included, called in to the radio station with contributions; others, including me, wanted to know where to sign up to fight.

Then, as always, the *bola* burst. Two days after Alabau's supposed return from Cuba, one of the city's American newspapers published photos exactly like those that Alabau claimed to have taken at Guayabal. Some intrepid reporter had invaded a toy store in Little Havana, where he commandeered a Tonka truck and a miniature building. He doused them with lighter fluid and put a match to them. Wild! The photographs he took were indistinguishable from those of the ministry building and the cement mixer.

There were other problems with Alabau's account. His "military communiqué" claimed that the attack had occurred at one o'clock in the morning; yet in his photographs the truck and the building cast long shadows. And if one looked closely, some of the soldiers in the photographs weren't wearing army boots but sneakers! Moreover, no one could find any record in Miami of José Rodríguez Zafra, the martyr whose body had been riddled by sixteen communist bullets.

In the next few days the whole truth came out—that there was no truth in the story at all. A member of Alabau's high command confessed that everything had been a fabrication. There had been no attack. Alabau had not been wounded. No buildings had been blown up. No one had been killed. Nobody in the United Invasion Movement had gotten closer to Cuba than Coral Gables. Alabau made the whole thing up—he had gone mad. Obsessed with the liberation of Cuba, he had spent too many years away from his homeland. It was rumored later that Alabau was terminally ill and that he had just a few weeks left to live.

The local *choteo* mill was quick to seize Alabau and grind him to a mango pulp. Wags remarked that in Cuban slang a *guayaba is* not only a fruit but a tall tale, a fib. No wonder, then, that the attack had taken place in a town called Guayabal! The story was nothing but a patch of guavas, an orchard of lies. Others compared him to Don Quijote, the mad knight who tilted at windmills and courted Dulcinea. Fidel was his evil giant; Cuba was his Dulcinea; he was determined to win her at any cost.

Like Don Quijote himself, Alabau was undaunted by all the ridicule. Resurrecting his old hagiographic vocation, he compared himself to Jesus Christ. Those doubting Thomases who didn't believe his story were free to stick their hands into the wound on his arm. Two months to the day after the supposed attack, Alabau began publishing a tabloid called *Invasión.* The first issue declared in big bold letters, "THE BATTLE OF GUAYABAL HAS JUST BEGUN." Undeterred by the incontrovertible proof that the attack had been a hoax, Alabau continued to speak of it as a great victory. This went on for two years, until Alabau fell ill and passed away. It was rumored that he died crazy.

But was Alabau really insane? Was he all that different from thousands of other Cuban exiles? Miami Cubans have never thought it crazy to recreate Havana at the edge of a swamp. We thought nothing of opening a store in the United States and putting up the sign "The same one from Cuba" or "Here since 1935." We take it as a matter of course that distance is not destiny, that our ways of life transcend geography. To one degree or another, haven't all of us enacted our own Guayabal?

Exiles live by substitution. If you can't have it in Havana, make it in Miami. The Cuban-American poet Ricardo Pau-Llosa writes, "The exile knows his place, and that place is the imagination." Life in exile: memory enhanced by imagination. Like Don Quijote, every exile is an apostle of the imagination, someone who invents a world more amenable to his ambitions and dreams. It's no accident that for over twenty years the most popular eatery in Little Havana has been the Versailles restaurant, which is all cigar smoke and mirrors. Surrounded by reflections, the exile cannot always tell the genuine article from the hoax, the oasis from the mirage. Exile is a hall of mirrors, a house of spirits. In that sense, Alabau may have been the quintessential exile.

During the 1960s and 1970s Calle Ocho, or Eighth Street, was a busy, bustling one-way thoroughfare lined with restaurants, supermarkets, gas stations, bakeries, florists, fruit stands, barbershops, car dealerships, furniture showrooms, appliance stores, *botánicas* (stores for religious artifacts used in Afro-Cuban rituals), funeral parlors, and schools. Anything one needed could be found on Calle Ocho, which was located in the heart of Little Havana. As sociologists put it, the community that sprang up around this street was institutionally complete. An individual who lived there could be delivered by a Cuban obstetrician, buried by a Cuban undertaker, and in between birth and death lead a perfectly satisfactory life without needing extramural contacts. Little Havana was a golden cage, an artificial paradise, the neighborhood of dreams.

Many of the establishments on Calle Ocho were *mami*-and-*papi* stores that supported and employed a whole family. While the grandmother stayed home with the small children, Mami and Papi worked the store. Once the children were old enough, they too came to work after school and on Saturday mornings. Some of the businesses in Little Havana had not existed in Havana, but others had been re-created in their Cuban image. One of the most prestigious private schools in Havana had been the Jesuit-run Colegio Belén, which many middle- and upper-class Cubans attended, including my father and Fidel Castro (Fidel graduated, Gustavo was kicked out). Shut down in Cuba, Colegio Belén resurfaced at the far end of Eighth Street in Miami, across the street from a Buick dealership. So it was with other well-known Havana establishments like the Rivero Funeral Parlor, the Centro Vasco and Casablanca restaurants, and radio stations such as Radio Progreso. La Ocho, as Cubans called it, was the location of Domino Park, as it was of the memorial to the soldiers who died at the Bay of Pigs.

Before the Cuban exodus began, Eighth Street had been a quiet, out-of-the-way street between Downtown Miami and Coral Gables; by the late sixties it had developed into the hub of a thriving community of energetic and ambitious exiles. Calle Ocho was where my father worked, where my mother shopped, where my grandmothers went to the doctor. When I was in college and went out on a date with a Cuban girl, that's where I headed, usually to the Pekín, a Cuban-Chinese restaurant that combined standard Cuban fare with Chinese dishes, so that you could begin your dinner with fried wonton and end it with guava shells and espresso. The Pekín was owned by two brothers, Rafael and Federico, who had been born in Cuba of Chinese parents and spoke Spanish with a thick oriental accent. As thin as bamboo reeds, they greeted their customers at the door, introducing themselves as "Lafael" and "Felelico." After dinner my date and I would go to a movie, perhaps at the Tower Theater a few blocks up the street, and then, if I got lucky, to *palito* beach (a whimsical name, because nobody ever got that lucky). If it was a special occasion and we stayed out really late, the evening would end with *café con leche* at the Versailles, which was open until four or five in the morning.

Since so many establishments in Little Havana had their roots across the sea, one tended to think of this neighborhood as a mirror image of its Cuban original. Cuba was everywhere—in the taste of food, in the sound of the voices, in the drawings on the place mats. You could walk into Lila's restaurant and almost pretend that you were still in Havana. Behind the counter was a map of the Cuban capital; on the walls, pictures of the Cuban countryside. All of the patrons, and all of the employees, were Cuban. The pungent smell emanating from the kitchen was vintage *criollo:* sweet plantains frying in olive oil.

At the same time, however, Little Havana was much more than a substitute city. Our neighborhoods didn't just emulate Havana, they completed it. Engendered by the coupling of memory and imagination, Little Havana was not only a copy but an alternative. Things that Havana lacked—food and freedom—Miami had in abundance. Some years ago a Cuban museum in Miami set up an exhibit detailing the history of the Cuban capital from its foundation in the sixteenth century. The striking thing was that the exhibit ended abruptly in 1958. There wasn't one artifact, one photograph, from the last thirty years, as if Cuba's largest city had disappeared from the face of the earth the day Fidel's *milicianos* marched in. To judge by the exhibit, on January 1, 1959, Havana vanished.

In one respect this view of Cuban history testifies to the exile's capacity for comforting delusion. We console ourselves with the thought that, while we have remained the same, it's our homeland that has changed. We often feel that we haven't abandoned our country, but that our country has abandoned us. Countless songs and poems play variations on this theme: Cuba changed, I didn't. Years ago an exile song told the story of a *guajiro,* a Cuban peasant, who visited Havana after the triumph of the Revolution. He found the place unrecognizable—the Malecón was deserted; the people looked different; no one sang or danced. The reason was that the son, the musical soul of the island, had left the country. With the son in exile, Cuba was no longer itself. From the *guajiro's*—that is, the exile's—perspective, the city that survived the Revolution was a different place.

But I don't think that this way of thinking is merely delusional. The exhibit ended in 1958 because in certain concrete, substantive ways the history of Havana ended with the Revolution. The break with the past was so sharp that the city acquired a new identity. Even the names of streets and buildings changed: Carlos III became Salvador Allende Avenue; the Havana Hilton became the Habana Libre; the Casino Deportivo was renamed the Sierra Maestra. Go to Havana and try to get directions to Club Náutico, and perhaps only an old-timer would be able to tell you. I ask myself: how much does the new socialist man who walks those streets and uses those buildings resemble his old *cubano* ancestor? Cuban exiles mockingly divide the island's history into A.C. and D.C., *antes del caballo* and *después del caballo* (a *caballo* is a horse, and the horse, of course, is Fidel—and never, ever confuse a Cuban *caballo* with an American *yegua*). This isn't only *choteo*. The changes brought by the aptly named Revolution have been so profound that one may well wonder whether it still makes sense to speak of Cuba as one country. Although I often wonder whether I'm still Cuban enough to pick up where I left off decades ago, I also ask myself whether the Cubans who didn't go into exile are themselves still Cuban enough to pick up where we all left off. One doesn't have to emigrate to become an exile—sometimes the most acute estrangement results from staying right where you are. Just as a man can look into the mirror and not recognize the face that stares back, a city can become a stranger to itself.

So it is with Havana: some of it has remained what it always had been, and some of it moved. Perhaps the Cuban museum's exhibit did not include a post-1958 display because that history was unfolding in the very neighborhood where the museum was located. To continue the overview of the city, all one had to do was step out on Calle Ocho. Little Havana U.S.A. was perhaps small in size, but it was large enough to contain some of what was best and most typical about Cuba. The diminished city, the truly little Havana, was the one that languished in the Caribbean. Compared to other Latin American nations, pre-Castro Cuba was a fairly prosperous nation. Pick the index you like—literacy, per capita income, the number of hospital beds or TV sets or Cadillacs or radio stations—and then compare the figures for fifties Cuba with those of other Latin American nations. My favorite stat: by 1950 Cuba had more movie theaters per capita than any other country in the Western Hemisphere, including the

United States. The Blanquita theater in Havana, which had 6,600 seats, was reputed to be the largest in the world. In the 1950s Cuba wasn't a typical third-world country; it became one only as a result of the Revolution, whose remarkable feat has been turning this formerly prosperous island into one of the hemisphere's poorest nations.

Exile mutilates the country that is left no less than the people who leave it. Even those exiles who arrived with only the clothes on their backs brought with them all kinds of precious baggage, a *cache* of expertise and talent whose loss changed the island, for the worse. Thirty-some years later residential Cuba is still paying the price of exile, and so are we. But the ultimate lesson of Little Havana is that, regardless of the costs, distance is not destiny. The true Havana is a movable city; its foundations slide on shifting grounds. The Little Havana of years ago, the one I grew up in, reminds me of Philip Larkin's definition of home: "a joyous shot at how things ought to be." Never mind that the words that wafted in the air weren't always intelligible. Never mind the cooler winters and the unusually muggy summers. Never mind that the sky was less blue and the sand less fine than in Cuba. In some ways Miami was closer to the heart of Havana than Havana itself. In Spanish there are two verbs of being: *ser,* which denotes existence, and *estar,* which denotes location. No matter how much geography may confine us, *ser* cannot be reduced to *estar*—a state of being cannot be reduced to a geographical place. Melding essence and residence, Miami Cubans picked up where history had dropped them off (or perhaps, where we had dropped ourselves off). Little Havana became the greater Havana.

By the early 1980s the Cuban enclave in Miami had expanded far beyond Little Havana. In April 1961, when the Bay of Pigs invasion took place, there were 135,000 Cubans in Miami; five years later, that figure was 210,000. By 1973 more than half a million Cubans had left the island and most of them were living in Miami. In the 1980s the number of Cubans in Miami swelled to about two thirds of a million.

As the first waves of exiles prospered, many sold their modest homes in la *sagüesera* and moved south or west to upscale suburbs like Coral Gables or South Miami; more recently they have moved farther away to Kendall or Perrine, which lie at the southern edges of Dade County. Hialeah, a working-class neighborhood located on the northwest portion of Dade County, grew into a large Cuban enclave, as did Westchester, Carol City, and other neighboring municipalities. When the first-wave Cubans moved out, more-recent arrivals moved in. Some were the so-called *marielitos*, Cubans who came to this country in the summer of 1980 via the Mariel Boatlift; others were immigrants from other parts of Spanish America, particularly Colombia and Nicaragua. The Nicaraguans, who began to stream into Miami after the triumph of the Sandinistas in 1979, have become the second largest Hispanic group in Miami.

Currently, Dade County has well over a million Hispanic residents, and about two thirds of them are Cuban. The influx of Hispanics of other nationalities has turned Miami into a more diverse, and in some ways a more interesting, city. Now, on a given Friday night, you can choose from the Colombian discotheque that plays *cumbia,* the Dominican one that plays *merengue,* and the Cuban one that plays *son* and *guaracha.* But I must confess that I miss the "old" Miami, the Miami of the sixties and seventies, which wasn't as Hispanic as it is now, but where every Hispanic that you met was certain to be Cuban. Now I can no longer go into a gas station in Little Havana and address the attendant with the familiarity that Cubans habitually use with each other; I may be talking to a Nicaraguan, who may not appreciate it if I address him as *tú* and call him *mi sangre.* These days you have to feel out the territory first, decide whether you are among Cubans or not, and act accordingly. Years ago Miami consisted of us, the Cubans, and them, the Americans. We were an upwardly mobile tribe, tightly knit and ambitious. Now things are more complicated, for it's not so clear where the "us" ends and the "them" begins. And to muddle things further, some of us Cubans, the younger ones, were actually born in this country. No longer the Cuban tribe, we're fast becoming part of the Latino community. We're making the difficult transition from exiles to ethnics. As an exile, I'm not sure I like it. Because I already lost Havana once, I don't want to lose my city again.

My trouble is that I don't see myself as Latino, but as Cuban— *cubano, cubiche, cubanazo, criollo.* To tell the truth, the Latino is a statistical fiction. Part hype and part hypothesis, the Latino exists principally for the purposes of politicians, ideologues, salsa singers, and Americans of non-Hispanic descent. The Latino's brown face has greenbacks plastered all over it, and in fact most of the people to whom the label is applied reject it, opting instead for a national designation: Mexican, Puerto Rican, Cuban, Dominican, Venezuelan, Colombian. (Ironically, the survey where these findings were reported was called the Latino National Political Survey—some professors never learn.) Although this diversity may be inconvenient for some, it reflects reality: Hispanics of different national origins have divergent features, customs, foods, temperaments, and traditions. A common language doesn't ensure a common culture. A Mexican is like a Cuban no more than an American is like a New Zealander or a Frenchman is like someone from Port-au-Prince.

As advertisers have discovered to their dismay, there's no such thing as a Latino market. There's a Cuban market (we call it *bodega*) and a Mexican market (they call it *mercado*) and a Puerto Rican market (they call it *colmado* and sometimes *marketa),* but there's no single, indivisible Latino market that can be reached with one sales pitch. Try to sell me a *coche,* the Latin American word for car, and I won't bite, for in Cuba *coche* is baby carriage. Try to sell me a pesticide that kills *gusanos,* worms, and I'll think you are my enemy. Put a lovely *mestiza* in your ad for skin cream, and Cuban and Dominican women won't pay attention. Like other Americans, when I want to eat exotic food I go for burritos and enchiladas. It's a pleasant experience, but it's not like having black beans and rice at a Cuban restaurant.

Not long ago I spent an afternoon walking around Little Havana with Roberto Fernández, a Cuban-American novelist who also grew up in the neighborhood. We went into a little restaurant on Calle Ocho that we both used to patronize, one that Fernández put into one of his novels. The decor and the menu hadn't changed much in twenty years, but the Cuban sandwich I ordered tasted nothing like the way it was supposed to. Roberto said it was because my Cuban sandwich had become a Latino sandwich. He's right. By now Little Havana is as much a part of urban American folklore as the French Quarter or Little Italy. The quaint lampposts on the street corners bear the names of politicians and patriots, Hollywood film crews shoot movies in front of coffee stands, and presidential candidates put in obligatory appearances at old-folks homes and cigar factories. But Little Havana, the Little Havana that I knew, doesn't exist anymore.

With its boarded-up storefronts and faded signs, Calle Ocho has become little more than a promotional gimmick for European tourists, who are invariably disappointed with what they find. You see them wandering up and down the streets, with their cameras slung around their necks, looking for something to photograph. Half of the places on their tourist guides don't even exist anymore. Casablanca is all boarded up and La Lechonera is falling apart. The monument to the Bay of Pigs veterans shares a block with a McDonald's, and my favorite Pekín restaurant has mutated into a Pizza Hut (which does, however, serve *chorizo*-lovers pizza). Because Little Havana was created in the likeness and image of Havana, it always did have an otherworldly feel; but these days it's a Cuban ghost town. Despite the best efforts of the local Chamber of Commerce, about the only time Calle Ocho comes alive is for the annual carnival, a multicultural extravaganza for tourist consumption. The real Cuban life now goes on in suburbs like Kendall and Hialeah.

Still, this place is the Cuba I know best. My parents still live there, in the same house that they bought in 1960. The Cuban grocer is a block away, and Dade Elementary, which has been converted into an English-language center for adults, looks pretty much as it did when I was in sixth grade. Because this place is home, it heals far more than it hurts. If I cannot find Cubans on Eighth Street, I look for them in Kendall or Hialeah. If they answer in English when I address them in Spanish, I'll remember that I'm in no position to criticize Anglophones. In Miami I seek what I find nowhere else— *communitas,* a word that has more to do with communion than with community, more with spiritual ties than with ethnic agendas. Actually, it's not *communitas* that I seek. *Communitas* is a word that I picked up in a book somewhere; I wouldn't know *communitas* if it hit me in the face. My word is *ambiente,* which I didn't have to pick up anywhere because it was bequeathed to me. *Ambiente* denotes congenial surroundings, a warm and friendly atmosphere. Miami gives me what I can only call *ambiente,* as in *"¿Hay ambiente, mi gente?"*—originally a phrase from a promotional jingle that turned into a proverbial way of asking whether a party is really hot, really hopping. As the rhyme suggests, the key to *ambiente* is *mi gente*— people who feel and think and sound like me. That's what I find in Miami, folks like me, people for whom my Cubanness goes without saying, who think nothing of the two cigars jutting out of my shirt pocket. In Miami I don't have to finish my sentences or explain my jokes or keep mum about my politics or spell out my name. When I was in sixth grade with Mrs. Myers, I couldn't hear well enough. Now, as a Cuban living in North Carolina, I sometimes feel that I'm screaming at the top of my lungs and nobody hears me. In Miami all I have to do is move my arms and open my mouth.

I seek *ambiente* not only among friends and family but also among total strangers who are, it turns out, not strangers at all. Such chance encounters with other Cubans can take place anywhere—in malls, gas stations, restaurants, bakeries, doctors' offices. Since they usually happen when I least expect them, they fill me with unanticipated joy. Take this one, for example, which took place last year, when I went to Miami by myself to spend a few days with my parents. I had just flown into Miami International Airport and, because it was late at night, the shuttle that took me to the rental car agency was empty except for the driver and me. She was a woman in her forties, Hispanic for sure but not necessarily Cuban. As we rode in the dark down the bumpy back roads, she said to me, in Spanish, "All these *baches* are enough to make your kidneys come loose." All of a sudden I'm thrust into a different world; all of a sudden I feel it, I have it, *ambiente.* From the way she speaks Spanish, I can tell that the lady is Cuban, a member of my ethnic group, of *mi gente* (add it to the census forms: African-American, Asian-American, Native American, Pacific Islander, Hispanic, Other, and *Mi Gente*). We strike up a conversation about kidneys, potholes, our families, and the hardships of life in exile. Although she doesn't realize it, her words have rescued me from my everyday American limbo, where human contact is often reduced to the formulaic How-are-you-today of the cashier at the supermarket, who doesn't even wait for an answer before she starts sliding my groceries past the bar-code reader.

Miami is different. Miami is full of voluble Cubans like me. In Miami lady bus drivers talk about their kidneys. In Miami renting a car can be a life-affirming experience. By the time, half an hour later, that I drive out of the rental agency in my red Tempo, I'm feeling that I never left. That brief encounter is all it takes to welcome me home.

∂ ∂ ∂

PART TWO
Family Ties

∂ ∂ ∂

FOUR

On the Corner of Paula and San Ignacio

Little Havana, 1991

The restaurant's name is La Habana Vieja, Old Havana. Decorated to look like the inner courtyard of a Spanish-style mansion, the interior has black and white tile floors, a stone fountain, and square columns. Each of the columns bears the name of a different Old Havana street, so that when you come in, you can take a seat at the corner of one of those narrow cobblestoned alleys with the wonderful theological names like Amargura (Anguish), Desamparados (Forsaken), or Merced (Mercy). Even without lampposts and balconies, the mode here is unmistakably retro. La Habana Vieja is a Little Old Havana, a miniature model of the colonial heart of the Cuban city. As sometimes happens in dreams, this place is more than one place. Walk in, and you begin to lose yourself in another world.

Nearly every time I go to Miami my father takes me to lunch or dinner at La Habana Vieja. Sometimes my mother and Mary Anne and my kids come along; but mostly Gustavo and I come by ourselves. Especially in the last few years, Old Havana has become a shared habit, a way of bringing out the moods and memories we have in common. Under the phony street signs and the kitschy murals, our disparate lives come together. La Habana Vieja opened sometime in the mid-1980s, but I had gone there several times before I noticed that my father always sits in the same section, by Paula Street. Then it dawned on me that this is where the *almacén* was located, on the corner of Paula and San Ignacio, and I realized what should have been obvious to me all along: that my father goes to Old Havana to revisit the business that he inherited from his father and that my brothers and I were supposed to inherit from him. Since he cannot take me to the *almacén* the way he did when I was a child, he takes me to its ghostly exile double. Sitting at a table for two on the corner of Paula and San Ignacio, he can imagine himself back at the helm of J. Pérez, S.A.

When we're there, on Paula and San Ignacio, the conversation invariably turns to Cuba. "Tell me, Gustavito, if Fidel fell would you go back?" As he says this he fidgets with the paper place mat, which has drawings of several Old Havana landmarks, including the church that stood just across from the warehouse (he never fails to point this out). Gustavo's question makes me squirm, for I never know how to answer it. Would I go back? Go back to what? To an eighty-year-old warehouse and a forty-year-old house? I don't know if I want to go back to that.

When my mother, Nena, is present, she comes to my rescue. "But chino," she says, "Gustavito has a career in this country. You can't expect him to drop everything and go back to Cuba. Your children's life is here." Then she turns to me. "Your father doesn't understand that you and your brothers have already made your life in this country. He thinks you can just drop everything and start all over." Hearing this, Gustavo turns sullen and goes back to his rice and chicken. It's not what he wants to hear.

But tonight Nena cannot come to my rescue; she has stayed home with her American daughter-in-law, Mary Anne, and her almost American grandchildren. They will spend the evening playing Scrabble or canasta and watching TV. Tonight I'm flying solo.

I decide that it does no harm to tell Gustavo what he wants to hear; who knows, I may want to hear the same thing myself.

"Yes, Papi, I would go back to Cuba if I could."

"And what about your career as professor?"

"I don't care; I'd rather work with you in the *almacén*."

Papi doesn't reply, but he's beaming.

"I wouldn't even have to quit my job," I add. "Just in case, I could ask Duke to give me a leave for a couple of years while we try to get the business back on its feet. Then I could resign my job."

Papi doesn't understand, he doesn't know sabbaticals from soup, but he's still beaming. That's all he needs to hear, that I'd rather work in the *almacén,* with him! The way it was supposed to be. He may not believe me, but it makes him happy to have me at least say that I would prefer to be an *almacenista* in Old Havana rather than a professor at Duke University. Since he never graduated from high school, he doesn't know much about professors. When I finished graduate school, he started calling me Dr. Pérez Firmat, but it was an ambiguous accolade, lament as well as compliment, a token of esteem but also a complaint about the parting of our ways. Two things about my title rankled with him—the "Dr." and my second last name, Firmat. There he was, plain old Pérez, surrounded by a Ph.D. and my mother's surname.

Sometimes he says to me, "You know, junior, I'm also a *literato*"—*literato* is Spanish for litterateur. I play straight man and ask how that can be. He unleashes the rhyming punch line: *"porque todos se arrodillan ante mi aparato,"* "because everyone kneels before my tool."

In asking whether I would return, Gustavo isn't only asking about the *almacén* or even about Cuba. He wants to be reassured that he and I are still alike. It's less a practical question about careers than a pained quandary about generational and cultural continuity. Behind his formulaic words lies a real conundrum: "Are you like me, Gustavito?" Those times that I have replied that I wouldn't return, when I have had a sharpened ax to grind, what I was really saying was, "No, Papi, I'm not like you." Often the tone of my voice added, "And what's more, I don't want to be like you."

But tonight I have left the hatchet buried in my backyard in Chapel Hill, and I find it easy to let Papi's wild dreams carry me away. After all, whether I like it or not, I am Gustavito, a chip off the old block. I've got the pockmarks and the happy feet to prove it. And who knows what the honest answer is? Perhaps I would go back after all. I'd certainly be glad to get back what was taken from us, as much for the principle as for the money. I'd love to get a chance to set history straight. Since Cubans have to eat, it probably wouldn't take long to get the *almacén* back up and running. Although I think of myself as too much of a loner to make a successful entrepreneur, once I got down there I surely would get into the groove. Maybe all it would take is a warm bath in my Cuban gene pool. Cubans are born chameleons. If I can pass myself off as a professor, I can pass myself off as a businessman equally well, probably better.

Once in Cuba the other parts of my life would probably fall into place. Mary Anne says she'd like living there, we fantasize about that sometimes. She could be the rich sexy *americana* in the flowered hat who walks down the streets of Old Havana turning heads. She'd drive a Lincoln, the way my mother used to. At the Casino Español, our beach club, her skimpy bikini would scandalize the Cuban women, and titillate the men. In her forties, my wife still knows how to work a crowd of onlookers.

I wonder what it would be like to make love to Mary Anne in Havana, how it would feel to come in Cuba, something I never did because I left at the age of eleven. A friend of mine has the theory that the place where you beat off for the first time, the soil on which you spill your first seed, determines your nationality. If that's so, I'm American for life. But maybe I can make up ground by making love to my American wife on Cuban soil.

As I spin elaborate and unlikely fantasies involving Mary Anne and me, my father voyages in worlds of his own. Now he's deciding who will do what at the *almacén.*

"When we go back, you could be the vice-president and work in the office next to mine, the one that used to belong to Gutiérrez. Carlitos can take care of the *viajantes,* the salesmen, because he's good with people and he likes to be on the go. He's got *jiribilla* in his ass, that's why he can't sit still. But we need to keep an eye on him. You know your brother. If Mari wanted to, she could be treasurer, the way Cuca was. And then there's your cousin José Ignacio, who's gotten a lot of experience working in New York for Jesús García."

The only one for whom Papi has a hard time finding a slot is Pepe, since of all his children Pepe seems to him the furthest removed from the old Cuba. Perhaps Pepe could stay in the United States and work for the company here.

"Your mother keeps saying that she's staying here, she's had enough of Cuba. If she stayed here, Pepe could stay here with her. That way you wouldn't have to travel to the United States so often."

In the wonderful world of Old Havana, everything goes together like black beans and rice. Papi knows full well that Pepe and Carlos and I are barely on speaking terms, but he doesn't say anything about this.

The arrival of dinner brings us back to reality. Because he can't bite too hard with his false teeth, Papi ordered *ropa vieja,* shredded beef, with white rice and a side order of fried ripe plantains, sweet and soft and chewy. I'm having *palomilla*—a large, thin steak seasoned with garlic and lime juice and garnished with chopped onions and parsley—and more white rice. Instead of sweet plantains, I've opted for *tostones*—green plantains cut into inch-thick slices that are then flattened out and fried in lard. When we were children, my brothers and I called them *plátanos a puñetazos*, punched-out plantains, because we had seen Caridad the cook beating down on them to make them flat.

Impatient with the waiter, Gustavo grouses about this and that. He complains that his drink doesn't have enough Scotch, that the rolls aren't warm enough, that he needs an extra plate for his rice. The waiter, who isn't Cuban, complies curtly with Papi's demands. Because my father comes here often and knows the owner, he thinks he should get special treatment, the way he would have in Cuba, thirty years ago. Although I try to play down his grievances, I realize that what he's really upset about is having to eat here at all. What upsets him is the disparity between the ordinary dinner and our extravagant dreams.

When the waiter picks up our plates, Gustavo chides him for piling one on top of another. Not good form, he says. Over a dessert of *natilla* and *flan*, custard and *crème caramel*, Gustavo brings me up-to-date on the latest news from Cuba. Meat is so scarce that they are making *picadillo* (beef hash) with banana peels. Imagine how that must taste. Things keep getting worse and worse. No lightbulbs, no gasoline, another pilot who defected, rumors of a purge in the army. There isn't even any soap, and I know what a hardship this is to most Cubans, for Cubans are sticklers for cleanliness.

"Imagine what Havana must smell like," he says. "When I was young, I used to shower three times a day. First in the morning right after waking up; then when I came home for lunch; and then before dinner in the evening. Now I shower maybe twice a week."

Although things in Cuba have been getting worse for thirty years, nothing happens. Somehow Fidel holds out; he may hold out for years still. But tonight Papi has different ideas. Earlier at home my mother had been feeding him Valium to douse his distemper, but right now he's flying high. The J&B has lifted his spirits—the J&B and me.

As he eats, he hums "Miénteme," his favorite *bolero*.

"Fidel is through," he says. "It's only a matter of time. It may be months, perhaps only weeks. The question is only when and how, that's all. What's so good about the situation in Cuba is how bad it is getting."

He has been saying this for many, many years.

After dessert, we have a cup of strong and sweet Cuban coffee and light our cigars. Where else but Miami can you go to a family restaurant, light up a cigar after dinner, and have no one give it a second thought? When the bill comes, I make a gesture to pay, knowing that he won't let me. Computing the tip, he rounds off the total to the nearest zero. The flourish on his signature is as rococo as ever, but his lettering has gotten much smaller. Pretty soon it won't be more than a *garabato,* a scribble. As a kid I used to spend idle moments at school attempting to reproduce his loops and curlicues, unsuccessfully.

Since it's not often that Gustavo and I go out by ourselves, he wants to make a night of it. We move to the lounge adjacent to the restaurant. Obviously, Papi has been here before, for Paquito the bartender isn't surprised to see him. Everything in the bar is winered except for the oak counter and the black upright piano, where a lady is playing Cuban music with the soulfulness of a robot. The brandy snifter on the piano has a couple of dollars and some coins in it.

I order an Amaretto and my father asks for a Cointreau. This is the first time I've ever seen him drinking anything but Scotch. At home he will have nothing else—only J&B and tap water with a twist of lime (never lemon). Jewish booze, he calls it.

It turns out that Paquito and my father are friends from Cuba. Paquito's family owned a grocery store across from the *almacén* and as kids they hung out together. "You should be aware," Paquito says to me, "that everyone in Cuba knew about J. Pérez, S.A. It was quite an important business. Wasn't it the biggest *almacén* in the island, Gustavo?" This isn't true, but my father doesn't deny it. Paquito is fond of my father, or he is a shrewd bartender. Maybe a little of both. He wants Gustavo to look good in front of his son.

Paquito used to spend days at the counter of his father's grocery store looking at the trucks going in and out of the *almacén.* He and my father spend a while arguing about the physical features of the warehouse. How many doors were there on the Paula side? Did the trucks go in through Paula or through San Ignacio? From the discussion I get the impression that Paquito remembers the *almacén* better than my father. Maybe I'm not the only one in the family with amnesia. Every once in a while Paquito reaches under the bar and takes a sip from a glass. Papi puffs away at his Padrón cigar and sips the Cointreau reluctantly, as if he didn't really like it. Somehow he doesn't look right with a snifter in his hand.

When he was young, Paquito tells us, he had dreamed of becoming a sales rep for Crusellas, a company that sold soap and toothpaste. Sales reps made good money, had guaranteed vacations, a pension plan, and health insurance. I'm struck by how modest his dreams were. But Fidel spoiled them too, and now he's not so sure he would go back. In a couple of years he can begin collecting Social Security and then he can retire. His daughter is married to an American who refuses to learn Spanish.

"He's a good boy," he says, *"un buen muchacho,* and he treats her very well, very well, much better than your father and I have treated our wives—isn't that right, Gustavo? He doesn't run around, he doesn't stay out late, he lives for Evelyn and their daughters. You know these *americanos,* all they do is work and work."

"As for me," Gustavo says, "let them try to take away all that I have danced."

"Then one day they drop dead of a heart attack and then what? The Americans, they're a great people, the most powerful people in the world, but they are not like us. We know how to enjoy life. Put three Cubans together, and they have a party. Can you imagine being young in this country today, Gustavo? *Coño,* nothing could contain us. Your father and I, we could tell you some stories."

This remark makes Gustavo uncomfortable and he shuffles over to the piano, drops a thrice-folded dollar into the snifter, and asks the lady to play "Miénteme"—"Lie to Me"—the song about a woman who asks her lover to lie to her about the fact that he loves her, because she can't bear to hear the truth. Every time Papi has a couple of drinks, he starts humming "Miénteme." He does it badly but with feeling.

"You know, junior, that was our song. Your mother's and mine. We heard Olguita Guillot sing it many times at the Tropicana. The first time ever that she sang it, we were there with Feluco and Hilda, your godfather and your godmother. I think that was the night Blanco Rico got shot."

I have heard this story before—my mother also likes to tell it—
how everybody hid under the baccarat and roulette tables when the
shooting started, but I have never understood how such a cynical
tune could have been any couple's theme song. Who was lying to
whom?

"Your father is too sentimental," Paquito says. "These *boleros*
are all alike. Whine and bitch. Whine and bitch. Forget sentimental-
ity. Let me tell you the story about Pinocchio and the prostitute.
Pinocchio gets in bed with a prostitute and wants to screw her right
away, but she says to him that first he has to let her sit on his face.
So he gets on his back and she sits down on his face. And then she
says to him, Okay, Pinocchio, now I want you to lie to me—*miénteme, miénteme*. That's my kind of *bolero*.

"Look, Gustavito," Paquito says, "people come here, they talk,
they have their drinks, they spend a couple of hours, and there is no
pain. What's the point staying home and fighting with your wife?
Here you talk, you sip a little Amaretto or Cointreau, you tell stories,
you reminisce about the good old times, and there is no pain.

"Look at me," he says. He has a slight build, and what little hair
he has is pasted sideways over his head to hide his bald pate. He's
wearing a black vest over a short-sleeved white shirt. He's got a
waiter's face, friendly but unreliable.

"Forty-five years ago I used to sit in the *bodega* and look across
the street at the *almacén*. And here I am now, in a different country,
having a few *traguitos* with you and your father, and there is no pain,
y no hay tormento. "

"Paquito," my father says, "how about the singer we used to call
Miss Cataclysm because of the way her hips shook? Remember
that?"

"Of course I do. She was Mexican."

"No, she had to be Cuban. No *charra* ever moved like that."

My father isn't in pain now. Sitting at the bar, with a few J&Bs
under his belt, which he's had to tighten a couple of notches in the
last few years, he's in his element. He's feeling expansive. Gustavo
is happy because we are out on the town together; it doesn't happen
often. I can't remember the last time Gustavo and I sat at a bar having drinks.

Paquito tells me that as a young man my father was robust like
me, and I feel flattered for both of us. All those hours grinding away

at the Nautilus machines haven't gone unnoticed. Although Papi is no longer robust, it gladdens me that he once was. I look at him now and his arms are thin and his shoulders are stooped and narrow. He looks threadbare. When I arrive from North Carolina now for a visit, he no longer even tries to get my suitcases out of the car. Sometimes I forget that he wasn't always this way. In old photographs from Cuba he's broad-shouldered, thick-chested, and big-bellied.

When Paquito finds out that I live in Chapel Hill, he wants to know whether there are a lot of *negros,* black people, there. But instead of saying the word, he rubs the back of his hand with his index finger. I tell him that there are black people everywhere.

"Cuban blacks are different from American blacks," he says. "Isn't that so, Gustavo?"

"There was no racism in Cuba," Gustavo says. "The day the *almacén* was confiscated, Mongo, the *negro* who was the head of the stevedores, came over to me with tears in his eyes and said how much he regretted what was happening. And he was a big *fidelista* and the head of the union. All that stuff about racism is communist propaganda. Paco, another Cointreau? Junior, want another one?"

I do. I'm feeling no pain myself.

"Every time they show pictures of Havana now, all you see are black and mulatto faces," Papi continues. "Sometimes I think there are no white people left in Cuba."

Content for once to be my father's son, I keep my thoughts to myself. I don't see the point in getting into an argument with him and Paquito about race relations. I know full well that there was racism in Cuba, but I could never convince my father of this. I do remember Mongo, a heavily muscled, mountainous black man with gaps in his teeth. When I used to go to the *almacén* as a kid, sometimes he used to pick me up and carry me around on his shoulders.

As Paquito and Gustavo talk on, I imagine that this is how it might have been in Cuba had it not been for Fidel. My father and I, in a bar somewhere in Old Havana, shooting the breeze after work and drinking. In Cuba I would have been his son in ways I'm not now. In Cuba Papi and I would have known the same people, frequented the same bars and brothels, eaten at the same restaurants, spoken the same language. In Cuba I wouldn't feel, as I have so often felt, that my choice of occupation was an attack on who he was; and my father wouldn't think, as he must often have thought, that by becoming a professor I was kicking him in the balls. I don't know about my brothers, but for me all roads led to the corner of Paula and San Ignacio. Having no choice but to be a chip off the old block if we had stayed in Cuba, I'd have chosen to be a chip off the old block.

But this night at the Old Havana restaurant Papi and I are making up for history's misdeeds. This night Gustavo and his son, Gustavo and his father, are bringing the past into the present. To hell with communism. To hell with Fidel. To hell with Miami. To hell with thirty years of waiting. Our world is right here and right now, our world is Old Havana and our *almacén* and having drinks and telling stories with Paquito the bartender, who has known my father since they were kids.

(But my father would say it differently—he wouldn't say "to hell," that's much too American for him, and he wouldn't say "Fuck Fidel" either, as I might. Cubans don't fuck with people, they shit on them. My father would say, *"Me cago en Fidel, me cago en la Revolución, me cago en la suerte, me cago hasta en la mismísima mierda."* "I shit on Fidel, I shit on the Revolution, I shit on fate, I even shit on shit itself.")

Although today is Social Friday, the lounge is deserted except for a couple of women off in a corner and a guy named Chucho, who says he is waiting for his *jebita*. With a double-breasted blue blazer, off-white linen pants, expensive loafers, and a pinky ring, Chucho looks every bit the aging Lothario that he would like us to believe he is. His gray hair is perfectly coiffed and the luster on his fingernails must have been put there by a manicurist. But *jebita* is an anachronistic word; when I was in high school, *jebita* is what we called the girls.

While Chucho waits for his date, he tells us his life story. He lived in Pennsylvania for seven years, twenty in California, and recently retired to Miami. He has two grown children who still live up North.

"My children have organized their own lives," he says, hinting that their organization chart doesn't include him. If Chucho is married, he doesn't mention it. He isn't wearing a wedding band, but that's not all that unusual among Cuban men. I don't either. But my guess is that he's divorced and regrets it.

When Paquito asks him whether he remembers J. Pérez, S.A., Chucho says that the name sounds familiar. It's obvious that he's lying, although Cubans have an extraordinarily loose definition of acquaintance. By Cuban standards, it's possible to be friends with someone without actually having met him; and if you have actually met the person, you must be nothing less than *socios*, best friends.

As we chat, Chucho keeps looking back and forth at my father and me.

"You can tell how proud your father is of you," he says to me. "Nobody can deny you're his son. It's wonderful that you and your father come here together."

I don't especially like this guy—he's more than a little bit smarmy—but I'm sorry that he has to spend his nights in Old Havana waiting for a *jebita*. He should be home instead with his wife and his children and grandchildren.

Gustavo doesn't like Chucho either. I think my father is jealous that Chucho has a *jebita*. It's been a while since Gustavo waited for a *jebita* at a bar. More than a few years ago, Gustavo may have been a lot like Chucho.

"Tell me, Chucho, how much did that watch cost?" Gustavo asks.

Although it looks to me like a Rolex, Gustavo will never admit that any Cubans made money in the States, at least not honestly. He assumes the watch is a cheap imitation like his and seizes the opportunity to ride Chucho a little bit. But before Chucho has a chance to answer, Paquito changes the subject by bringing up a new operation to restore men's potency.

"They put a little pump into your thing," he says, "and when the time comes you inflate yourself by squeezing. You have a choice about how big you want it. Small, medium, large, or extra large."

"Hey, Chucho, do you think you are going to need a *bombita*, a pump, tonight?" Papi is still trying to get Chucho's goat.

Chucho shakes his head, knocks twice on the oak bar, and says, "Thank God." Apparently he won't need one.

"And your son here doesn't need one either," he adds.

"But *I* will," Papi says, laughing.

Strangely, the only personal topic about which Gustavo isn't reticent is his own impotence, which he wields like a club, sometimes to disarm and other times to titillate. But perhaps impotence is my father's metaphor for exile. Joking about his lack of virility, real or imagined, may be his way of expressing the abiding feelings of powerlessness that overtook him when the *almacén* was confiscated and he had to leave his country. Once, when I told him that impotence was psychological, he replied that his problem was that, after so many years in the United States, his mind and his body no longer spoke the same language.

What I know is that, for my father, good humor is a species of courage. Never a stoic, he copes with adversity not with a stiff upper lip, but with a loose tongue. His way of being heroic is to make off-color wisecracks. When he was diagnosed with glaucoma, he remarked that if his vision kept getting worse, he was going to have to look at the world *por el ojo del culo,* with his red eye.

When Chucho's date shows up, he waves her over to the bar. She is at least forty-five and trying a little too hard not to show it. Although her body has seen better days, she is still pretty, but Cuban women keep their faces longer than their figures. Don't snipe, I think to myself. The plain truth is that Gladys is a knockout, and I wouldn't mind being seen with this *jebita* myself. Since Chucho is probably past sixty, he has good reason to preen his blowdried feathers. After the introductions, he excuses himself and takes Gladys to the end of the bar, sitting between her and us so that we can't ogle. Chucho is a sly silver fox.

They sit there, off in a corner, whispering and giggling for a few minutes. Then Chucho announces that he and Gladys are going dancing—we're going to move our skeletons, he says—and settles his tab by placing a hundred-dollar bill on the counter.

"Hey, Paquito," Gustavo says, "tell him we don't have change for that around here."

Afraid to prejudice his tip, Paquito pretends not to hear.

A few minutes later, Gustavo and I decide to leave because Nena must be getting worried. It's almost midnight. He lets me settle our tab, which depresses me a little because it shows how little money he has. I leave Paquito an outrageous tip. He shakes my hand and says he looks forward to seeing us again.

In the parking lot Gustavo hands a dollar to the Nicaraguan attendant, who opens the car door for us and jokes that it's time to go home and watch TV. My father replies that first he has to move *la Dama,* the Queen. He means that first he has to go home and screw, but from the way he talks I seriously doubt that my father has made love to my mother in years.

For once, Gustavo lets me drive. This depresses me more, for it's a sure sign that he's getting old. Years ago he would have insisted on driving himself no matter how much he had drunk; and he would have done it well too, gotten us safely back home.

My father used to love car rides. Sunday evenings after dinner he would pack all of us into the car and take off for a long *vuelta* to Miami Beach. That was back in the days before the expressway, when it took at least an hour to get to Ocean Drive and back. It didn't matter how tipsy he was or how much my mother complained when he drove too fast. But old age has made him careful. Now he's afraid of getting his license taken away if he gets stopped. And he doesn't know Miami as well as he used to.

In the car Gustavo says how much he's enjoyed our evening together. For him, this amounts to a whole speech. I mumble that I've had a good time too, but I want to say much more. I want to say that I'm sorry about everything, that I want to do the last thirty years all over again, that I really do love him. I want to say that I don't give a damn about teaching, or Duke University, or the United States. I want to say that I'd like nothing better than to be a chip off the old block. But I'm too afraid or embarrassed to say anything.

As I pull up on the white gravel in front of the house, which is dark by now, he remarks that the years of exile have gone by very quickly.

"Life is short," I say.

"Life is shit," he corrects.

I am assessed with a mystery man—my father. As a child, I didn't need him; as an adolescent, I looked and couldn't find him; as a young man, I tried to avoid him. But in my middle age, he has become inescapable.

Like the God of the theologians, Gustavo is everywhere. I can be talking about the birds in the trees and I look up and there's my father hanging from a branch. I can be at the pool enjoying the company of the beautiful young moms and there's my father eyeballing along with me. When I back out of my driveway, he guides my hand around the mailbox. When I'm dancing, he lives in my hips and my legs. I sip J&B and smoke cigars and my father dwells in the taste and the aroma.

This man with whom I thought I had nothing in common never leaves me. Just as I cannot look at my son without seeing myself, I cannot look at myself without seeing my father. I used to glare into the mirror wishing to erase my father from my face. Wishing to efface him. I used to think that my worst features came from him, while my best were mine alone. No more. Gustavo, Gustavito, Cuba, *el almacén:* they're all coming back, but not with a vengeance. They come back like a gift, a gift I didn't know had been given me, but which has been in my possession all these years. I spend hours now mining my memory for Gustavo's words and I feel a surge of happiness when I retrieve a phrase or a sentence—there aren't that many of them—which I then share over the dinner table with my wife and my children.

"As my father says," I say, *"P'alante y p'alante y al que no le guste que se tome un purgante."* I have to explain to them what this means, and my pleasure increases. "If you don't like what I'm doing, go take some Ex-lax." When they still don't understand, my pleasure increases some more. "It's a way of saying that you have to keep on forging ahead without worrying about what other people will think." Papi and I are secret sharers. We know things that others ignore. Not momentous, life-and-death things, but little details, crucial details: the premise of a joke, the connotation of a word, the humor in a rhyme. *Literato-aparato*—who else but us, but me and him, would think this funny?

Entering middle age, I need to make my father more than he was, than he is. As I write this sentence, I cringe a little, fearing that he may read it, apprehensive that I'm undermining one of the pillars of my life. But I know that unless my mother reads it to him, he won't read it himself, and I doubt that she will. I don't think every son harbors this need to magnify his father. I have friends who have spent their lives doing the opposite, hacking away at their fathers in an attempt to cut them down to size. But my project is to build my father up, to make him grow, to exaggerate him if I have to. I labor to give Gustavo mass and dimension. For many, many years he seemed to me insufficient, smaller and fainter than he should have been. Now I want to enlarge him, I want to make him robust, bigger than our life.

It's also possible, I know, that all I'm doing is restoring him to the stature he always had, and that I refused to grant him. The irony

is that Gustavo has become a robust presence in my life at a time
when he's becoming more and more feeble. Now in his seventies,
he's beginning to sputter, to *cancanear,* as he says. With his health
on the slide, his normally good spirits tumble down with it. Some
days I call and when he answers the phone I can tell that he has been
crying. If I ask my mother what's going on, she'll say that he gets
grouchy and dejected for no reason. Because the roots of his depression run deeper than neurons, the drugs his doctor prescribes don't
help much. One day when she confronted him with his bad temper,
his reply was, "How can I *not* be in a bad mood?" He would say
nothing else. "How can I *not* be in a bad mood?" With this rhetori-
cal question Gustavo summarized thirty years of exile.

It amazes me how little I know about my father. Most of it comes
from my grandmother Constantina, who has been dead for almost
fifteen years. Now I wish I had asked more questions, for when she
passed away, my fountain of information dried up. Gustavo is a paradox: a gregarious man who hates to talk. He loves to kid, to
carouse, to dance, to drink, to whoop it up, but he avoids conversation as if it were ragweed. When the family is gathered around the
table and the after-dinner chitchat begins, Gustavo instantly heads
for the cover of the newspaper or the TV. He doesn't tell personal
stories, hardly ever reminisces, and he certainly doesn't want to hear
somebody else's stories or reminiscences. For him, all of this falls in
the category of *hablar mierda*—talking useless shit. When you ask
Gustavo about Cuba or his youth, he claims that it was so long ago,
he doesn't recall. If you insist, he refers the question to Nena, who
somehow remembers things she never even saw. Cuba is ever-
present in his thoughts, but he can't be pressed on the specifics of his
life there. Don't ask him why he got kicked out of high school or
who his friends were, because he'll say he doesn't remember.
Although Cuban men tend not to be self-disclosing, my father's
reserve verges on muteness.

These are the facts that I know. The youngest of three children,
Gustavo went to work at the *almacén* when his older brother, Pepín,
who was being groomed to take over the business, died of peritoni-
tis as a young man. According to Constantina, the doctor who oper-
ated on him was an alcoholic and botched the operation. The couple
of pictures that I have seen of Pepín show a pale, thin young man
with jet-black hair and a serious expression. Although my grand-

mother talked about Pepín often, I have not once heard my father utter one sentence about his only brother. Either they didn't get along or Gustavo finds it too painful to remember him. In 1937, when Pepín died, Gustavo was sixteen years old and attending Bowles, a military academy in Jacksonville, Florida. For reasons I don't know, he had been thrown out of Belén, a Jesuit academy in Havana. In order to punish him, as well as to make him learn English, his parents sent him to study in the States. He learned English at Bowles, though it's not the only thing he did. Constantina also once mentioned that my father found a bookie in Jacksonville who made it possible for him to put to better use the money they were sending him for winter clothes.

After Pepín's death, Gustavo was needed at the *almacén* and went back to Cuba without finishing high school. A couple of years later, in 1942, he met my mother on a blind date and married her, over Constantina's objections. Not only was Nena the daughter of divorced parents; worse, her family had no money.

During most of World War II Gustavo and Nena lived in the States, traveling here and there buying merchandise for the *almacén*, a lot of it on the black market. Their base of operations was Crowley, a small town in the rice-growing region of Louisiana, where they had befriended some of the mill owners. According to my mother, they were a good team—a young, attractive, English-speaking couple that the Americans found easy to do business with. The other Cuban *almacenistas* with whom my father had to compete for merchandise didn't speak English as well and weren't accompanied by their lovely wives. In the fifties our trips to the States always included a stop at the Egan Hotel in Crowley, where my parents rented a room year round.

When his father, my *abuelo* Pepe, passed away in 1954, Gustavo became the head of the company. Only thirty-three, he must have felt the *almacén* weigh heavy on his shoulders, for in photographs of those years he often looks tense or tired. He had to be steady like Pepe, serious like Pepín—his sister, Cuca, and his mother depended on him. Constantina used to tell me that it took Gustavo a couple of years to get the hang of the job. One year when the *almacén* lost a lot of money, she surprised him in his office with a gun in his hand, contemplating suicide. This sounds so out of character that I'm not sure I believe her, but in any event, by the late fifties the business was again thriving. Only a few months before the nationalization, the office building had been renovated. The new third floor housed Gustavo's elegant, spacious office suite, which had both a bar and a bathroom, his two favorite rooms. Sitting in his new office, my father must have been a happy *papi*.

When I was eight or nine, Gustavo began taking me to work on Saturday mornings and in the summers. He did this not only for the companionship but because he wanted to get me used to the idea of going to the *almacén* every day. Waking up when it was still dark, we tiptoed out of the house together while everyone else was still asleep. It was a twenty-minute drive through deserted streets from our house in the Reparto Kohly to where the *almacén* was in Old Havana. After opening up the office, we walked down the block to a *fonda,* or coffee shop, where we had slices of Cuban bread with butter and *café con leche* to dunk them in. The rest of the day, while Gustavo worked at his desk, I made confetti with a three-hole punch in an empty office or roamed around in the warehouse. Several times during the day we would walk over to the coffee stand on the corner. While Gustavo sipped espresso, I drank a Coke or *guarapo*, a syrupy drink made by crunching sugarcane stalks.

But nothing was as sweet as the warehouse, with the constant loading and unloading of the antiquated orange trucks, which had cranks jutting out of the front end. At the entrance to the warehouse, my grandmother's cousin Vicente usually stood behind a lectern checking the shipments that came and went. The floor was covered with sawdust, and the pungent smell of *bacalao*, or dried codfish, was everywhere. By folding an empty rice sack, the stevedores like Mongo made a little pad that they placed on their shoulders to serve as a cushion. Then they picked up and carried the fifty-pound sacks of rice as if they were feather pillows. Every once in a while, a large flour sack fell to the floor and burst into a white cloud. While the workers went about their business, I built forts from empty boxes and scaled the mountains of rice and bean sacks.

At the end of the day, men would gather in Gustavo's office to have drinks and talk into the evening. They talked about politics, about business deals, and sometimes about women. I sat and listened. My father's cousin Joseíto was always full of grand, get-even-more-rich schemes, but always with somebody else's money. One time he wanted my father to buy a nail factory; another time he talked him into buying a yacht, the *Red Fox,* another casualty of the Revolution. We usually didn't get home until nine in the evening, after my brothers and my sister were asleep.

In person a man of few words, on the phone Gustavo is nearly aphasic. Since I don't see him often enough, for the last several years I have tried, intermittently and with no small amount of trepidation, to get him to talk to me when I call. Although he's the one who normally answers the phone, he isn't interested in conversation. I'll say hello and ask how he is. Depending on his mood, he'll answer that he is fine or barely coping. Sometimes he says, with his lovely thick Cuban accent, "Hanging on, as the Americans say." Then he will ask me a sequence of quick questions: How are you? How is Mary Anne? How are the children? Not given to small talk myself, I answer his questions with monosyllables: I'm *bien,* Mary Anne is *bien,* David and Miriam are muy *bien.* But before I have had a chance to sneak in another word, Nena is on the phone telling me about my sister's miscarriage. Gustavo may live another twenty years, and I will probably never know any more about him than I do now. The Cuban Revolution cost many people many things; sometimes I think it cost me my father.

Growing up in Miami, I was too wrapped up in my own adjustments to pay much attention to what exile was doing to him. When I was fourteen or fifteen and Nena reminded me of how much my father had left behind in Cuba, how much his life had changed in Miami, I heard her words, but they didn't register. I didn't linger on what he had lost, couldn't feel sorry for him. I had a score to settle. Most of my life I've viewed the Cuban exodus as a bad idea, at best improvident and at worst cowardly, and I have said so to my father. I said, "You should have stayed and fought. By leaving, you made it easy for Fidel." What must he have thought, listening to his son say that exile was the coward's way out? If he was a coward, what did that make me? Although I believed that I held this view as an intellectual position, I was venting personal grievances. I was really saying to him, "You tricked me by bringing me into exile; you let me down by taking me out of my country." And yet over and over I heard my parents explain that they left Cuba because of their children, and primarily because of me, since they feared that once I reached my teens, the Cuban government would conscript me into the military. To this day,

I'm not sure what the truth is about why we left. I'm not sure they know it themselves. We left because they didn't want their children indoctrinated. We left because the *almacén* was confiscated. We left because the bank accounts were frozen. We left because Fidel was communist. We left because we could, because my parents spoke English and had lived in the States before. We left because everybody else was leaving. Who knows why we left?

Gustavo was exactly forty years old in October 1960. It wasn't until I turned forty, at a time when I was caught up in revolutions of my own, that I began to understand how hard it must have been for him to change lives at midlife. His anguish and disorientation were no longer foreign to me, for I could feel them inside my own skin. Until then, I bitterly (but quietly) resented his detachment from my life. Gustavo never gave fatherly advice; Gustavo didn't tell stories; Gustavo didn't teach by precept or example. Only once, on the eve of my first marriage, did he take me aside and counsel me: "Gustavito," he said, "if you don't keep women in their place, they will walk all over you." That was the extent of his wisdom, which at the time I ignored, of course, since I was young, foolish, and college-educated.

What I didn't realize was that if Gustavo gave no advice, it was because he had none to give. Rudderless himself, he could not steer me. I know something of the puzzlement of displacement; I know what it is to start from scratch in unfamiliar surroundings; I know how it feels to work among strangers. But I have no idea what happens when you put your life into something like the *almacén* and it is taken away. It's not the money, mind you. The issue is not net worth but self-worth. In Spanish the word for soul is *alma;* Gustavo put his *alma* into his *almacén*. Take that away, and you unsoul him. Lose that, and you lose yourself. I write books and I teach young people to speak Spanish and appreciate literature. I view myself as a writer and teacher, meaningful occupations both. It's embarrassing to admit this, but I didn't always understand the obvious: that selling sacks of rice and boxes of *turrón* are meaningful occupations too. I thought that being a professor was the higher calling. But in fact my ivory tower rises no higher than his hill of beans, and at this moment I'd trade all of my degrees for a shot at the *almacén*. Like me, my father took his identity from his work. Take that away, and the damage done is incalculable.

This damage didn't show up all at once. All things considered, I suspect that the first years of exile may not have been the toughest on him. Cuban history, with its constant political upheavals, gave him every reason to be hopeful of return. For centuries now Cubans have been going into exile and coming back. Cuba's great liberator, José Martí, lived in New York almost as long as he lived anywhere else; our very first president, Don Tomás Estrada Palma, spent over twenty years in the United States (as a Spanish teacher!). Before Castro, no Cuban ruler had been in power for as much as ten years in a row. Even Batista had not been able to hold on very long. Cubans like to think of themselves as a restive, freedom-loving people. Why should they put up with Fidel any longer than they put up with Batista or Machado, fearsome dictators both? And then there was the United States, which in the past had often meddled in Cuban affairs. Throughout the decade of the sixties, the following proposition was etched in stone in the soul of most Little Havanans: the Americans will never allow a communist regime ninety miles away from their shores.

It didn't turn out this way, of course, but Gustavo and countless others like him have never come to terms with reality. He has never reached the point of conceding, at least openly, that the U.S. Marines are not coming to topple Castro, that his *almacén* is gone for good. To this day he speaks of the *almacén* as if it were still his company. A monolith of brick and mortar, it rises before us as the irrefutable measure of our family's achievements in Cuba, where achievement really counted. Periodically, my father trots out thirty-year-old financial records showing that the *almacén* was a million-dollar enterprise. "Not now," he says, "when a million dollars is nothing. But back in the days when a million really counted." Every once in a while Gustavo takes these sheets to work and shows them to his American bosses. It's his way of saying, I may be an underling now, but in Cuba I was somebody. It's his way of saying, if you want to know who I am, don't look at my clothes, don't look at my car, don't look at my house, don't look at me now, look at my 1960 bank statement.

His feelings about the *almacén* parallel his attitude toward Cuba. Although deep in his heart he must know that he has lost Cuba forever, he doesn't concede this to others, perhaps not even to himself. Still claiming possession of a place that he no longer owns or inhabits, he continues to pretend that three decades of residence abroad have not made any difference. With somebody else, all those years could have killed the exile and given birth to the immigrant. But not with him. Inside every exile there is an immigrant that he tries *not* to let out, and Gustavo succeeded in stifling the ingrown immigrant within him, perhaps because his own parents were immigrants and he was determined not to slip backward. He never wanted to start over; he never wanted to become someone else. At the car lot where he works, the Americans have always called him Gus and he accepts the moniker cheerfully, as if it had nothing to do with him. He knows who he is, and he isn't a Gus. When I get called Gus, I go bananas, for the name hits too close to my homelessness. Gustavo knows who he is—he is who he was, and nothing can change him. I believe that my father wakes up every morning with two incompatible thoughts: I'm one day closer to regaining my *almacén* and I'm one day further away from having owned it. The time of dispossession lengthens and shortens simultaneously. As the *almacén* recedes in his memory, it comes closer in his dreams. Is the hourglass half-empty or half-full?

I don't know what my father genuinely thinks about return. I know what he says, I know the assumptions beneath his sentences and his sentiments. Every time I ask him to visit me in North Carolina he replies that the only place he's going to visit is Cuba. But I have no idea what he mutters to himself in the dark. A Spanish proverb says, *el que espera, desespera*—he who waits, despairs. After three decades of waiting, despair must have set in. The *almacén* must have been carved out of his soul brick by brick, shingle by shingle. I'm not sure that "loss" is the right word for such a slow evisceration, since loss suggests an abrupt, definitive rupture. Gustavo hasn't lost the *almacén* yet, but he has been losing it for decades. In my mind's eye, I see the warehouse where I played as a kid and I imagine it being dismantled one brick at a time. I see the shingles on the roof lifted off, the doors unhinged, the orange trucks with the crank driven away to nowhere. I see the whole structure gradually coming down until finally only a vacant lot remains. I'm certain that if I were to go back to Old Havana the way my brother Pepe has done, I'd be shocked to see anything at all on the corner of Paula and San Ignacio.

Gustavo's emotional investment in the *almacén* gave our years in Miami a provisional, makeshift character. Life was elsewhere. While we waited for elsewhere to get here, children had to be fed, parents and relatives had to be looked after, the family had to be kept together; but this was all marking time. My father somehow believed that once Castro was deposed, the clock would be set back to 1960 and he'd get a chance to do it all over again. I'd be eleven years old again, he'd be at the head of the *almacén* again, we'd have a house with servants again, and everything would go back to the way it was. This wait-and-see (or perhaps, wait-and-not-see) attitude made the initial years of exile easier to take, but in the long term it damaged him and us in ways that he couldn't have foreseen. It was not just that he was too depressed or distracted to monitor the tremors of his children's adolescence. When he did notice that something was amiss, his and Nena's solutions always consisted of stopgap measures. If I locked myself up in my room and didn't come out for days, they looked the other way. If my brother Carlos, lost in a different kind of world, ripped off a store, they put the money back. The thing was to get by, to *resolver* as they liked to say, until the hard years of exile ended. Both as a family and as individuals, we had no project, no overriding sense of purpose or direction. There was no point in saving money; after all, we were rich—in Cuba. There was no point in steering the children into one profession or another; after all, we had the *almacén*—in Cuba. There was no point in acquiring property; after all, it would be nothing compared to what we had—in Cuba. Accustomed to the best, good enough was not enough. Gustavo, who has worked for over thirty years in an automobile dealership, doesn't even own a car. Why should he settle for a Nissan when he can drive a Cadillac—in Cuba?

I want to understand, not blame. It was difficult enough for him to put food on the table from day to day, let alone formulate a plan, a vision, establish a set of goals for himself and his children. In Cuba my brothers and I were too young for my father to have much to do with us; by the time we became old enough, we were exiles and he was a nobody. How could he have helped us get somewhere when he was nowhere himself? Clinging to history's promise, he never developed American expectations for his family. Whatever we did here, good or bad, was inconsequential. Nena proudly distinguished between immigrants and us. Time after time she said, "Remember, we are exiles, not immigrants." Unlike the immigrants, we did not come to this country to start all over—we came to wait.

Had we considered ourselves immigrants, we may well have fared better in the long run. The exile and the immigrant go through life at different speeds. The immigrant is in a rush about everything—in a rush to get a job, learn the language, set down roots, become a citizen. He lives in the fast lane, and if he arrives as an adult, he squeezes a second lifetime into the first, and if he arrives as a child, he grows up in a hurry. Not so with the exile, whose life creeps forward an inch at a time. If the immigrant rushes, the exile waits. He waits to embark on a new career, to learn the language, to give up his homeland. He waits, perhaps indefinitely, to start a new life. If immigration is an accelerated birth, exile is a state of suspended animation that looks every bit like a slow death. For the exile, every day is delay, every day is deferral. He may hear the seconds ticking away on Radio Reloj, that Miami radio station that ticked off the time minute by minute, but the timer inside his head never moves. If his life were a painting, it would have to be a tableau. If his life were a symphony, it would be played lentissimo.

The still-life of exile made it too easy for my brothers and I not to grow up and move on. Living in exile was comfortable. It gave me an identity and justified my unease, the nagging sense of not belonging anywhere. I wasn't Cuban, I wasn't American, I wasn't a professor, I wasn't a businessman—I didn't have to be anything because I was an exile. When I moved away from Miami in 1973, I convinced myself that I was going into exile a second time, since now I lived far from both Havana and Little Havana. Not even the birth of my children anchored me. When my son was born in Chapel Hill in 1981, I felt more estranged than ever. It seemed incongruous, even cruel, to have to raise children in North Carolina. What did North Carolina have to do with me? I hated autumn—all those red and ocher leaves. What did these colors have to do with me? I wanted to go back to Miami, my cozy, green exilic cocoon.

Now I realize that the roots of these feelings go all the way back to the Miami of the sixties. I know many other Cubans who at some point, in their everyday lives if not in their hearts, began to behave like immigrants. The hope of returning did not stop them from making a life in the United States. In my own family I have aunts and uncles who arrived in the States and planned out a life for themselves; none of them got rich, but most of them lived peacefully and comfortably. My uncle Pedro left Cuba in 1961 and went directly to New

York, where he found a job as a painter (in Cuba he had been an accountant). After a month of painting houses and buildings, he figured he had learned enough to start his own company. The business did well, the years went by, and Pedro put his money away. When his two children finished college, he retired to Miami with his wife.

I'm not sure why my father was never able to do something like this. His temperament—hardworking but hedonistic—had something to do with it; the financial demands of an overextended family had something to do with it; the years of pressure at the *almacén* had something to do with it. And certainly, my brothers and I had something to do with it. Nothing would have stopped us from following in his footsteps, from retying the knot cut by expatriation. Had we wanted to, we could have helped him find himself again in us.

But exile seems to foster discontinuities, and not just geographical and linguistic ones. To judge from what I have seen with Cubans of my generation, the children of exiles often don't follow the vocational patterns of their parents and grandparents. This happens in part because the family's traditional occupation is sometimes unprofitable or irrelevant in the new land, and in part because sometimes the older generation doesn't provide enough guidance. But it also happens out of spite. The exiled child lumps together the old country and the old occupation, and ditches them both. The exiled child says to his father, "Since you made me leave Cuba, I'm going to leave you." In my immediate family this occurred three times. My brothers and I all had our own individual ways of leaving, but we all left. One-and-a-halfers can be an angry bunch. When you deprive children of something dear, they resent you for it, especially if they don't quite understand the reasons for the deprivation. Their revenge is to deprive you in return, not necessarily of their affection—that's much too hard to do—but of something just as valuable: their companionship. So my businessman father has one son who's a literature professor, another who's a left-wing political activist, and a third who doesn't know what he is.

Most of my life I've held a grudge against Gustavo for not being with me enough, physically and spiritually. Now I see that I wasn't there for him either. We could have saved each other for each other, but we didn't. Probably each of us thought that the other one didn't want to be saved. Perhaps this is why, even now, Gustavo doesn't answer my questions about his life. For a long time he thought that once Fidel disappeared, we would get a chance to do it over. Maybe I thought that too. Later I convinced myself that there was nothing to do over because we had nothing to do with each other. He and I didn't even speak the same language. But now, in these last few years, my anger at my father for having failed me is matched only by my anger at myself for having failed him.

Anger—that's another one of those fashionable American words that I hear and use all the time, a word that spreads out over my life like an all-purpose salsa but somehow doesn't resonate with me. I don't want to express my anger; I want to live my *empingue*, a vulgar Cuban slang word whose closest equivalent is "pissed off." A *pinga*, you see, is a prick—not a penis, not a phallus, not a sex organ, not a member, but a prick. When you're *empingado*, totally and irremediably pissed off, it's as if you became engorged with rage, as if you yourself turned into a stiff, throbbing prick of fury. You don't feel an *empingue*, you embody it. The *empingue* is you. And that's what I feel these days, a tremendous, raging *empingue* toward myself and my father and my brothers for not seizing the opportunities that exile offered us. Gustavo, my brothers, and I—we could have been a family together, if only we had given ourselves the chance.

One hears a lot about Cuban success stories. But for every Cuban success story there's someone like my father, who survived but did not overcome exile. In his old age neither a rich nor a happy man, my father still lives on dreams of Cuba.

FIVE

Domino Theory, Canasta Klatch

Various places, at different times

In my family, when I had a family, the men played dominoes, while the women and children favored canasta.

The wooden tabletop for dominoes has raised borders so that the ivory tiles won't fall over the edge. The tiles are half red and half white, with the two slabs of ivory fastened together by a rivet that juts out a little on the white side. The pips are painted black. Nobody except a truly expert player wants to draw the double nine, whose darkness makes it look like a casket. Tucked into the corners of the tabletop are dirty ashtrays. Each of the four *atriles*, or domino holders, fits exactly ten tiles. The men, as they play, smoke cigars and drink—Scotch for my uncle Pepe, rum and Coke for my uncles Octavio and Manolo, and seltzer water for my grandfather Firmat. Standing a few steps away, my uncle Mike, thin and gaunt, studies the progress of the game. Following domino decorum, the players hardly speak to each other. The only noise is the whacking of the tiles as they are slapped onto the table. The afternoon light slants in through half-closed venetian blinds.

In the next room, my grandmother Constantina and three of her Spanish friends entertain themselves playing canasta. The game takes place on a square tablecloth secured under the corners of the folding table by a strip of elastic. The tablecloth has a flower pattern and pockets for the cards, which have a flower pattern also. The plastic card tray holds the discard and the take-up piles. The joker placed sideways under the discard pile means that the pack is frozen. Green-tinted glasses with soft drinks, ashtrays with cigarette butts, and a canasta score pad cover the tabletop. Constantina is so large that she spills out from her chair.

The people who played dominoes and canasta at these tables are for me the "purest" Cubans in my family, those least affected by exile. Some of them never left Cuba; but even the ones who lived in Miami for years, like my grandmother Constantina and my uncle Mike, seem not to have been damaged by exile the way my father has been. All of them are dead now, and some died in Cuba, which means that I knew several of them only as a child. Still, I treasure my recollections of them. As someone who has grown up straddling cultures, I feel a special need for those members of my family who weren't American at all. I look at them and see important pieces of myself. Reflecting on their lives, I understand how I would have fit in Cuba and why I don't completely fit in America.

Not all these people were model individuals. Some of the men, especially, lived according to a set of rules that many of us today, including me, would find objectionable. And yet these men and women, who come from a world so foreign to our own, continue to teach me lessons that I ignore at my peril. When I need advice, I have them talk to me; when I feel lonely, I imagine myself in their presence. In my heart and mind, these older Cuban relatives, the oldest relatives whom I remember, provide the company and direction that my father, whom exile has diminished so much, has not been able to give me. Although I wouldn't necessarily want their lives to live, I need their lives to lean on.

In the United States dominoes has never been more than a diversion for children, but in Cuba it is second only to baseball as a national pastime. Cuban men have been playing dominoes avidly for two hundred years. Cuban firemen, in particular, are said to be indefatigable domino players, and there is even a devil-may-care way of beginning a game known as the fireman's opening. By the twentieth century Cubans had developed their own version of the game, which uses a set of fifty-five pieces rather than the customary twenty-eight. It's an easy game to play, but a difficult one to master. (I have in my library a 560-page manual detailing the intricacies of *dominó cubano.*) Not even exile could break the domino habit. One of the best-known spots in Little Havana is Domino Park, a small lot at the corner of Calle Ocho and 15th Avenue that began as a meeting place for old men who just wanted to play dominoes, and that by now has become a historical landmark, complete with patriotic name, memorial plaques, and a tall chain-link fence. (A few years ago, as I was showing Mary Anne the Antonio Maceo Domino Park, we were asked to leave by one of the old men in *guayaberas,* who said that the park now was reserved for members only.)

Dominoes is a game of conquest. Using the tiles, or *fichas,* as instruments of empire, a man playing dominoes is a Pizarro of the tabletop. By laying down his tiles, he tries to turn the table surface into his dominion, his domain. When he is about to play his last domino, when he's about to win, he slams it forcefully on the table and crows, *"¡Dominé!"*—I have dominated. Believe me, it's a great feeling. Although historians have speculated that the name may go back to the Dominican friars, who helped popularize the game in Europe, the sobriquet is particularly apt, for dominoes is all about domination. Among Cubans, the game is played almost exclusively by men, perhaps because it furnishes a harmless outlet for aggressive impulses traditionally associated with male behavior. But the interesting nuance is that, in dominoes, conquest requires collaboration. Although each player strives for a free hand, for the leeway to place his tiles without interference from the other players, your rivals' tiles are needed as pegs for your own. Dominoes on the table are said to be *pegados,* stuck or glued to one another, and only by "gluing" your pieces to others can you achieve victory. Skilled players know how to elicit a certain tile from their opponents so that they can then use it to place their own pieces. The domino-male connects and conquers at the same time. When Cuban men play, it's bond and bump, clasp and clash. Yet I wonder whether this blend of conquest and camaraderie isn't also true of men in general—American football players congratulate each other by bumping chests and clashing helmets. By fusing the contradictory impulses of competition and collaboration, dominoes may tell the truth about all men.

The shuffling of tiles between games is termed *hacer agua,* to make or turn into water. Facedown on the table, the virgin stock of dominoes is envisaged as a shapeless liquid from which the arboreal patterns will emerge and back to which they will collapse. It's no coincidence that the pile of leftover tiles is called *monte,* wilderness. Because dominoes transforms the fluid into the fixed, because it freezes water into sculpture, it may be a metaphor for civilization itself. To the eyes of the adept, the zigzag design of the tiles on the table is a work of art, testimony to the triumph of man over nature.

So at least goes the domino theory of my uncle Mike, who loved to philosophize about dominoes, and just about everything else. In Cuba Mike had been a dentist and in the United States he became a jeweler. In reality he was a philosopher, a *mono sabio,* or wise monkey, as Cubans call someone who knows a lot. Of all my uncles—about a dozen, if I include the great-uncles (but they were all great)—he was the speculative one. Mike didn't dance and he wasn't much given to partying, but he loved to think about the workings of the world. A dilettante in the true sense of the word, he delighted in knowledge for its own sake. Although his reading did not extend far beyond *Scientific American* and *National Geographic,* he was always ruminating on one thing or another. Recording his theories in pocket-sized notebooks, Mike speculated about God ("the great atom"), Cuba ("a worthless country"), and Fidel ("Batista with a beard"). During the parties at Nena's house in Miami, he would grab me by the elbow and, lowering his voice as if he were disclosing a secret, say, "Let me tell you this, Gustavito, because it's something that I think you should know. Cubans are a disaster. I have always thought this. I know what your father thinks, but for myself I don't plan to return to Cuba. The day I left La Habana, I said farewell to Cuba for good. Fidel, Machado, Batista, Grau—they are all alike. You mustn't let your patriotism cloud your judgment. Cuba is a worthless country. It will never change."

Tío Mike was one of those exiles who, undeterred by the shock of displacement, carved out a good life in this country. Born at the turn of the century, he descended from a prominent family of dentists and physicians. His father, Benito Vieta, had been the dentist of the king of Spain, Alfonso XIII; his eldest brother, Ángel, was the dean of the University of Havana Medical School. As a young man Mike had wanted to be an architect, but his father refused to pay for any nonmedical career. I remember going as a child to his *consulta,* or office, which was located in El Vedado, one of the oldest and most elegant neighborhoods in Havana. While my mother had her teeth worked on, I sat outside by a moss-covered stone fountain full of fish and yellowed leaves.

Since Mike was nearly sixty years old when he arrived in the States in 1960, instead of trying to get a license to practice dentistry in this country, he found a job making jewelry, an old hobby of his. Setting a diamond, he always said, was no different from filling a cavity. For the next twenty-five years, he worked as a jeweler in New York and Miami. Although he never earned a lot of money, he and my aunt Mary put away enough to retire to Miami Beach and travel around the world a couple of times. Gustavo and Pedro always made fun of them because, in order to save for their trips, they often ate at fast-food outlets. (Gustavo and Pedro would rather eat sirloin steak once a week than hamburger every day.) But Mike and Mary were quite happy with their Big Macs and sausage biscuits. Mary, my mother's older sister, was a big, busty, and somewhat blowsy woman who never sat still except when tutoring one of the children. In Cuba she had given English lessons to me and my brother Pepe; twenty years later in Miami, she taught Spanish to her granddaughters.

Anytime Mary stood still long enough, Mike gave her little pats on the rear, which she always ignored. Not given to macho bluster, he didn't flirt like my father, he courted. Mike never tired of telling anyone who'd listen how beautiful Mary was and how lucky he was to be married to her. He had fallen in love with her at first sight when he was a young dentist and my fourteen-year-old aunt—who was actually a distant cousin—had traipsed into his office as a patient. He waited a few years for my aunt to grow up, and when she did, he made his move and won her heart.

Mike was short, sunken-chested, with pencil-thin arms and spindly, hairless legs. He once bragged to me that he had never in his adult life weighed more than 135 pounds. In Cuba he used to design extravagant high-heeled platform sandals for my aunt, and every year he created new costumes for the masquerade dances at the Casino Español. One time he painted on a goatee, put a patch over one eye, a scarf around his head, and a scabbard and sword around his twenty-eight-inch waist—a regular Cuban Bluebeard. Decked out in a strapless gold-lamé gown so tight that it was almost a bodysuit, Mary was his treasure, towering above him in five-inch heels. Another time he dressed up like a pasha with Mary as his slave, shackles and dog collar and all. If Mary Anne and I showed up at a Duke party dressed like this, we'd probably be run out of the town, but I'm not

sure what the fifties-vintage Cuban bourgeoisie thought of these displays of kinky affection.

Because of Mike's frail appearance and gentle manner, my father
and my uncle Pedro regarded him as a wimp; but to judge from an
exchange I overheard some years ago, Mike was still making love to
Mary long after Gustavo had started cracking jokes about his lack of
virility. One afternoon, my father, Pedro, and Mike were sitting in the
Florida room of my parents' house in Miami, chatting and having
drinks. Gustavo was telling a joke about a seventy-year-old *viejito*
who had enrolled in a sexology class. One day the teacher asked how
many in the class made love every night. Two or three people raised
their hands. Then he asked how many made love once a week, and
how many once a month, and some more people raised their hands.
Finally, he asked how many in the class made love only once a year.
The old man, who was sitting in the last row, started waving and hol-
lering. When the professor asked him why he was making such a
ruckus, the *viejito* answered, "Because tonight's the night!"

After the story, Tío Pedro said, "Miguel, that *viejito* is like you."

"No," my father joked, "Miguelito belongs in the first group
because he's one of those who screw every night—isn't that so,
Miguelito?"

To which Tío Mike replied, with not a trace of vainglory, "Well,
no, not *every* night." Who knows what the magic was between Mary
and Mike, but it was obvious the two were very much in love.

Only after Mike had died and Mary was in a nursing home did I
discover that the one couple in my family who seemed genuinely
happy had not been married by the Church. Mike, who was more
than ten years older than my aunt, had been previously married to a
woman who had left him for another man, and with whom he'd had
a daughter named Athenais (only my uncle would think of such a
curious name). As a child, I had never understood why Mary and
Mike never took communion like everybody else or why neither had
been chosen as a godparent. The reason was that since they had only
been married in a civil ceremony, they considered themselves
excommunicated. It wasn't until 1986, after Mike's first wife died,
that my aunt and uncle were married at St. Hugh's Catholic Church
in a private ceremony, which they timed to coincide with their forti-
eth wedding anniversary. In my book, that's amore.

Most of my other male Cuban relatives, the ones I'm related to by blood rather than marriage, were not nearly as happy or well adjusted as Mike. Some had an unmistakable neurotic streak; others were self-centered rogues, what Tío Pedro would call *jodedores,* half-pranksters and half-hedonists, with a pinch of lunacy thrown in. Foremost among them was my grandfather Firmat, who was an enigmatic, sometimes rotten human being. During the years when he served as the Cuban consul in Norfolk, every six months or so he would get fed up with his wife and children and think up some excuse, some literally diplomatic excuse, to return to Havana, where he kept a mistress. Eventually, he would go back to Virginia for another stint with the family, until he got fed up again and negotiated another furlough. Years later, when he finally left my grandmother for good (her own good, I think), he would send her notes saying, "I have no money this month. You're on your own." Even though he was a hopeless hypochondriac, he always gave himself the benefit of the doubt. When he developed cancer of the prostate, he convinced himself that what he had was a hernia, trussed himself up, and took morphine. When he was dying and my mother brought a priest to his bedside, his grateful last words were, "Nena, how could you do this to me?"

I don't remember these incidents with pleasure. How can I love my grandfather when he was such a lout? When he neglected his wife, who was my grandmother? When he abandoned his children, who included my mother and my aunt Mary? What I have often wondered is whether he had another side that I know nothing about. Because he died in 1954, when I was five years old, my own recollections are so dim that I have to rely on the picture that has come down to me from the children he abandoned, who paint him as an arbitrary and embittered man, someone who felt that he never received the honors that he deserved and coveted. But since I'm not sure how well his own children actually knew him, this portrait may be partial. Abuelo Firmat never did spend much time at home, and for the last twenty years of his life they rarely saw him. I believe that my grandfather may have had another life, inward or outward, that his children weren't privy to. When I turned forty, my mother's birthday present to me was Abuelo Firmat's New Testament, one of the very few books from his library that he allowed her to keep. This man who never went to church and resented having a priest at his deathbed had carefully marked many passages, including the statement in the Epistle of Saint James that a man is justified by works rather than by faith alone, as well as Jesus' pronouncement, recorded in Luke, that anyone who doesn't hate his mother and his father and his wife and his children cannot become His disciple. I don't know why he highlighted these passages, but they suggest that his decision to separate himself from his family perhaps obeyed a purpose other than freedom from responsibility. Did he imagine a higher calling than father and husband?

One of the intriguing details about Abuelo Firmat is that his favorite pastime was to cultivate carnations in the rooftop garden of his house in Havana. According to my mother, he spent much more time with the carnations than he ever did with her or her siblings. By deftly combining different strains, he eventually developed over forty different varieties of this flower. One of his tricks was to water the seedlings with indigo dye, resulting in white carnations with a blue fringe. When he was angry at my grandmother, who didn't like to garden, he used to bark at her, "What can I expect from a woman who doesn't grow flowers?"

For me, Abuelo Firmat's carnations are a symbol of his dedication to activities that others may have thought frivolous or incomprehensible, but that to him were charged with meaning. An economist and journalist by training, he was known in his day for espousing unpopular, even slightly off-the-wall causes. In his columns in the *El Heraldo de Cuba* he repeatedly argued for the diversification of the Cuban economy through the cultivation of rice, a crop that had never grown well on the island. On other occasions, he started campaigns in favor of potatoes and coconut oil. Whatever my reservations about Abuelo Firmat as a husband and father, I find something admirable in his single-minded, if mysterious, devotion to uncommon causes and trivial pursuits.

Of the men of Abuelo Firmat's generation, the ones I got to know better in the flesh were my grandmother Martínez's three brothers, Pepe, Manolo, and Octavio. Every Cuban my age seems to have a syphilitic great-uncle, and Pepe was mine. The disease, which he contracted as a teenager, left him not only half-deaf but sterile, although his wife, Josefina, didn't know this when she married him. Nevertheless, she stuck by him for forty-some childless but more or less contented years. A great *jodedor,* Pepe wasn't about to let marriage or pangs of conscience change his bachelor ways. As he once told me, "A man is only as good as his secrets." After he married, he turned his medical condition into an ever-ready excuse to escape Josefina's vigilance. He and his doctor, a man named Segurola, belonged to an informal organization called *El club de los anaranjados,* the Club of the Orange Men, a reference to canker sores that many of the members suffered. The orange men, who had all been casualties of the wars of love, wore their scars like Purple Hearts. Anytime Pepe wanted to go on the town, he said he was going to visit his doctor, and off they went to a brothel. Among the members of the club, Josefina was known as la *perseguidora,* the patrol car, because she was always chasing after her husband.

By the time I really got to know Pepe well, the orange days were behind him, and his only remaining passion was baseball. In Miami he and Tía Josefina lived in a small efficiency a few blocks down from Eighth Street and spent most of their time at a community center in Little Havana playing dominoes and bingo with other exile old-timers. The one luxury they allowed themselves was a TV set so that Pepe, a lifelong Yankee fan, could watch baseball games. While living in Cuba, he and Josefina would travel every fall to the United States for the World Series. In Miami a black-and-white TV set with rabbit-ear antennas had to suffice. However exciting a game might have been, watching Tío Pepe watch was more fun still. Hunched forward only a few feet away from the set, he reacted to the plays on the screen with the glee of a child at the circus. A missed swing was enough to provoke a loud guffaw. A line-drive single made him break out in expressions of wonder. "Did you see that, Josefina," he would scream to his wife, "did you see that *batazo? Coño,* what a tremendous *palo!*" For him there was no such thing as a routine out or a dull game. A man on the moon was nothing compared to Clete Boyer on third.

One of those unlucky people who, instead of just dying, get slowly dismantled, Pepe spent his last years in and out of hospitals. The last time I visited him, at the Mercy Hospital in Miami, he was such a wreck that I could hardly stand to look at him. His weight had dipped to under one hundred pounds. His heart was failing, his kidneys had stopped working, he had tubes up his nose and an IV in his arm. Josefina, looking almost as bad, was at his side as always. Dummy that I am, I asked the obvious, oblivious question—how was he feeling. Instead of shaking his head and mumbling something trite or pious, as someone else would have done, he pointed to his heart and made a seesaw movement with his hand, as if to say, "This one's not so good." He pointed to his liver and made the same motion—it wasn't so good either. Then he pointed to his kidneys and his bladder and did the same thing again. Finally, he pointed to his prick and then moved his hand up to his neck pretending to slit his throat with his finger, as if to say, "But this one, this one's totally worthless, they might as well chop it off." Josefina, who had witnessed the whole performance, said with a blush, "Oh, the things that occur to my Pepe."

The most important thing I learned from my uncle Pepe, a simple but indispensable lesson, is that a man is not his body. Destroy the body, and the spirit remains. Whether he was watching a baseball game with Josefina or making deathbed jokes with me, Pepe was all spirit. He loved life even when life did not love him back. Neither exile nor illness got the best of him. According to Josefina, one of his last acts before slipping into a coma was to pinch a nurse.

Unlike Pepe, his brother Manolo was a stuffed shirt who didn't go in for Pepe's bawdy humor or his indiscreet philandering. I remember Manolo impeccably dressed in white linen suits, always talking about the sugar company for which he kept the books. But what the family didn't know, or at least pretended not to know, was that Manolo had secrets too, for in his spare time he wrote pornographic plays for the Alhambra, a famous burlesque theater in Havana. I found this out by accident in the most unlikely place—the Duke University Graduate Library—while poring over a dull book on Cuban vernacular theater. Buried in a list of half a dozen playwrights who had achieved "great theatrical triumphs" at the Alhambra, I came upon my uncle's name. Later, Pedro confirmed that Manolo did indeed write for the Alhambra under the pseudonym of Manolo De Más (Manny Too Much). His hit play, *Los farolitos rojos* ("The Little Red Lights"), poked fun at a law that required brothels to identify themselves. Although some people in the family knew about Manolo's moonlighting, Pedro said, no one ever talked about it very much, just as they didn't talk about the fact that Manolo, a lifelong bachelor, kept two concubines, one white and the other mulatto. Although I don't know what to make of the fact that my one literary forebear was a shy pornographer, I'm glad at least that the books in Tío Manolo's life weren't all ledgers.

The third brother, Octavio, who was almost deaf from diphtheria (or perhaps syphilis, I'm not sure), owned an instrument and record store in Old Havana called the House of Music. Although it's doubtful how much music he was able to hear, he found other uses for his wares. As a young man in the 1930s he was a member of the ABC student coalition, which led the resistance against then-dictator General Gerardo Machado. Hiding sticks of dynamite inside the big Victrola radios, he helped the urban underground carry out bombings and other terrorist acts. Although the House of Music was a known meeting place for the rebels, Octavio was able to escape the clutches of La Porra, the dictator's feared secret police, because Ricardo Firmat, his *concuño* (his sister-in-law's brother), a career army officer who was one of Machado's assistants, kept the goon squads away from the store. In 1933 when Machado was finally toppled, Ricardo was spirited out of Havana in Octavio's car, which was flying the ABC safe-conduct insignia.

By American standards, Octavio and Ricardo weren't even related, but Cubans tend to have a stronger and more far-ranging concept of family than Americans. Our idea of family is molecular rather than nuclear. That's why we have several kinship terms that don't even exist in English: *concuño,* which refers to the relationship among siblings of a married couple; and *compadre* and *comadre,* which names the bond between parents and godparents. Although Octavio and Ricardo didn't come from the same biological stock, they considered themselves family nonetheless. As *concuños* they had to look out for each other regardless of political differences.

These are my ghosts—my domino-playing, cigar-smoking, Cuban-coffee-sipping ghosts: cankerous and cantankerous, hardworking and hedonistic, obstinate and loyal. You may have reservations about my ghosts, you may think they are a pretty sad bunch of scoundrels, but I cherish them. I'm their sum, or perhaps only their remainder. Without knowing it, each of them has given me something precious. My great-uncles Ricardo and Octavio taught me to place family loyalty above political alliances; Manolo and Pepe, to love life at all costs. From Uncle Mike I learned a different way of being a Cuban man; and from my grandfather Firmat, the value of stubborn self-absorption. My Cuban ancestors are like a spectral council of elders to whom I go for inspiration and advice. In Spanish, when there aren't enough players for a card or domino game, one says that a *pata,* or leg, is missing. These people are my missing leg, another phantom limb of exile. At times I have thought that they are more me than me.

When I look around me now, I seldom see men with the spirit and fire of Ricardo or Pepe or Octavio. In Chapel Hill, at the mall or the video store, too often I see men who, by the time they reach their middle age, shuffle around with hunched shoulders and a quiet, devastated look. Don't middle-aged American men ever strut? Has life so thoroughly tamed them? Sometimes I imagine my uncle Pepe sitting with me on the bench outside J&J's deli, watching these men emerge from the supermarket with bags of groceries under their arms, saying in his loud deaf-man's voice, "You know, Gustavito, what's wrong with these *americanos* is that they are like roosters shorn of their spurs. They have forgotten the pleasure of conquest. I bet you old Pepe could teach these Americans a few tricks."

Although I talked about dominoes with Mike, I played it mostly with my father and Tío Pedro. We play less now than we used to, but my pilgrimages to Miami usually still include one or two sessions of dominoes with them. Typically, we begin after lunch and don't stop until Nena makes us sit down to dinner. Sometimes we pick up again after dinner and continue late into the night. Since often it's only the three of us, we can't divide into partners; instead we play the variant called *guerra,* war—that is, each man out for himself. While we play, we smoke cigars and drink Scotch. Sometime in the afternoon one of us goes out for Cuban sandwiches and coffee, since Pedro refuses to drink his sister's home brew. The only Cuban coffee worth drinking in Miami, he says, is at Versailles or La Carreta, and then only the one from the coffee stand on the street. According to him, the coffee they serve inside the restaurant tastes different. When we play, I always lose more than I win, but since the stakes are low (five dollars per a hundred-point match), the damage is negligible.

Gustavo and Pedro are both incomparably better players than I am, but neither one is willing to share his expertise. Old Cuban codgers both, when I ask a question—how did they know that I was going to pass with fives?—they refuse to disclose their secrets. Just lucky, they guess. And no, of course they had no idea that I had a run of fours. In this way they routinely attribute to luck outcomes that I know result from skill. The reason is not pettiness, but their unspoken belief that dominoes should not be taught but learned. Although we talk a little while we play, it's mostly formulaic banter about the course of the contest. My father and Pedro underscore their moves by naming the tile they have just played. When Gustavo places a nine on the table, instead of saying *nueve* he'll say *Nuevitas Puerto de mar,* which is the name and description of a town in Cuba. At least as it's played by Cubans, dominoes is for the sticky silent types, a collaborative competition of mute males. Any player who gets a little too loquacious will be silenced immediately with the proverb "Dominoes was invented by a mute," a reference to the legend that the originator of the game was a mute Italian monk by the name of Antonio Dómine. Pedro once did this line one better by replying to my insistent questions with a phrase in *ñáñigo,* an Afro-Cuban dialect: *"Mundele quiere bundanga,"* "White man wants to know mysteries."

Like the visits to La Habana Vieja restaurant, these domino games with my father and my uncle ferry me to the past. The sessions turn into séances. The shuffling of *fichas* calls up my gallery of old-country ghosts: Grandfathers Pérez and Firmat; Great-uncles Manolo, Pepe, Octavio, and Ricardo; my father's brother Pepín and his cousin Joseíto; my uncles Richard, Mike, and Tony; my and my siblings' godfathers—Feluco, Mario, Abelito, Orlando. As we play, even Gustavo and Pedro acquire a ghostly mien. When my father puts down a domino and says *Blanquizal de Jaruco,* a Cuban town that doubles as the nickname for the double-zero tile, his words transport me back to Cuba. I visualize the large playing hall at our beach club, the Casino Español, with its granite floors and windows looking out on the beach and the ocean. I see the row of domino tables, with the drink glasses and ashtrays in the corners. I see those men from whom I descend, some lively, some sullen, slapping down the tiles or contemplating their next move. And in my imagination I see myself, drinking and joking, turning the tiles into water and back again. Like those men, I know how to work my hand, I know how to disguise my weaknesses and how to exploit a *data,* a run of several dominoes with the same number. No one could tell me I don't belong.

Growing up, however, I didn't play dominoes but canasta, a game that was invented in Uruguay around the time I was born. During the 1950s in Cuba, while men preferred dominoes or poker, canasta was the game of choice for women and thus for the children. At the Casino Español, next to the domino salon, there was another large hall filled with canasta-playing women. Although few people play canasta today (for months I've been trying unsuccessfully to find a canasta scoring pad), when I was growing up, canasta decks and implements were everywhere.

Unlike dominoes, canasta isn't a game of domination or war. In Spanish a *canasta* is a basket, and the goal of the game is to complete as many canastas as possible. When you come down to it, canasta is basket-weaving by other means. If domino responds to the aggressive impulses of males, perhaps canasta flows from the more social and cooperative impulses of females. Everything about the game smacks of hearth and home. Like baskets of laundry, canastas come in two kinds, "clean" and "dirty." The cards themselves are held in a tray, and the tablecloth on which the game is played is lined with pockets like an apron. A card that stops your opponent from winning the pile is called a *tapón*, a sink stopper. A stack that cannot be won is said to be "frozen." The red threes are called "flowers," and if you are lucky enough to get all four (canasta is played with two decks), you have a *florón*, a big flower. Seven cards of the same number will make a basket, and whoever "closes" the most baskets wins the game. Whereas dominoes uses fighting words—parrying your opponent's move, you taunt him by saying, *Eso no es puñalá pa' gallo guapo,* "You can't hurt this rooster with such a feeble stab"—the language of canasta is conciliatory, even amiable. In canasta one doesn't stab, one "melds" (the English term for closing canastas). At the end of a hand of canasta, you don't crow *dominé;* rather, you politely ask your partner, "May I leave?" Unless she agrees to let you, the hand must continue. If dominoes is a game of conquest, canasta is a game of consensus.

The most avid canasta player in my family was my grandmother Constantina. In Cuba she played almost every afternoon at the Casino Español. In Miami she couldn't play as frequently, but she and her Spanish friends got together two or three times a week. Her approach to the game was businesslike, and she never played much with her grandchildren. She didn't have the time or the temperament for children or grandchildren, hers or anybody else's. Only in Miami, after many of her friends had died, did she condescend to play canasta with younger folk, most of whom were no longer so young.

Not a centimeter over 4'9" and tipping the scales at about 220 pounds, Constantina was a ball of fat and fire. She was so short and so round that in her later years when I took her Christmas shopping at Sears (the only store she would patronize), we had to use the freight elevator to go up to the second floor because her wide body didn't fit on the escalator. Although her blood pressure and cholesterol were always sky-high, when her heart finally gave out, she had been in good health for most of her ninety years. A happy, hearty eater, she loved fried foods and rich pastries. One of her specialties was *arroz con manteca,* rice with lard, which I ate with delight and trepidation. In spite of her size, though, she was light enough on her feet to dance a lively *jota,* a Spanish folk dance. Snapping her fingers above her head, she would take graceful little hops and steps to the imaginary music, which she accompanied with a small, squeaky voice. She looked and sounded like an overfed canary on a tightrope. She also liked to do the *pasodoble* with my father, though between her girth and his, their arms barely reached around each other.

In Cuba, Constantina had been the heart of the *almacén.* Averse to fuss or turmoil, my grandfather Pérez was a quiet, industrious soul who minded his own business. Unlike him, Constantina loved a good fight and thrived in the spotlight. Anytime there was any hassling to be done, she was the one who did it. When they needed a zoning change to build a new warehouse, she was the one who made the rounds of inspectors and bribed whoever needed to be bribed. When they were sued by a disgruntled client, she was the one who went to court. It was thanks to her that the government indemnified them for the old *almacén* that had been built against the city walls. When the government at first demurred at the high price she asked, she sued. When the court did not issue the judgment she wanted, she refused to give up, telling the judge that her maiden name was not Mulas (mules) for nothing. Eventually she got her way. When I was a child in Cuba, she was the only woman in my family who worked outside the home. A strong-willed, liberated woman long before such roles were acceptable, somehow she raised three children and helped build a large business. And all of this with only an elementary school education. Knowing how to count, she liked to say, was better than knowing how to spell.

Although in Cuba she had lived next door to us, I only saw her once a week, briefly. Every Friday at noon my brother Pepe and I would go over to her house to show her our *boletín,* our weekly report card. Entering through the kitchen, we'd usually find her sitting by herself at the head of the large dining table, surrounded by steaming plates of food, with a napkin tucked under her chin. We had been taught by our mother that it was bad manners to tuck the napkin inside your shirt collar, but Constantina had a manner all her own. Since our American-raised, health-conscious mother disdained fried foods, the aroma of Constantina's kitchen was unlike anything we were used to at home. There is no scent more comforting than that of well-marinated pork chops frying in olive oil. When you walked into Constantina's kitchen, it enveloped you like a warm embrace. But Pepe and I didn't go there for her pork chops, but for her pesos. We walked over to where she was sitting, gave her the obligatory kiss on the cheek, and showed her our grades. If they were good enough, she wiped her mouth on her napkin and asked us to get her black purse from a nearby chair, from which she pulled out one or two dollars as recompense. Then Pepe and I walked back to our house and our mother's *bistí* and mashed potatoes and sirloin steaks. Because she spent her life either at the *almacén* or playing canasta, the only other time I saw Constantina was when I accompanied my father to work. During the mornings, she was always at her desk counting money and putting it away in the wall safe next to the desk.

I'm not sure what kind of a life my grandfather Pepe and Constantina had together, since he died when I was six years old. When I was already a grown man, she once told me that the day my father was born she informed Pepe that from now on if he wanted sex he should go to see the *putas* (whores) because she had had enough. Another time she said that by the time Pepe was fifty "his joints had rusted" and they didn't have to sleep together anymore. Although she wasn't prudish about sex, it was clear that she thought of it as a nuisance that distracted her from a higher calling—selling bags of rice and playing canasta.

After we left Cuba I had little to do with my grandmother for several years; although she was still around (and still round), I was busy with friends and school. By the time we connected again, I was in college and she was well into her seventies. Although she had lived off and on in tiny efficiencies, in the late sixties she settled into the upstairs apartment at my parents' house. She still played canasta several times a week with the same group of friends with whom she had played in Cuba, and she still liked to eat, except that now she cooked for herself. When she wasn't cooking or playing canasta or hassling on the phone with the Spanish old ladies who were her friends, she read the exile tabloids and listened to talk shows and other political programs on the radio. Sometimes she called in to recite poems that she said she had composed, but which were often schoolbook rhymes by Campoamor and other nineteenth-century Spanish poets. I don't know whether she actually believed that she had written these poems herself, and I didn't want to tell her otherwise.

Although Constantina lived in the States for twenty years, she never learned one word of English, or *inglis,* as she called it. For a while she and her friends went to the English Center to take classes; but the teacher has not been trained that could teach my grandmother to say even "yes" or "thank you." Her vocal cords simply refused to emit anything that sounded remotely like English. Although she tried over and over, she never did pronounce correctly the one syllable in my cousin's American husband's name, Jeff. On her purple frog lips, Jeff always came out "Yes." But when she tried to say "yes," it sounded like "chess." She wasn't proud of her impediment, but accepted it as inevitable. The way she looked at it, it wasn't that she resisted acculturation, only that she was incapable of it. "Gustavito," she used to tell me, *"inglis* just doesn't enter me. God must not want me to speak *inglis."* Somewhat the same thing had already happened to her in Cuba; though she had left Spain when she was a teenager, all her life she retained a thick Castilian accent, with its hard *z*'s and soft *d*'s (both similar to the *th* sound in thimble). On her lips Pérez was always "Péreth" and Madrid was always "Madrith." She also kept the old peasant names for many household objects—ice was *nieve,* snow; butter was *manteca,* lard; a little bit of something was always a smidgin, *una miaja.*

Because old people are the least prepared for exile, they are often the ones least affected by it. Paradoxically perhaps, their deeply grooved habits act as a cushion against the shock waves of expatriation. And so it was with Constantina, who lived in Miami as if she didn't. Since she never thought that she would die here, she didn't take exile all that seriously. Her nonchalance stemmed in part from political naïveté, which made her think that the Revolution was

ephemeral, and in part from the wistfulness of old age, which shield-
ed her from a more realistic assessment of Cuban politics. As a
result, her dreams of Cuba, unlike my father's, remained as fresh and
untarnished as her Castilian *z*'s. America didn't stand a chance of
changing her Old World ways.

In 1970, when I began attending the University of Miami, Constantina and I developed a partnership that lasted until I got married
and went away to graduate school: she cooked and I ate. After spending my mornings in crowded auditoriums listening to lectures about
the Elizabethan stage or the Russian novel, I would come home to
her *fabada* and *caldo gallego.* The college education that distanced
me from my father had just the opposite effect on my relations with
his mother. Since I was an English major, she didn't have the foggiest idea what I did at the university either, but she wanted something
to do and I needed somewhere to eat, so our destinies merged.

Going to her house at lunchtime was like living in Cuba again.
Although the dining room and kitchen of her Havana home. were
now combined into one small area, the aroma of garlic and olive oil
remained intact. By the time I got there around noon, Constantina
was already sitting at the table, napkin tucked under her chin.
Because most of the burners on her range were broken, she cooked
on a portable electric stove that she placed next to the dining table,
which allowed her to keep an eye on the food without having to get
up from her chair—a major undertaking at her weight. On top of the
refrigerator—she called it a *nevera,* snow box—she always kept a
white enamel casserole filled with the *escabeche,* pickled swordfish,
that we ate as an appetizer. The clean pots and pans were stored
inside the oven, which she hardly used. I tried to get her to cook with
as little fat as possible, but without much success. Throwing a couple of heaping tablespoons of lard into the rice pan, she would say to
me, "You see, Gustavito, you see how little *grasa* I'm using?" My
one big accomplishment was to get her to fry my eggs in water rather
than olive oil, although they tasted so good that I'm sure that she
cheated. For dessert we had either a Spanish dessert like *torrejas,* the
Castilian version of French toast, or guava shells and cream cheese.
I picked the guavas from a tree in the yard, which unfortunately my
mother decided to cut down one day because she couldn't stand the
pungent smell of the rotting fruit. Every lunch ended with a scald-

ing dose of Cuban coffee, which Constantina drank from the saucer rather than the cup.

While we ate, we listened to the radio and talked about the family or Cuban politics. When she received a letter from my aunt in New York, she'd read it aloud to me, providing commentary as she went. When she laughed, which she did often, she cackled like a big fat beautiful hen, with the folds of skin under her chin slapping against her swollen chest. Convinced that we would go back to Cuba someday, she didn't find it painful to talk about the past, which she did endlessly. In most of the stories she was the star, with my father or grandfather cast as a supporting player. Yet from what I have been able to gather from others, Constantina exaggerated her achievements only slightly. A sweet and gentle soul she was not. With her hooked nose, jutting jaw, and massive body, she was both immovable object and irresistible force. If you got her dander up, she was capable of ripping your heart out with her tongue.

Even at her meanest, however, Constantina had a sense of fairness that I admired. One time, for some reason I don't remember, she and my mother got into an especially nasty quarrel. Constantina's definitive, irrefutable insult, which she saved for just the right moment in the fight, was to call my mother "the daughter of divorcés." My mother replied that at least she had not descended from illiterate Spanish peasants. Constantina countered by telling her that those illiterate Spanish peasants had made it possible for Nena to drive around Havana in a Lincoln Continental. Nena answered that at least she, Nena, had taken Constantina in, which is more than her own daughter in New York had done. One time, after listening to the volley of insults for a while, I became upset that Constantina was getting the best of my mother, and I intervened on her behalf. At this point the fight had spilled over to the backyard, where the laundry room was located. While Nena changed loads in the washing machine, Constantina stood a few feet away berating her. I confronted my grandmother on the steps to the back door. Towering over her short broad frame, I screamed, "¡¡Basta!!"—Enough! Constantina snarled at my mother a moment longer but soon retreated upstairs. A few days later over lunch, Constantina said to me, "Gustavito, I was hurt that you screamed at me the other day because you know how much I love you, but I understood that you stuck up for your mother because that's what a son should do. I'm proud of you for that." I believe that she actually meant what she said.

In the evenings around nine, I would usually go back upstairs to visit with my grandmother for a second time. We would watch a Spanish-language soap opera or two, make Cuban coffee during the commercials, and I would help put the glaucoma drops in her eyes. Administering the drops was quite an undertaking. First Constantina had to get settled into her folding rocking chair, which had several handkerchiefs tied to the armrests. Then she untied one of her hand-kerchiefs with the lace fringes and dried her eyes with it. Then she bent her head back as far as she could, which was about an inch and a half, and I bent over her with the drop dispenser. After I carefully put two drops into the corner of each eye, she batted her eyelashes several times—this she was good at—in order to let the liquid seep into the eye. Finally, she dried her eyes with the handkerchief and asked me if I thought the drops had gone in. Invariably, I answered, *"Sí, Abuela."* Then it was time to watch the soap operas. During my college years, I spent more time with my grandmother than I ever did with my mother or my father.

In return for her *escabeche* and her hospitality, I ran errands and drove my grandmother around, though probably not as often or as willingly as I should have. Constantina didn't go out much, and when she did it was always to the same places: the Cuban grocer and butcher to buy food for our lunches, a friend's house to play canas-ta, and the doctors. The latter were legion—she had an eye doctor, an ear doctor, a heart doctor, an arm doctor, a stomach doctor, a foot doctor, and a G.P. Most of them were youngish Cuban physicians who treated *viejitas* like my grandmother kindly and patiently, since I think they understood that the purpose of the frequent visits was social as much as medical. Constantina reciprocated their attentions with a mixture of affection and irreverence. She called them her *novios,* her beaux, and bought them little presents. Sometimes I would drop her off at a doctor's office early in the afternoon and not pick her up until several hours later. Usually, she had agreed to meet one of her friends there, and they spent the afternoon catching up on old news and new ailments.

In fact, Constantina was extraordinarily healthy for most of her life. She always used to say to me that she was immortal, like the saints. It was only a couple of years before she died that she began having medical problems, and this only because she fell and broke a hip. At that point her excessive weight became a handicap, especially because one of the American inventions that she never mastered was the walker. Instead of letting it wrap around her and sliding it forward as she walked, she turned it sideways and dragged it behind her. There was no way anyone could convince Constantina that walkers were to be used otherwise.

The one ailment Constantina did suffer from was periodic depression, or *neura,* as she called it. The *neura* would come and go unexpectedly. One fine morning she would wake up with the *neura,* which automatically turned her into a vegetable. She couldn't cook, couldn't clean, couldn't get dressed, couldn't comb her hair, couldn't put on rouge and lipstick, couldn't go shopping, couldn't talk on the phone. Normally a coquette (she was especially proud of her thick hair and smooth skin), under the influence of *neura* she moped around the house teary-eyed, wearing only a sleeveless *bata* (bathrobe) and slippers. Pinning several handkerchiefs to the shoulder straps of the bathrobe, she made sure you saw her drying her tears, which weren't all depression-induced, since she also had a chronically clogged tear duct. But the tears and the handkerchiefs hanging from the straps added to the overall effect. The only activity that was *neura*-proof was canasta, although during severe depressions even canasta suffered. When Constantina passed up an opportunity to play canasta, you knew that the *neura* had hit her really bad.

The bouts of depression would last for days or weeks and then, as abruptly as they had appeared, they would vanish. She usually had a supernatural explanation for her sudden recovery. "I was lying awake in the middle of the night and the Virgin of Carmen appeared to me. She said that she was going to cure me of the *neura.* When I woke up, the *neura* was gone and I was full of *ánimo.*" At other times the apparition would be the archangel Gabriel or a favorite saint like Joseph. They always came to her in the middle of the night. On the days immediately following her miraculous recovery, she became a whirlwind of activity, catching up on the things she had neglected during the *neura*-cooking, cleaning, getting herself prettied up, talking on the phone, shopping for groceries, making the rounds of doctors, playing canasta. It was all I could do to keep up with her. Times like these I prayed to *my* favorite saint (Jude, patron of hopeless cases) for a mild relapse of *neura* so that she would slow down a bit. But once her spirits were lifted by the spirits, there was no way to bring Constantina down to earth. The manic pace lasted until the next onset of *neura*.

My grandmother and I were certainly an odd couple, unlikely lovers thrown together by exile. Our relationship was the ultimate May-December romance, an affair of the heart and the intestines. One thing that made the romance possible is that she liked men better than boys. As a young man in Miami, I was far more interesting to her than I had been as a little boy in Cuba. Constantina didn't bake cookies, read stories to her grandchildren, take us to the movies, care for us when we got sick, or stay with us when our parents went on vacation. Those traditional grandmotherly tasks were reserved for my other grandmother, Abuela Martínez, who performed them gladly and lovingly because, unlike Constantina, she liked boys much better than men (remember, she had been married to my grandfather Firmat). It was Abuela Martínez who actually taught me to play canasta when I was seven or eight years old, and who took us to the movies and bought us toys. Constantina never did any of these things, which worked out well in the end, since this way I didn't run out of grandmothering when I reached adulthood. Where one *abuela* left off, the other one picked up.

Not that Constantina and I, like all lovers, didn't have our spats. One day, out of the blue, or rather, over a bowl of Galician stew, she declared that the girl I was dating at the time was a *puta,* a whore. When I asked how she knew this, she said, "She is twenty-three-years old and unmarried. She must be a *puta.* Besides, I'm half *bruja. I* know these things." A *bruja* is a witch. Anytime that she revealed knowledge of any detail of someone's life, usually mine, she said the same thing, that she had supernatural powers. "It's that I'm half *bruja*, you see." I was furious and stormed out of her apartment without finishing my lunch.

Since I've always had the courage of my conniptions, I then spent several weeks without eating or watching the soap operas with her. During this period I used to come home from the university in the afternoons to find Constantina leaning out of the window of her apartment like some forlorn maiden, begging for a reconciliation: "Gustavito, Gustavito, don't you love me anymore? Why won't you talk to me, Gustavito?" I would go right past her into the house without looking up or saying a word. Eventually, I broke down under the barrage of affection (and the need to eat) and Constantina and I made up. She once even went to the Spanish movie theater with me and my girlfriend, who did turn out to be something of a *puta* after all. Anytime I started going out with someone new Constantina would say, *"Tú eres un poco veleta como tu abuelo,"* "You're a weather vane like your grandfather." She was right on the mark about that too; I have never been as constant as Constantina.

Her death in April 1979 carved a big hole in our family. Although we had experienced other deaths in the family before, this was the first time I thought that something irrevocable had happened, that exile had maimed us permanently. Not only had she been a daily part of my life for years, but she was my principal conduit to people and events that I didn't know firsthand or that I remembered only faintly. Death is always plural; who dies takes not only herself but those we knew through her. Large in every way, Constantina was a multitude, a whole canasta of people. She was the one who made the *almacén* come alive, the one through whom I found out about my father and grandfather, the one who told me about her uncle the bishop or my tubercular cousin from Spain. I experienced her death as depopulation, as a thinning out of my mental society. She occupied so much space that when she passed away, the family became noticeably smaller, much less inhabited.

Over the last three decades, demographers and sociologists have repeatedly counted the number of Cubans living in Miami. But has anybody ever counted the exiles who have *died* in Miami? Has anybody taken a census of the city's Cuban dead? Miami is a little Havana not only because of the Cubans who still live there but because, perhaps primarily because, of those who have died there. The living can always move away; it's the dead who are a city's truly permanent residents, for once they stop living there, they never stop living there. Castro could fall tomorrow, every Cuban in Miami could go back to the island, and for me the city would remain as Cuban as it is today. Thousands and thousands of exiles like my grandmother have made it so. The irony is that because Constantina's gravestone records the place and year of her birth and death, it omits any reference to Cuba, the country where she spent most of her life, where she married and had children, where she helped my grandfather build the *almacén,* where she played canasta every day.

When Constantina fell ill, I flew down to Miami, but since at the time I was rushing to finish my first book, after a few days I decided to return to Chapel Hill. When I went to the hospital to say goodbye, on Saturday, she was still in intensive care but apparently doing better. I told her that I would see her later that summer. She blew me a kiss and batted her eyelashes in her typical coquettish way. Monday morning my mother called to say that Constantina had died the previous night. I flew back to Miami. That evening at the Rivero Funeral Parlor in Little Havana I was surprised by how comfortable she looked. Her blubbery body had settled into the open casket like rice pudding. For the first time, my grandmother looked almost angelic.

Gazing at her, I remembered the Constantina I had known as a child in Cuba, who always seemed either to be counting money at the *almacén* or playing canasta at the Casino Español. Then I thought back to our years together in Miami, all those trips to Sears and all those lunches of *escabeche* and all those evenings of Cuban coffee and glaucoma drops. I couldn't believe that she was dead, this woman who had lived so long and whom I had loved so much. As I stood there, lost in my recollections, I began to hear her soft cackling laughter, and then I heard her voice saying to me, "Don't be sad, Gustavito; you know that I am immortal, like the saints."

SIX
The Ghosts of Nochebuenas Past

Havana-Miami, on Christmas Eve

El hombre manda y la mujer gobierna—man rules and woman governs. This Spanish proverb accurately describes the balance of power in our family when my siblings and I were growing up. Although our father was the titular head, our mother ran the household and made most of the day-to-day decisions. If Gustavo was king, Nena was the prime minister. Both in Cuba and in Miami, she was the one who answered our questions, the one who solved problems and averted catastrophes. Perhaps because she herself grew up in a storm-tossed household, she governed with a loving and steady hand, always making sure that, whatever else happened in our lives, we had peace and stability at home.

When I reflect on my mother's life, I always think about Nochebuena, the Cuban Christmas Eve, a celebration of family togetherness. In my mind, my mother has always been the spirit of Nochebuena. When I was a child in Cuba, Nochebuena (literally, the Good Night) was the most important family gathering of the year. As far back as I can remember, relatives and close friends always gathered at my parents' house on the evening of December 24. Bisected by midnight mass, this night oscillated, sharply but predictably, between the sacred and the profane, between religious observance and secular mirth-making. Since in the 1950s Catholics were still required to fast before receiving Holy Communion, the party that accompanied the religious observance was not supposed to begin until one or two o'clock in the morning, after everyone got back from *la misa del gallo,* midnight mass, whose name goes back to the

115

Roman custom of holding mass at dawn, when the *gallos,* or cocks, crowed. But cultural differences being what they are, the Cuban roosters began crowing long before the Roman cocks. By the time midnight mass rolled around, my aunts and uncles had been celebrating for hours. Some of the men, who typically were less devout than their wives, were already well into their Bacardi cups. When they accompanied their wives and children to midnight mass, many remained on the steps of the church while the women and children went inside to pray. It was a curious sight: from inside the church you could see the crowd of men, impeccably dressed in their long-sleeved *guayaberas* with bow ties, milling around outside and talking. The hubbub was such that sometimes Father Spirali, the Italian-born pastor of the San Agustín parish in Havana, had to interrupt the service to hush the men congregated outside. I looked out jealously from within the church and couldn't wait to be old enough to join them.

Cuban Nochebuena was essentially a feast for grown-ups. Since in Cuba most children got their holiday gifts on January 6, the Feast of the Epiphany, nothing that happened on Christmas Eve had to do directly with us. At our house my brothers, my baby sister, and I went to bed before *la misa del gallo.* The last couple of years in Cuba, Pepe and I were allowed to attend midnight mass, but since our American-tinged household was visited by both Santa Claus and the Three Wise Men (Santa brought the better gifts), we were still packed off to bed sooner rather than later, with the pretext that Santa wouldn't come until all of the children were asleep. But it was hard to get to sleep on Nochebuena, a good but not a silent night.

After the dinner of roast pig, *yuca con mojo* (yuca root with seasoning) and *congrí* (black or red beans and rice cooked together), which usually wasn't served until two o'clock in the morning, the celebration went on for several more hours. Those years when my parents skipped midnight mass, they and their friends would troop off directly from our house to a 5 A.M. mass at the Sacred Heart Church. From there they would go to breakfast. When my brothers and I woke up Christmas morning, my father would be sleeping, but my mother stayed up so that she could be with us when we opened our gifts. For her, Christmas morning with the children was no less important than Nochebuena with the grown-ups (for Gustavo, who slept until one or two in the afternoon, Christmas was the bleary day that inevitably followed the long good night). As we tried out our new toys, Vargas and the maids went about straightening up the house, which had that desolate post-party look, with smudged glasses and dirty plates and crumpled napkins strewn everywhere.

At least for me, the best part of Christmas wasn't Nochebuena or Santa Claus, but the preparations that preceded the festivities. Like other Cuban couples, my parents had an uneven division of festive labor: Nena prepared, and Gustavo partied. Her job was to set everything up; his job was to make the most of her arrangements, for the benefit of others as well as himself. If Gustavo was the life of the party, Nena was its soul. Her preparations for Nochebuena began weeks earlier with the arrival of boxes of Spanish nougat, marzipan, filberts, sparkling wines, and other holiday staples, gifts from the people my father did business with. We'd buy the tallest Christmas tree available at a nearby American-style supermarket, and then spend several afternoons putting up the ornaments and setting up the nativity scene. The fake fireplace in the living room was just the right size for the large plaster figures of Baby Jesus, Mary, and Joseph, and made a marvelous manger. Under the tree we built a replica of Bethlehem, complete with river, bridge, shepherds, and sheep. Off to one side, somewhat in the distance, the Three Wise Men approached on their camels, bearing gifts. In the foyer my mother placed mirrors and cotton swatches to simulate snow and a frozen lake, which she surrounded with little cottages with red roofs and lights inside. Between early December and the second week in January, this incongruous wintry landscape was the first thing one saw as one entered our Cuban house, where even the walls were painted a leafy green.

Compared to the bushy Carolina balsams that I later became accustomed to in the States, the puny imported pines that reached the Ekloh Supermarket looked like malnourished third-world imitations of the real thing. They shed needles like rain, and no amount of watering could cure their wan, skeletal look. But to us they were marvelous. Other kids in the neighborhood, whose parents didn't believe in Christmas trees, came to our house for awed stares. The point was not the tree, anyway, but the decorations, whose abundance more than made up for the gaping holes in the foliage.

Because Americans think of Christmas trees as natural objects, often their idea of decoration is a red ribbon with a pinecone or some paper cutouts that their kids bring home from school. For us, Christmas trees were cultural artifacts that provided an opportunity to demonstrate once again the triumph of man over nature, and so we smothered them with decorations: lights, endless rosaries of shiny marble-sized balls, and box upon box of ornaments, including some odd ones like a blown-crystal *bohío* (thatched hut). Any residual holes we buried under a canopy of *lágrimas*, literally tears but in fact tinsel. Tears blanketed our sagging tree like kudzu. The crowning touch was a large, brightly lit figure of the archangel Gabriel, who presided over the living room with arms outstretched. It was usually Vargas who got up on a ladder and, tottering above Nena's watchful eye, skewered the angel into the tree. By the time we were through, several days after we had begun, our formerly spindly tree looked splendid—an anorexic wrapped in jewelry and furs, and with an angelic tiara to boot.

When we got to Miami in October 1960, we stopped celebrating Nochebuena. It seemed pointless to observe this feast in exile, with our unsettled situation and the family scattered all over—some relatives still in Cuba and others in New York and Puerto Rico. That first Christmas in Miami we put up a tree, though a smaller and greener one, but the only créche we could afford was a cardboard stable with fold-out figures. Instead of Nochebuena dinner, we had Christmas lunch; instead of the traditional roasted pig, Nena baked a turkey. My parents kept hoping that we would be back in Cuba in time to celebrate Nochebuena the way we always had, but it didn't happen. Sitting around the table on Christmas Day, we weren't so much gloomy as dazed. We had been living in this house only a few weeks, everything was topsy-turvy, it wasn't clear what we were supposed to think or say. There we were, just my parents and us four children around the table, suddenly transformed into an American nuclear family. Instead of the noisy bacchanals we had been used to, our Christmas celebration was brief and muted. Earlier that morning Santa had left gifts for those of us who still believed in him, but two weeks later the Three Wise Men didn't show up.

After a few years, our family reinstituted Nochebuena. By the late sixties everybody in our family had left Cuba, and if they didn't live in Miami, they were able to come down for Christmas. Since the family had been brought together again, it no longer felt inappropriate to celebrate in exile. Indeed, the opposite thing happened: distance from the homeland made us celebrate the occasion all the more vigorously, for Nochebuena became one of the ways of holding on to Cuba. Although the Nochebuenas in exile were less splendid than the Cuban ones, the essentials remained the same. During these years Little Havana was full of Cuban markets that carried all of the typical foods. *Turrón* and *sidra* (Spanish champagne) were easy to obtain; and if a family didn't have the time or the equipment to roast a pig at home, an already-cooked pig could be bought at the corner *bodega,* along with containers of *congrí* and *yuca.*

Like the food, the faces in our family gathering hadn't changed much. Our Miami Nochebuenas from the 1970s included many of the same relatives that had attended the gatherings in Cuba. Tío Mike always arrived early to set up what he called his "intellectual laboratory," where he concocted mysterious martinis by looking up the proportions in one of his pocket notebooks. While Mike experimented, his wife, Mary, minced around in her gold high-heeled thongs with the furred straps. Tony, an uncle who had been a cabaret singer in Havana and was now a waiter in New York, crooned *boleros* accompanied by my sister on the guitar, while Gustavo danced randy rumbas with any willing (and sometimes unwilling) partner. Tío Pepe and Josefina came, as did Tío Pedro and his wife, Amparo, and Joseíto and his wife, Encarnita. Also present were assorted boyfriends and girlfriends and current and prospective in-laws—all Cuban—and the one American in the family at this time, my cousin Evelyn's husband, Jeff, the one whose name Constantina never mastered. And, oh yes, Constantina. At some point during these evenings, with her eyes sparkling from a glass or two of *sidra,* Constantina did her famous *jota,* which was followed by the ritual *pasodoble* with my father.

In spite of the similarities to Cuba, though, these lively parties weren't really clones of the old Nochebuenas. Even if we went to church, pigged out on roast pork, and drank and danced, the holiday had begun to change. Without anyone being overly aware of it, the Cuban Nochebuena and the American Christmas had started to get acquainted, to negotiate a compromise. Not only was Christmas sneaking up on Nochebuena; Nochebuena was converging on Christmas. Like Constantina doing the *jota* next to the Christmas tree, Cuban customs began to merge with American ways.

On the face of it, the merger was not an easy one. As a *prospective* celebration of the birth of Christ, Nochebuena has a high-strung, restive feel. Many Cubans spend the night in perpetual motion, going from one house to the next, a custom that supposedly goes back to the biblical story of Mary and Joseph wandering around Bethlehem looking for a place to spend the night. On the evening of December 24, Cubans divide into two camps: the squatters and the roamers. The squatters stay put, cook, stock plenty to drink, and keep their doors open. The roamers make the rounds. Since we were always squatters, part of the fun of Nochebuena was having people show up at our doorstep at any hour of the night, have a couple of drinks, eat, dance, and then move on to their next house. Needless to say, it's safer to squat than to roam, but it's the roamers who give the evening that extra burst of *embullo,* that extra hit of festive fuel.

By contrast, the spirit of Christmas is neither raucous nor nomadic. As befits a family holiday, Christmas is merry but not movable, joyful but not extravagant. Whereas Nochebuena is a nocturnal feast, Christmas is a daytime celebration, a holiday in the full sense of the word. If Nochebuena is all motion and commotion, Christmas is peace. On Christmas families gather to exchange gifts and spend time together, not to hoot and howl. Children are a big part of Christmas, but during Nochebuena they are little more than a nuisance. Our Nochebuena photographs show bunches of grownups living it up; our Christmas photographs show parents and children gathered around the tree. When Christmas encounters Nochebuena, American days run into Cuban nights.

In our house the marriage of day and night occurred when my siblings and my cousins and I grew up and then began to have children of our own. By the mid-seventies and for several years thereafter, we had achieved a rough balance between the "Cuban" and the "American" ends of the family. The older Cubans, mostly men like my father and my uncles, celebrated Nochebuena; Nena and her American-born grandchildren did the same for Christmas. As a member of the one-and-a-half generation, I swung back and forth between one and the other, sometimes playing Cuban son to my father and at other times playing American dad to my son. During these balanced years, the prospect of Christmas morning made Nochebuena a little more sedate, and Nochebuena made Christmas a little more lively. Since the adults had to be up at the crack of dawn to open presents with the kids, we couldn't—as Nena always reminded us—stay up all night and then go for breakfast to La Carreta or Versailles. Besides, the house was too small for the kids to be able to sleep while the adults carried on outside. Since by the 1970s the Church had slackened its rules on fasting, most years Nena served dinner before midnight mass. By two or three in the morning Nochebuena was over.

I loved these hybrid celebrations, half day and half night, for they seemed to combine the best of both worlds. The problem, though, is that biculturalism is a balancing act that topples with the passing of generations, and by the end of our third decade in exile, our Nochebuenas had changed again. Tío Pepe, Constantina, Abuela Martínez, Joseíto, and Tío Mike passed away in the 1970s and '80s. Other aunts and uncles were either too old to travel to Miami every December or became too infirm to leave their houses. When his wife died, my uncle Pedro stopped celebrating holidays altogether. (Now he gets on a plane on the morning of December 24 and spends Christmas Eve at the blackjack tables in the Bahamas; a *noche buena* for him now is when he doesn't lose too much money.) Then also, those in my generation have our own lives and can't always make it to Miami for Christmas. My sister, who lives in Chicago with her husband and three children, has started holding Nochebuenas of her own; so has my brother in Atlanta. Maggie and Armandito, my cousins and drinking partners, now live in Mexico City. My younger cousin Anita is gay and doesn't feel comfortable bringing her lover to the party, so she doesn't come. Once every few years some of us still coincide in Miami for Nochebuena, but it seems to happen less and less often.

Every Nochebuena for the last four or five years, Nena has been grumbling that this will be her last, that she's getting too old for all of the preparations, but come the following year she roasts another leg of pork, cooks another pot of *congrí,* and tries to get the family together. However Americanized she may say she is, she doesn't seem willing to give up this Cuban custom. Old Havanas are hard to break, but for Nena and Gustavo, Nochebuena has become a mournful holiday, a reminder of how much things have changed in their lives.

For exile families, the impact of change is not only personal but cultural, for the passing away of a generation spells the extinction of a culture. As a friend of mine puts it, Cubans are not assimilating, they're dying. The ones who are still alive, he and I among them, are the ones who weren't totally Cuban to begin with. With every first-generation exile who passes away, we in the younger generations lose words, turns of phrase, habits of thought, gestures that are distinctively Cuban. No one could pack more devilishness into a wink, for example, than my father's cousin Joseíto, and no one could exclaim *"¡Oye, niña!"* like my uncle Pepe. The personal loss is inevitable, but the cultural loss, a consequence of prolonged exile, is much harder to accept. Every culture evolves, and the culture of children is never identical to that of parents and grandparents, but extinction is not evolution. Nochebuena used to be a time to remember and celebrate things Cuban. The ritual toast, "Next year in Cuba," set the mood for the evening, a mood both nostalgic and hopeful, for the Nochebuenas of yesteryear were a warrant on the Nochebuenas of tomorrow. During those very good nights in the 1960s, 1970s, and 1980s, everything harked back to Cuba—the celebrants, the food, the music, the customs. Every year we heard my father's favorite chanteuse, Olga Guillot, singing "White Christmas" with a Spanish lyric. Every year we danced to "La Mora," an old Cuban song whose questioning refrain was uncannily relevant: *"¿Cuándo volverá, La Nochebuena, cuando volverá?"* "When will they return, those old Nochebuenas, when will they return?" Soon, we all thought, very soon. At no other time of the year did Cuba seem so close, did *regreso* seem so imminent.

With the death of the old-timers, Cuba is dying too. Our Miami Nochebuenas have become more and more American. It has been years since anybody showed up at my parents' doorstep at two o'clock in the morning. If they did, they would find the lights out and the family in bed. As the celebration has become geared to the American grandchildren, Nochebuena has become Christmas Eve, more an anticipation of the next day than a festivity in itself. With the arrival into our family of non-Cuban spouses, even the *lingua franca* of the night has evolved toward English, a language that my mother handles comfortably but that my father doesn't like to speak.

Gustavo and Nena have adapted to these changes with a mixture of resignation and good cheer. Although he sorely misses the company of his contemporaries, Gustavo compensates as best he can by showing off his dancing skills to his American daughters-in-law. He flirts with them with almost as much *embullo* as he displays flirting with the waitresses at his favorite Cuban restaurants, and somehow he now manages to come up with bilingual dirty jokes. At the same time, however, he drinks less than he used to and gets bored or tired quicker. Sometime in the evening his mood will modulate from merry to melancholy; then he settles into his chair and turns on the TV.

For Nena, the most difficult part hasn't been the Americanization of Nochebuena—after all, she grew up in Norfolk celebrating Christmas, not Nochebuena—but the fragmentation of our family. Until the last few years, she had been fairly successful in keeping everyone together. Both in Cuba and in Miami her house was our oasis, our hospital, the haven to which we repaired in times of trouble, the temple where we celebrated birthdays, baptisms, graduations, engagements. Even during difficult years she bore this burden lightly. No occasion was too insignificant, no party too big, no demand on her time or energy too onerous. In these tasks my father was an onlooker; once he stocked the bar and bought the bag of ice, his job was over. Nena was the one who cooked, who cleaned, who set everything up, who extended invitations and organized logistics. She was the one who kept finding reasons and occasions to gather children and cousins and aunts and uncles and nephews and nieces. For thirty years her project has been keeping the family whole. She spun the thread that kept us tightly knit. As she says, give me a roof over my head and enough beds for my children and I am happy. I think she loved the Christmassy Nochebuenas even better than the Cuban ones.

But this doesn't mean that exile has been easy on her. If my father experienced exile as loss of wealth and status, she has experienced it as the diminishment of the family. Nena complains about exile when something goes wrong with the family, when it frays at the edges or comes loose at the seams. She complains when she cannot be at her daughter's or daughter-in-law's side during childbirth, when one son gets divorced and another gets into trouble, or when her sister-in-law has to be eulogized in English by a priest who doesn't know her. At times like these, she intones her eternal question, "Why has exile been so hard on us? Things would have been so different in Cuba." She views exile not as economic deprivation, but as an assault on her family. For her, the Cuban Revolution has been less a political than a cultural cataclysm. Compared to the dispersal of thousands upon thousands of families, financial hardship and expatriation are nothing. Fidel's greatest crime, she likes to say, the one for which he will roast in hell like a suckling pig, is the breakup of the Cuban family.

For Nena, the human cost of the Revolution must be measured in Nochebuenas, for it is then that the fractures in our family show up with the clarity of an X ray.

This is why her adaptation to exile followed a very different curve from my father's. For him, losing the almacén was the decisive blow. For my mother, however, exile was manageable so long as the family stayed together. If my father fantasizes about returning to his business, my mother dreams of a time when the family was whole. In spite of the plethora of day-to-day problems, for years Nena was basically happy in Miami. Even as she complained about the hardships of life in exile, she balked at the idea of returning to Cuba immediately after the fall of Fidel. She always said that what she missed was not Cuba but Kohly, the neighborhood where our house was located, and that Kohly would never be the same. She once told me, "Remember what Scarlett O'Hara says—she doesn't say she wants to go back to Atlanta. She always says, 'I want to go back to Tara.' Kohly was my Tara."

In Cuba my mother's life had been a roller coaster of Friday nights at the Tropicana, Saturdays on the yacht, Sundays at the racetrack or the baseball stadium. The money that made possible the big house and the servants subsidized a lifestyle that she sometimes found unbearable. When my parents quarreled in Cuba, it was usually about partying. Gustavo wanted to, Nena did not. Being the king of the house, Gustavo usually got his way. In Miami all this changed. With the money went the maids as well as the fast-track lifestyle. No longer able to spend his evenings gambling or dancing, my father became a homebody. If he went out at night with his cousin Joseíto, it was to ride around Little Havana and have a cup of espresso at the Casablanca restaurant on Calle Ocho. In Cuba it hadn't been so easy to track him down.

Once in exile, my father and mother made common cause. Old wounds healed and long-standing frictions subsided. When my father is out of earshot, Nena says that exile saved her marriage. But when my mother is out of earshot, Gustavo says that exile ruined his life. Both exaggerate, but neither one is lying. Enervated by his losses, in Miami Gustavo became a spectator in his own family. He worked and he watched. Although he remained the principal breadwinner, Nena took care of everything else. Partly by default and partly by design, she became the family's sole solid center. Juggling husband, children, parents, and relatives, she never let any one of us drop. In Cuba she had never worked outside the home; in Miami she held a full-time job as a school secretary and served also as cook, chauffeur, financial planner, daughter, wife, mother, and maid. "Who could have told me," she says, "that I would have to spend the rest of my life pulling hair out of the bathroom sink?"

With my father emotionally disengaged, Nena picked up the slack. Because we asked her all of the questions, she got good at having all of the answers. Many of her answers were wise, and some were cockeyed. Soon after arriving in Miami she made my father turn down a job offer in the Dominican Republic. Why? Because she wasn't about to raise children anywhere where they didn't have *papel de aluminio,* aluminum foil, which for her is a symbol of the advances of American civilization. (Don't ask me how she decided that there was no aluminum foil in the Dominican Republic.) When my brothers and I were adolescents, she counseled us against marrying black women. Why? Not because she found anything wrong with interracial marriages, but "because the United States is not ready for mulattas."

In times of crisis, Nena always shone. In my family, as in so many Cuban families, the women like my mother display a strength and stability that their husbands seem to lack. I have observed this pattern over and over in other exile families, each anchored by strong, resourceful women. Nena never cracked, or at least never let it show. Always on call, she seemed tireless. The accidents, the illnesses, the poverty—she could deal with them all. For years Nena nursed her mother at home, long past the time when Abuela Martínez, who not only was blind but suffered from Alzheimer's (which we called only *chochería),* stopped remembering who or where she was. But putting her mother in a home was something that Nena couldn't do. According to her, this is what Americans did, while Cubans took care of their own.

When Nena went off to work in the morning, an old lady who lived down the block sat with my grandmother. At noon Nena came home to fix my grandmother's special lunch, a tricky undertaking since Abuela Martínez had a tumor in her stomach the size of a grapefruit. After work Nena spent the rest of the afternoon picking up and distributing children. When she wasn't cooking or cleaning or patching blue jeans or taking down cuffs or fending off Constantina, she was looking after her mother, who—because of the Alzheimer's—was not only recalcitrant but cruel. I remember that often Nena had to dodge insults and wipe shit from the floor at the same time. Years went by without my mother being able to take an afternoon off to go to a movie or visit a friend.

When Abuela Martínez became so feeble that she needed a full-time nurse, Nena finally relented and put her in a convalescent home, but only after being persuaded to do so by her confessor. She visited her mother almost daily, returning home in tears. Even today, when she talks about having put her mother in a home, she starts to cry. I should be ashamed to say this, and I am, but I don't know whether I would be able to do for my mother all that she did for hers.

No family survives exile intact, and in spite of Nena's extraordinary exertions, things happened that undermined ours. As decade succeeded decade, the extended family distended. Taking care of her mother was an ordeal but an expected one. Other things were tougher to countenance. Siblings who had been raised to be *uña y carne,* as close as fingernails and flesh, hardly talked to each other. Relatives who in Cuba would have been living nearby, died in distant places. Children whose children she expected to raise moved away. Today, the older Nena gets, the more alone she is, the fewer people she has to care for. To her, a woman's work is cyclical mothering. In her youth a woman mothers her children; in her middle age she mothers her children and her parents; in her old age she mothers her children and her grandchildren. By sundering the family, exile broke this cycle, and eventually Nena had to confront what she regards as American problems—separations, loneliness, divorces, family strife. Contented for many years in Miami, she has in the end come to bear the brunt of exile as fully as my father. My mother knows that those Nochebuenas of old will not return.

In all the years I have resided away from Miami, I've missed only one Nochebuena there, and that because one year my parents decided to spend Christmas in North Carolina, an experiment that didn't turn out well and won't be repeated. As long as Nena and Gustavo are alive and willing, I'll go to their house for Nochebuena. Although the celebration and the celebrants have changed a great deal throughout the years, more than my parents and I would have liked, Nochebuena remains for me the holiest—if no longer the happiest—night of the year.

But I have no illusions. Our Miami Nochebuenas have come to resemble those skeletal Christmas trees from Cuba. I wish it were different, but the time to do anything about it may have passed. I could make a joke and say that you can't make roast pig from a sow's ear. But this is no joke. After my parents have passed away, I hope many years from now, I will celebrate Nochebuena in Chapel Hill with my American wife, my almost-American children, and my American stepchildren. Instead of going to Miami, I'll be staying put. I'll be a squatter, not a roamer. But I will be squatting far from home. I know that in Chapel Hill my Nochebuena traditions will suffer a further attenuation, and when this happens I'll find myself in the position that my father occupies now—I will be the only Cuban rooster in the house. The Good Night, which became less than good in Miami, may well not be good enough in Chapel Hill. My reluctant but hopeful wager is that the not-so-*buena* Nochebuena will be followed by an excellent Christmas.

SEVEN

Billita, Who Am I?

Chapel Hill, 1982

Exile is a heavy weight. The family is a muscle that grows stronger by lifting heavy weights, or tears in the attempt. In our family, but I'm certain that it's not just our family, the muscle has torn, and none of us is quite sure what to do about it.

Our early years in Miami, which I still regard with fondness, were in fact disastrous. On the outside the family stuck together like glue, the way Nena wanted, but deep down we were coming apart. In Cuba my brother Pepe and I had been almost twins—we were the same height, had the same haircut, wore identical clothes. I was two years older, but you could never tell. Yet once in Miami, we quickly separated. We still slept in the same room and attended the same schools and wore the same-size trousers, but each of us went his own way. No longer Gustavito and Pepito, we became Gus and J.G. (Pepe's baptismal name is José Gilberto, and in Miami he shortened it to Jay-Gee). Pepe read voraciously, classified the constellations through a telescope, dissected insects, performed chemical experiments in the backyard, and did extraordinarily well in school. I played sports, studied enough to get decent grades, and tried to be a *ligador,* a teenage stud. He felt superior to me because I was a jock; I felt superior to him because he was clumsy.

Meanwhile, my sister, Mari, and my youngest brother, Carlos, banded together. Like Pepe and me, they looked the same age, although they, too, were two years apart. Putting up a common front against parents and older siblings, they kept to themselves, developing their own routines and groups of friends. Don't ask me whether they had a happy childhood and adolescence, because we didn't talk enough for me to know. Although we lived in very close quarters, and although I was only four years older than Carlos and six years older than Mari, somehow we managed to lead separate lives. As we grew up, we grew apart.

With a distracted father, a do-it-all mother, demanding inlaws, and confused children, that little house in Little Havana was not a paradise but a pressure cooker. All of us lurching from one crisis to the next. All of us waiting, always waiting. Growing up and marking time. Eventually, the pressure became too much, and Pepe, Carlos, and I exploded out in different directions. (Of the four of us, Mari seems to be the only one to have emerged from exile unscathed, perhaps because she was too young to have memories of Cuba.) Pepe left Miami as soon as he finished high school and never returned. Caught up in the turmoil of the sixties, he dropped out of college, lived for a while in California and New York, and then surfaced years later promoting in Nicaragua the kind of revolution that had disenfranchised us in Cuba. For several years, my parents' only contact with him was the signature on the back of canceled checks. If they sent him a check and he cashed it, at least they knew he was alive and well enough to sign his name. During this period, I had no contact with him. We became strangers. There are ten years of my brother's life about which I know next to nothing. In an American family this may not seem so uncommon; in a Cuban family this is remarkable. The few times Pepe came home, Nena and Gustavo tried to make light of his long hair and radical politics, but of course the Cuban Revolution was also made by *barbudos,* grungy men with long hair and beards.

To this day Pepe says that he doesn't begrudge the Cuban government for having taken our house and the *almacén.* It's not theft, he says, but expropriation. When I hear Pepe extol the merits of the Cuban Revolution, I want to strangle him. When I hear him justify our dispossession, I want to eat his flesh and drink his blood. How can my brother talk this way after what the Revolution did to our family? Doesn't he see what a shell of a man our father has become? After his last trip to Havana not long ago, Pepe gave my parents copies of the photographs that he had taken of the house and the *almacén.* Lovely, heartbreaking photographs that I refused to look at. When I told him that I wanted to keep intact my memories of our home, he replied, "Junior, you haven't changed in thirty years."

Unlike Pepe, I lived at home until I got married. By the time I finished high school, however, I was boiling with anger and resentment. I spent my late teens and early twenties seeing Nena and Gustavo every day while barely exchanging a word with them. In some respects my behavior was more cruel than my brother's, for Pepe just took off, while I took my revenge by living right there with them. Every time I refused to eat at the table or greet an old friend who came to visit or get on the phone with a relative, I made Nena and Gustavo pay for what I thought they had done to me. Cooped up in my room day after day watching TV or playing chess or working on a term paper, I sent the message that I wanted no part of the life they had given me. I blamed them not only for exile but for their inability to get beyond it. And yet there I was, an inhouse hermit, as much of an exile as either one of them. The one family thing I did was go upstairs and spend time with my grandmother Constantina; otherwise, I lived by myself. When I got married right out of college, Nena was delighted. Marriage to a nice Cuban girl was going to make me leave my room, rejoin the family. As it turned out, in some ways it did and in other ways it didn't.

Did exile make all the difference in the world to me and my brothers, or does it make no difference whatsoever? Is Nena right— would none of this have happened in Havana? Or would the family have been rent there too? As I write and think about my troubled family that I love and loathe so dearly, I agonize over these questions, but I can't answer them. What is certain is that exile pushes us to the limit. There, at the limit, we find our best and worst selves. Given to heroism, we become heroic. Given to listing, we keel over. Leaving Havana was more of a blow than any of us ever realized. I know that we wouldn't have been perfect brothers in Cuba, but I also know that exile sapped our strengths and fed our frailties, that it made us weak rather than strong. My brothers and I grew up distrusting and blaming each other as much as we distrusted and blamed our parents. Moving to the United States made it more difficult for my father to be a good father and for us to be good brothers and sons. Instead of sticking together and helping each other cope, we flew off in separate directions.

Our estrangement culminated in a bizarre and painful episode involving Carlos and me. This is a difficult story to tell, for the episode has deepened the rifts in our family and caused our parents much unhappiness. I'm sure my mother would not want me to write about it; as she always says, dirty laundry should be washed *en casa,* at home. Nonetheless, I have decided to recount what happened between my brother and me because these incidents illustrate in a striking way what can befall a family overstressed by exile. I don't write out of spite, but rather with love toward Carlos and sadness at the gulf between us.

In 1982, on a sunny and chill October morning in Chapel Hill, I get a call from Carlos in Miami, who says he has to leave Miami right away. He can't explain why, but he needs a place to stay for a while. Cuban family being what it is, what it should be, I say yes, and the following afternoon he pulls into our gravel driveway in his Trans Am, loaded down with his most precious possessions—a large-screen TV set, a Yamaha stereo with oversized speakers, and about two dozen records and tapes. We have rented a fold-out bed for his visit and he moves into the room that is my study.

For several weeks Carlos spends his days in that little room, surrounded by my books and filing cabinets, the door shut and the TV or stereo blaring. He emerges to eat a couple of times a day and every once in a while baby-sits for my one-and-a-half-year-old son, David. By the end of November, almost two months later, the situation hasn't changed, and I decide to have a heart-to-heart talk.

"Carlos, you know that you're welcome in this house and that you can stay as long as you need to, but don't you think you need to start looking for a job?"

"*Ya sé,*" he says, "I know, I know." He had gone through a rough time in Miami, he tells me, without offering specifics—he needed some time to regroup. But now he's ready to get back on track.

A couple of weeks later he lands a job at Radio Shack. Carlos always had a knack for electrical gadgets, and he's very good with people. A few weeks after that, however, Carlos still shows no intention of moving out. So I decide to speak with him again.

As I inform him that he needs to get his own place, I feel guilty. A part of me, my Cuban side, doesn't think that it's right to place convenience—I need to regain use of my study—above family obligations. Another part, my American side, wants him out of my hair and my house. I've helped him for the last few months; now he needs to help himself. Although I don't know exactly what problems Carlos was having in Miami, this isn't the first time he has been in trouble, and I'm less patient than I otherwise might be.

Sometime in January Carlos finally does move out, though I see him a couple of times a week either at the Radio Shack where he works or when he comes over for dinner. Almost thirty years old, he has started dating a teenage girl who works at the Burger King on Elliott Road.

In March my wife and I take our son down to Miami for spring break. Before we leave we arrange to have Annie, our maid, clean the house while we are away. But when Annie walks in on the Friday before we are to return, the house is a mess. There are dirty dishes everywhere, the windows are ajar, the mattress from our bed is on the floor of the living room. Annie thinks that someone has broken into the house and leaves without cleaning up. When we return on Saturday, however, the house is neat and orderly. It turns out that during the ten days that we were away, Carlos moved in. He had planned to clean up and move out the day before we returned, but didn't know about our arrangement with Annie.

Family is family but this is too much. Furious, I ask Carlos to return the key to our house. Afterward I change the locks, just in case. A month later I hear from my mother that Carlos has moved back to Miami and is now living with them. A mildly unpleasant episode with my brother seems to have drawn to a close.

Out of the blue, a year and a half later, I receive a phone call from a furniture rental store in Miami. The man on the phone tells me that my check bounced. I have no idea what he's talking about— I've never rented any furniture in Miami. I get the number of the bank account on which the check was drawn, and the next morning I call one of the Miami branches. Sure enough, I've had a checking account with them for the last several months. Right now the account is overdrawn.

When I receive copies of the furniture rental agreement and the bank application, I discover that the personal and financial information about me is accurate, except that according to the applications I have retired from Duke University and am now part owner of a pizzeria in South Miami. The Credit Bureau in Chapel Hill has received the same information: as far as they are concerned, I have retired from Duke and moved to Miami.

The tiny, crabbed handwriting on the applications is familiar, in the fullest, most fearsome sense of the adjective: it's my brother Carlos's.

After I get over the shock, I realize I have to face various problems, some practical, some spiritual. But my initial dilemma is legal: I need to show that Carlos is not me and that I am not Carlos. I soon find out that Aaron Rents is not the only place where I have bounced checks. Bad checks were also given to supermarkets, laundries, restaurants, and utility companies. Carlos has a credit card in my name, with an outstanding balance of several thousand dollars (which he spent on gold chains, a watch, and a stereo system), and has taken out a two-year lease in my name at Fontainebleau Park, the fashionable, mostly Cuban development in Southwest Miami.

Why is Carlos doing this? And more important, why is he doing this to *me,* his own brother? Is this his retaliation for my banning him from my house? Or is he envious of me? Although Carlos didn't do well in school, he was the one among us who became self-supporting first. The business world that threw a fright into me did not faze him in the slightest. Gregarious like my father, he began working as a salesclerk when he was still a teenager, and got married and moved out right after he graduated from high school. With his wife he purchased a condominium at Fontainebleau Park, the same place he was now renting an apartment in my name. Carlos may have envied my scholastic achievements, but I envied his life, which, in my twenties, I always thought was far more normal and happy than mine.

But apparently Carlos wanted to be me. Is it because I'm the firstborn and bear our father's name? Or because, to my parents, I was the model son and model husband, and as of two years ago also the model father, as well as a tenured professor? In any case, thanks to my brother's confiscation of my life, I'm no longer a professor at Duke; instead, I live in Miami and own a pizzeria, which later turns out to be a front for a money-laundering operation. Carlos and I have traded places: he's the professor and I have become the *marimbero,* the drug dealer.

But which of the two am I really? And which of the two is he? Carlos is certainly not the only impostor in the family—in a sense, we're all impostors, all chameleons of one kind or another, changing

colors to match the leaves. My brother Pepe pretends to be a socialist. Mari pretends to be a banker. Carlos pretends to sell dope. I pretend to be a professor. But professorial poses suit me as poorly as
they suit Carlos. In truth I'm no more a professor than he is; and he's
no more a *marimbero* than I am.

There's a wonderful moment in *Don Quijote* when the mad
knight of La Mancha, at the giddy heights of his lunacy, thunders to
Sancho, "*¡Yo sé quien soy!*"—"I know who I am!" Can Carlos and
Pepe and Mari and I say as much? I doubt it. We may be possessed,
but we're not self-possessed. What I am is dispossessed. I don't even
own my name. Heck, *yo no sé quién soy.*

By mid-July I receive the rest of the financial records from
Miami and call the Coral Gables police department, telling my story
to a Detective Noyer, who doesn't quite believe me but promises to
look into it. He tells me to stay away from Miami until the situation
is cleared up. Later I call my parents to tell them what has happened.
When I blame everything on their habit of covering up for Carlos,
which goes way back, we get into a fight. They defend Carlos, saying he needs to be helped, not hounded.

Several days later I discover from the Credit Bureau that my
credit history has also entwined with my father's. Now there are at
least three Gustavo Pérez's in Miami, though only two of them live
there and only one of them is me and I don't live there (even though
I have always wanted to). Six or seven more credit inquiries from
Miami stores have come in. Carlos is still using my identity.

The next day I call my father and when he asks how I am, I reply,
"*Bien con jota,*" a Cuban expression that means "pretty fucked up."
When he asks why, I tell him that it's because of Carlos.

"Don't give it so much importance," he replies.

His words send me into a rage, and the *empingue* brings out the
best and the beast in me. "What do you mean, don't give it so much
importance? Of course I have to give it importance. It's *my* life. It's
my money. It's *my* name. That's always the problem with you, nothing is ever important. Nothing is ever done about anything."

Two days later Detective Noyer, who by now has satisfied himself that I am telling the truth, calls to inform me that "Gustavo
Pérez" showed up at Avis to rent a Datsun 2802, which he's going to
pick up on Monday. The Avis clerk got suspicious because his cus-
tomer didn't sound like a college professor. Noyer is going to arrest

Carlos on Monday when he shows up to pick up the car. The irony is overwhelming: for twenty years my father has made a living selling Datsuns. Maybe it's Gustavo Sr. that Carlos really wants to become after all. As it turns out, today is July 26, the thirty-first anniversary of Fidel Castro's attack on the Moncada barracks, which started the Cuban Revolution.

My uncle Pedro calls a day or two later to tell me he has spoken to Carlos and actually gone to see him, telling him that if he was a man he would turn himself in. Running into my uncle on the way up from the pool, Carlos apparently looked as if he didn't have a care in the world. It doesn't seem to Pedro or me that the appeal to Carlos's sense of honor is going to get us anywhere.

On Noyer's advice I go to the Chapel Hill police station, where more surprises await me. It turns out that Carlos is wanted in North Carolina for robbing an appliance store in Chapel-Hill. In addition, a few months ago Carlos was arrested in Miami for running a red light and driving without a license, but before the police in Chapel Hill had a chance to verify his identity, he convinced them that he was me, Gustavo. What really takes me aback, however, is that the file states Gustavo Sr. showed up at the Miami police station and vouched that my brother was his eldest son, Gustavo. One Gustavo vouching for a second Gustavo who is really Carlos. My father apparently doesn't know his own sons.

Someone else might be shocked by my father's behavior, but I realize he was just acting according to his philosophy, which is to improvise, make do. Find a way out of the jam and worry about the aftertaste later. With his son about to be extradited to North Carolina to face robbery charges, Gustavo chooses the easy way out. As Nena says, the thing is *resolver, poner parches,* to cover the wounds with Band-Aids. Life here, in his mind, is always short-term, for in the long term there's Cuba.

I can't bring myself to tell my father what I have found out. He'd just apologize and start crying that he was doing what he thought best. After the close call at the police station in Miami, Carlos must have figured that he could get away with the imposture of me on a more permanent basis. "In Coconut Grove you can buy a fake driver's license for fifty dollars," Noyer told me the first time we talked. A license with your picture, but somebody else's name and numbers.

Once you get that, you can open a bank account, get charge cards, find a job, deal dope, and start a new life.

On Monday I call Noyer to see if he's arrested my brother.

"He's sitting right here next to me," Noyer says. "Picked him up this morning at seven. Waited outside his home and grabbed him when he came out. He's being very cooperative. Wanna talk to him?"

"No," I reply, "I can't think of anything I want to say."

"He says he wants to talk to you."

"Tell him that if he wants to talk to me, he can talk to himself."

When I tell my mother that Carlos has been arrested, she begins to sob and can't say another word. A son in jail—this would never have happened in Havana. My father dourly remarks that I should be happy now that I got what I wanted.

On this July morning in Chapel Hill, I realize that there's an immense frozen sea between my brother and me, between my parents and me. According to my mother, family loyalty comes before everything. Many times when we were growing up she told us how Uncles Ricardo and Octavio saved each other's life during the Machado dictatorship. Unlike my great-uncles, I have betrayed my family by turning my brother in to the police. No matter how good the reason, brothers shouldn't do this to each other. I'm beginning to feel as if I'm the criminal, and my conscience is killing me. All those years of Nena's gentle indoctrination have left their mark.

In the car on the way to Miami I'm so spaced-out that I keep calling my son, David, by my brother's name. My mother always did the same thing—Gustavito became Pepito became Carlitos became Gustavito. As kids there were always two things we could count on: Nena would lose her keys and get her children's names mixed up.

We stop for the night in Brunswick, Georgia, the halfway point between Chapel Hill and Miami, but I can't sleep. While I lie awake in a motel bed at a Howard Johnson's, my brother is spending the night in jail. So far as I know, this is the first time anybody in our family has gone to jail. In my mother's eyes, this disaster is a result of exile. In Cuba she wouldn't have had troubled children. In Cuba brothers wouldn't have betrayed one another. In Cuba they had money to get Carlitos out of whatever trouble he got himself in. In Cuba. Always in Cuba. Meanwhile, I'm in Georgia, not in Cuba, and I can't sleep.

Have we been in exile too long? A few years earlier my mother had received a card from her brother Ricardo, who lives in New York and had been out of touch for many years. In 1959 Tío Richard was in the last year of law school at the University of Havana. The Revolution interrupted his studies and he left for New York. For a few years he kept in touch with his mother, but after Abuela Martínez went into the nursing home he fell silent. For ten years no one knew his whereabouts, until one day a card addressed to my mother arrived. On the inside flap Tío Richard had printed one short sentence in squiggly block letters: "BILLITA, WHO AM I?" Billita was the name of his maternal grandmother. Not only didn't Richard know who he was, apparently he didn't know who my mother was either.

Names and more names. Names, proper and improper. Nena and Billita. Junior and Gustavito. Gus and Gustavo. Carlos and Gustavo. Gustavo and Gustavo. I have counted seventeen different names to which I have responded at one time or another in my life. The trouble is that the names you respond to are not necessarily those you call yourself. Perhaps we should change names the way we change spouses. Sue your name for divorce on the grounds of irreconcilable differences, or mental cruelty, or adultery. If I'd known my name was going to two-time me, I would have dumped it a long time ago!

Like my mother, I transform the episode into a morality play on the evils of leaving home, or into a Cuban-exile Cain and Abel. Turning my brother in was the course of action dictated by considerations about credit ratings, bank accounts, mortgages, individual responsibility. It was the American thing to do. Minding my own business and making sure that Carlos minds his, I'm acting like the naturalized American citizen that I am. America, to me, is a society of autonomous individuals, not of sticky family entanglements. Maybe in Cuba family came before everything else, but not here. "Internecine" is a word I first learned in English, always in tandem with "warfare." I don't even know whether the adjective has a Spanish equivalent. A famous stanza from the national epic of Argentina, a poem about gauchos, states that the first law of nature is for brothers to look after each other. If brothers quarrel, the gaucho singer says, they will be devoured by outsiders. But who are the outsiders who are sinking their teeth into us?

Our summer in Miami turns out to be a season in hell. My mother hardly speaks to me; nobody wants to baby-sit David. Since my father cannot hear to see his son behind bars, Tío Pedro accompanies my mother to the building that houses the county jail and that Cubans call *cielito lindo,* pretty heaven. It's the same building where I was sworn in as a citizen in 1977.

When Nena and Pedro come back from their first visit, it's ninety degrees outside, but Nena's cold stare could have given me frostbite. Without saying a word, she locks herself in her room and doesn't come out until the next day. Nena became so agitated in jail that Tío Pedro thought she was going to have another heart attack. (She had her first a month after putting her mother in a nursing home.) She brought my brother a crucifix and a rosary, and has asked one of the priests in her parish, the young Cuban one, to go see him. She wants Carlos to make a confession, repent for his sins. When we first got to Miami in 1960, we knelt in front of a backlit portrait of the Sacred Heart every night and said a rosary for the liberation of Cuba. Now she has to say a rosary for the liberation of my brother.

At the jail Carlos gave my uncle the key to his apartment. The next day Pedro and I go to the apartment. The bedroom is littered with canceled checks, receipts, unpaid bills, all in my name. All signed by Gustavo Pérez in an ugly, uneven script. It's strange to realize that I have been leading a double life without knowing it. I laundered pants I never wore. I cooked steaks I never ate. I talked to people I never met. I snorted coke and never got high. After wishing for most of my adult life to live in Miami, finally, in a way I did. As I go through the pockets of Carlos's dirty laundry, I hear two voices inside my head. One asserts, "Gustavito, this is your life!" The other asks, "Billita, who am I?"

After two weeks in Miami, I cut our vacation short and return to North Carolina. When I get back home, I bury myself in my books. It will take many months to disentangle the financial knots. In the end I go to the Credit Bureau so often that I get on a first-name basis with the women who work there. "Goose-tai-vough," they call me, "Goose-tai-vough," just like Mrs. Myers in the sixth grade. Is that who I really am?

After several months in jail, Carlos was released without ever coming to trial. Overburdened with really serious offenders, the

Miami courts couldn't bother with small fry like him. He moved to Orlando, where he lived for a year before returning to Miami. Since then Carlos has held a variety of jobs, none for more than a few months at a time, and has lived with my parents on and off. I suspect he's continued to have his troubles, but I don't know for sure, since Nena and Gustavo won't talk to me about him—they're afraid that I would turn him in again. I do know that a couple of years ago my parents took out a new mortgage on their house, and I would bet that as sure as I am Gustavo, Carlos is the reason. Whatever the truth is about Carlos, I can do nothing to change old habits. Ten years have gone by, and not once have I spoken with my parents about what happened. It's another of those catastrophes of exile that will be undone magically someday.

Only once have Carlos and I talked about his impersonation of me. I was married to a Cuban woman for fifteen years; a few years ago, when I divorced Rosa and married Mary Anne, most of my family, including my parents and my sister, boycotted the wedding. Other than my children, the only relatives who attended were my brothers, Pepe and Carlos. Because the wedding took place on a Saturday afternoon, the one justice of the peace we could find happened to be Lieutenant Sumney, the same cop who several years earlier told me that Carlos had ripped off the store in Chapel Hill. He married Mary Anne and me on the lawn outside the police station, with my brother nervously standing by.

At the reception at my house afterward, Carlos, Pepe, and I got drunk. After the dancing and the eating ended and the few guests left, we sat down on the living room sofa and began to talk, at first about nothing in particular but eventually about ourselves. The conversation lasted into the next morning. We had never talked like this before, and we have not talked like this since. Rancors and regrets that had been simmering since childhood bubbled out. Each of us felt misunderstood and scorned. Each of us feared and distrusted the others. Each of us had a puddle of hate in our hearts. Carlos told me that he realized that he had screwed me over, but that all his life he had been made to feel inadequate. It was always, Carlitos, why can't you get good grades like your brothers? Carlitos, why aren't you going to college? Carlitos, why can't you be like junior and Pepito? In retaliation, he began stealing when he was still in high school. Then came the drugs, a failed marriage, and more problems. Eventually, he wound up in Fontainebleau Park living as someone he wasn't, because he could no longer afford to be who he was.

Carlos didn't know that one of my books contains a poem about his imposture. I took the thin volume from the shelf and read the poem aloud to him. In the poem I imagine Carlos going into a bank or a supermarket and signing my name to a check, his hand trembling. Then I imagine my hand also trembling when I sign my own name. Because of the imposture, my brother and I have finally become as one. As we both sign "Gustavo," we're closer than we have ever been before. The imposture was not a crime, it was an act of love, a desperate embrace. Since the poem is written in Spanish, I have to translate it as I go along—I never realized that Carlos doesn't know Spanish well enough to read a short poem.

Understanding may bring peace, but it doesn't bring intimacy. Our wedding-night conversation felt good—we vented and ranted until there was no more to vent or rant about, but it didn't change a thing. After letting it all hang out, we packed it all back in. Although Pepe, Carlos, and I are somewhat closer than we were a few years ago, we will probably never be any closer than we are now. Certainly, we will never be as close as when we were small children in Cuba. The tough truth is that, as grown-ups, we make each other squirm. None of us wants to look the other in the eye. None of us wants to expose himself. None of us wants to reopen old wounds. Our cure for too much closeness has been too much distance. Instead of seeking contact, we shy away from it. When I get to Miami on vacation, Pepe has just left. If I go down for Christmas, he goes down for Thanksgiving. The convenient excuse is that the house is too small to accommodate more than one family at a time, but obviously there's more to it than that. If I'm staying with my parents and Nena invites Carlos for dinner, I find an excuse not to show. If Carlos is living with my parents, I rent an efficiency across from the University of Miami, my old haunts.

By now all of us realize that our best chance to have a real family is to start one, to bet on the future rather than the past, on the United States rather than Havana or Little Havana. My sister, Mali, lives in Chicago with her husband and three children. In spite of his troubles, Carlos has remarried and is trying to start a new life. Pepe, who now works as a journalist for the Spanish branch of CNN, got tired of making revolution and has settled in Atlanta with his wife and three-year-old daughter. And I've come to accept, grudgingly, that my life is in Chapel Hill, not Miami.

Poor Nena still exerts herself to bring us together, but to no avail. What exile has put asunder let no mother join together. As the years go by, my brothers and I see less and less of each other. "Fortunately, I won't be around to see it," Nena says, "but the day will come when you and your brothers will forget each other's names." I could say to her, "That day already came, Mami."

PART THREE
Discovering America

EIGHT
The Gusano as Bookworm

Ann Arbor—Little Havana, 1973-89

When I left Miami in 1973 to attend graduate school, I felt that I was both entering and escaping exile. Growing up in Little Havana, I had learned that home was elsewhere, and I took this lesson with me to Ann Arbor. The moment I moved away, I began to long for Miami much as my father, living in Miami, had always longed for Cuba.

At the same time, I knew that a university teaching career would probably spoil my chances of spending my life among Cubans in Little Havana. But in those days I wasn't thinking about where I wanted to live. For me, life was exile. I wanted a retreat from life, a refuge from exile, and I believed I had found it in books. Since I felt betrayed by history, I turned my career into a reason not to face the world around me. I didn't leave Miami for Ann Arbor, but for the Hatcher Graduate Library of the University of Michigan, where I spent most of my days and nights during the five long, cold years it took me to get a Ph.D. in comparative literature.

Since my wife Rosa, whom I had married right before coming to Michigan, was also a doctoral student in literature, anytime we weren't in class or sleeping, we tramped off to the library, usually in frigid weather and several feet of snow. Outside, it always seemed to be dark and dreary—a shocking contrast to the climate I had known all my life; but inside the library, it was warm and bright. I got to know this massive, windowless building that houses several million books better than I knew my own apartment. I could tell you where every bathroom was, the exact location of every Xerox and change

145

machine, the fastest way to get from one point to another, the out-of-the-way corners where you could find undergraduates necking. The labyrinth of floors and basements and levels and sublevels held no mysteries for me. I got so good at it that often I didn't have to use the card catalog to find a book. Without meaning to, I had memorized whole chunks of the Library of Congress numbering system.

And yet, regardless of my plans, by going to graduate school at the University of Michigan, I wasn't really turning my back on the world, but starting on a winding path that would eventually take me to a new life. Although it took me years to notice, once I moved away from Miami I began to become a different man from what I had been up to then. Whether I knew it or not, I was embarking on a protracted but irreversible voyage of discovery, and of self-discovery. Even the Hatcher Library was not what I had anticipated. Rather than a safe haven, an academic branch of the Cuban Refugee Center, it turned out to be a perilous, unpredictable book world.

By the summer of 1977 I was itching to finish graduate school. I had completed my courses with excellent grades and had already published half a dozen articles in well-regarded scholarly journals. Since my dissertation was progressing quickly, I decided to go on the job market in the fall. By then I would have finished several chapters. My dissertation topic was Hispanic vanguard fiction, a shelf of all-but-forgotten novels written in the 1920s and 1930s in Spain and Latin America. For me, as for other graduate students, the price of admission into the professorial fraternity was writing a book that nobody would read about other books that nobody has read. Not coincidentally, my favorite novel in the group was *El profesor inútil,* "The Useless Professor," about a bespectacled, bookwormy thirty-something who spends most of his life reading. In spite of the obscurity of the topic, or perhaps because of it, vanguard fiction appealed to me. I identified with the useless professor, and I liked the fact that these novelists had never been widely known, even during their lifetime. When I took out a novel by Benjamin Jarnés or Jaime Tomes Bodet, it often happened that the book had not been checked out of the library before—a wonderful feeling. Being the first borrower was almost as thrilling as being the first reader. And if I actually had to separate the pages with a penknife, which I sometimes did, it was like making love to someone for the first time. When you keep checking out books that nobody else has borrowed before, you know either that you're onto something or that you're totally wasting your time. Usually, I knew both things at once.

I worked on my dissertation in a carrel on the fourth floor of the library. Cramped but cozy, my carrel felt more like home than any other place except my parents' house in Miami. Under the desk I kept a little portable heater, with which I warmed my Cuban cold feet after the trudge through the snow and the sludge. The best thing was the carrel's location right across from the PQ section of the stacks, which contained Spanish and Spanish-American literature, my scholarly turf. Usually, all I had to do to find a book was take a few steps down the hall.

By the beginning of June I was brimming with bright ideas. I had gathered reams of material and had begun outlining several chapters. All my notes were scribbled on hundreds of 3-by-5 and 4-by-6 index cards, my most precious possession, which I kept in a couple of boxes in the carrel.

One Thursday afternoon, when I came in to continue working, I noticed several things were missing from my locked carrel: a textbook with which I was teaching myself to read German; a pocket German-English dictionary; several pens and pencils and other office supplies—and my two file boxes, each of which had been filled to the hilt with the sum total of my research and writing on Hispanic vanguard fiction. In an instant I felt my career collapse like a stack of index cards.

I was always careful to lock the carrel, but since the partitions between carrels did not rise all the way up to the ceiling, it was possible to climb on one of the portable book ladders and descend into a carrel. But it had never crossed my mind that anybody would have designs on index cards containing doctoral dissertation notes. After I got over the shock, I panicked. No notes meant no dissertation, no dissertation meant no job, and no job meant failure. It was bad enough that I was headed toward a career as a professor rather than an accountant like my great-uncles or a businessman like my father; now even that would be denied me! Fleeing the dispossession of the exile, in the ivory tower of academe I unexpectedly encountered a different kind of dispossession.

I had read about other scholars who had worse catastrophes befall them. During World War II the great philologist Erich Auerbach had to flee his native Germany, leaving many years of research behind. He ended up in Turkey, where he wrote *Mimesis,* one of the classics of modern literary scholarship, largely from memory. Knowing about Auerbach provided little consolation. I was Cuban, not German; I lived in Ann Arbor, not Istanbul; and although I too had left my homeland, I was certainly no Auerbach.

And yet, like him, I had lost all of my research. My carrel mate, a doctoral candidate in history, also kept her cards and notebooks there, but none of her material, except a stapler, was taken. I had a couple of extra index card files with nothing in them; those too were left behind. Except for the textbook and the dictionary, which could be resold, none of the stolen items was worth anything to anyone not writing a dissertation on Hispanic vanguard fiction. And who but me would want to do that? Who else could decipher my handwriting? Who could make any sense out of the morass of illegible sentences and inchoate paragraphs? The conclusion was inescapable: whoever broke into the carrel was out to get me, the Cuban-exile Auerbach.

It occurred to me, of course, that the card heist might be a mean-spirited prank by a couple of fellow students. Although I didn't have any declared enemies among my peers, I also didn't have many friends. Because I spent most of my time working, I didn't socialize very much, which earned me a reputation for aloofness. In addition, my personal history and conservative politics set me apart from many of my professors and most of my peers, who looked up to Fidel Castro and who spoke of the Cuban Revolution as a model for the rest of Latin America. As someone who had lived through the Cuban Revolution rather than only read about it in books and newspapers, I knew the reality was otherwise; but in the eyes of many of my graduate school colleagues, I was just another right-wing *gusano* from Miami towing the party line. It was certainly possible that the theft was motivated by academic jealousy or ideological spite. Perhaps my cards had been confiscated by a thesaurus-brandishing Che Guevara.

After I tired of searching every inch of the carrel over and over, I called Paul Ilie, my dissertation adviser, a famous Hispanist scholar whom I both feared and admired. I used the old wooden phone booth on the fourth floor, where my carrel was, and it was like going to confession. I had never called Professor Ilie at home before.

The phone rang several times before he answered. Ilie had a hollow voice, the kind that seems to emanate from someone else's throat. The first time I had ever spoken with him, when I went in for advising upon my arrival in Ann Arbor, he told me that I talked too fast and suggested that I take speech lessons, as he himself had done. "I know you could never tell," he said, "but I used to pronounce my name Paul Oily." The lessons had indeed erased his Brooklyn accent, leaving in its place an eerily affectless monotone. When he said hello, it sounded as if he were speaking from the bottom of a well.

"Professor Ilie, this is Gustavo. I'm sorry to bother you at home but something terrible's happened. I just went to my carrel and somebody took all of my notes for the dissertation. Everything, even my bibliography. It's all gone. I was here yesterday and when I came back today someone had taken it. I can't write the thesis without my notes. I don't know what to do."

Usually, I found Ilie's voice unsettling—talking to him was like shaking a plastic hand—but that afternoon over the phone the hollow voice became soothing, like a neck rub, just the right palliative for my mile-a-minute, Cuban-accented raving, which no amount of speech therapy could ever correct. After hearing me out, Ilie tried to calm me down. There must be some mistake, he said. He would talk to the head of the library and see what could be done. He suggested that I contact the campus police, send letters to the local papers, and offer a reward for the return of my cards. I did as he told me, and also posted signs on every door of the library asking if anyone had seen two file boxes full of index cards written mostly in Spanish.

Friday morning my ad, offering a reward if the cards were returned to the circulation desk, appeared in the *Michigan Daily* under the headline "Help!"

Saturday and Sunday went by and nothing happened. Several times during that weekend I was on the verge of packing my bags and going home to Miami. I had never felt at home in Ann Arbor, but now this midwestern university town had turned into enemy territory—not only foreign but treacherous. By Monday morning I had decided instead to follow Auerbach's example and reconstruct what I could from memory. I holed up in my apartment over the next several days and nights, regurgitating phrases, sentences, ideas, titles, names. Even though I felt dizzy the whole time, by the end of the week I had a decent draft of the first two chapters. I began to feel better. It's surprising to realize how much of a scholar's research is superfluous. Books get in the way of books, and sometimes the best way to write them is to stop reading them.

That Friday, somewhat relieved but still dizzy, I went to my carrel as I did every day, hoping against hope that my cards would magically materialize. Inside the carrel, on the desk, I found a note:

I found your cards and a stapler with name Norris on it. They were in a brown bag in a 3rd floor carrel June 1. Do not trust your promise of no questions asked. If you want the cards back do the following: 1) write how much the reward is and 2) how the transfer can be done without us meeting. Put your reply in a book on the 3rd floor.

Cinemania Filmic Creation
Alfred Gordon Bennet
808.29
B 469 ci

Sandy

P.S. I found out where your carrel was because I work here. I did not steal them. I found them! Also two cards are attached. Are they yours? After you put your reply in book put sign on door of 3rd floor saying Roger, I am in carrel #21, Barbara.

I didn't quite know what to make of this. The note was printed with a felt-tip pen on a piece of lined loose-leaf paper. The lettering was shoddy, as if it had been written in a hurry. The postscript was awkward in a way that could mean that Sandy was on the level, but I had no idea how my cards could have ended up in a paper bag in a third-floor carrel. I checked with the head of the library and there was no Sandy on the staff. I wrote back:

I found your note today (Friday June 10) at 2 p.m. I've managed to get together $30, of which $10 are enclosed. If you leave the cards in my carrel I will put the other $20 in this book. As soon as I have my cards I'll leave the rest of the reward (say where).

Gustavo

P.S. I'm leaving town next week so we have to do this now.

After leaving the note inside *Cinemania: Aspects of Filmic Creation,* an early history of the movies written by an Englishman, I posted a sign saying, "Roger, I'm in carrel #21, Barbara." The next couple of days were not easy. Everyone hates to wait, but as someone whose very life has been waiting, I hated it more than most. I thought of all the years my father had waited to get his business back. Compared to his *almacén,* my cards were trivial, but I felt that history was repeating itself.

I must have looked behind *Cinemania* twenty or thirty times, to no avail. Sandy wasn't talking. Finally realizing that I had been conned out of ten bucks, I went back to re-creating the third chapter, the most difficult one yet, since it required a lot of documentation from secondary sources. That afternoon, on another of my hourly visits to *Cinemania,* I found the note I had been expecting.

Dear Gustavo,

30 dollars is not enough. This is six months work for you etc. Make it $50 and the exchange can be made. Put the money in the book, either $20 at a time or all of it and I will return your cards to you. You seem to forget who has the cards. It is up to you to trust me. To show I am acting in good faith I will leave 1/5 of the cards in a place in the library which I will specify tomorrow. Hurry up because I am leaving soon. Keep away from the library. Check only at 5:00 and 9:00. If I even get a suspicious feeling about this I will just throw the cards away. Oh yes, one more demand. I am short of a few necessities. I want 2 pair of bikini panties, a bra, a nightgown, preferably a babydoll nightie, and a box of tampons or a few sanitary napkins. These should be of high quality material. I need this right away. My measurements are 36-25-35. C-cup. An exact fit is not necessary but should come close. Put these articles in a brown paper bag and leave them in the library. I don't care how you get them just get them. These are my final and last demands. If you fulfill them I will return all your cards. If not I will throw them out. Hurry.

Sandy P.S. Received your 10 dollars. Thank you. When you have done this put a sign on the 5th floor door, same as before. Your cards will be in the same place where you should deposit the articles I want. So when you pick up cards deposit the articles. Put behind this book:

A.L.A. Library Education Newsletter
Lib Sci
z 668
.A54

There are no negotiations.

Dear Gustavo? What does she mean, dear Gustavo? And what sort of measurements are those, Miss America's? Whoever had my cards, if she really did have my cards (and if she really *was* a she), was having fun with me. Up to now I had felt like a character in a story by Borges, but this PG-13 twist was unlike the Argentinian bibliophile, who wouldn't have known a C-cup from a teacup if it hit him in the face. Sandy had pulled me out of *Dream Tigers* and plopped me down in *True Detective*.

My wife offered to get me the necessities, perhaps because she was beginning to get jealous of Sandy, whom I imagined tall and with sunlight in her hair, as in the sixties song. But this was something I had to do myself. Note in hand, furious but also a little bit titillated—talk about *empingue*—off I went to the mall. In the midst of my rage and panic, I found my relationship with Sandy unexpectedly exciting. Whatever her motives, she was giving me a glimpse of a different, perhaps more vital, existence—for which I secretly yearned. Sometimes I thought of her extortion notes as perverse valentines.

It was my first time (though not my last) buying women's underwear—and for an *americana!* Although I didn't splurge, I tried to get good-quality stuff, as Sandy had asked. The items I liked best were the bikini panties, which had a lace front decorated with tiny pink and green flowers. The bill for everything came to less than forty dollars.

The next day, eager to make the exchange, I located the *A.L.A. Newsletter,* which was shelved in a remote nook of the library. Instead of my cards, there was another missive from my cruel mistress:

Dear Gustavo,

A change in plans has occurred. Leave my things on the 5th floor of the new building behind a book DC611 M57 A46. Do not try anything. Your cards right now are sitting in a waste paper basket not in this building that is due to be dumped tonight if I don't save them. I will get them after I pick up the package. I will leave a message there telling where the rest of the cards will be. Put your package in 5th floor behind the same book. I will leave the cards at the specified place. Do not come near the library until 9:40.

Sandy

I headed for the new location, which was in a different wing of the library, and there I found one of the staplers, a box of staples, and a few dozen cards. Following instructions, I dropped off Sandy's things and left. At 9:40 that night, twenty minutes before closing time, I came back. There was nothing behind DC611 M57 A46. I searched every book on that set of shelves—still nothing. I was furious, frustrated, in despair. But as Cuban luck would have it, on my way out of the stacks I noticed a familiar sign on the door: "Roger, I'm in carrel #28, Barbara." Same message as before, but with a different carrel number. A Borgesian clue! Twenty-eight was the number of my carrel, the one from which the cards had been rifled. Sure enough, on the floor of my carrel I found a slip of paper with still another message:

Gustavo,
      I'm sorry but I think I forget where I said I would put the cards so I put them in the 1st floor West of the old library behind this book

PA6207
A7
1914

Sandy

By now it was close to ten and the lights in the library had blinked on and off a couple of times indicating it was closing time. Rapidly navigating darkened stairwells and deserted corridors, I hurried to the oldest section of the library, which housed the books with the PA call numbers. Behind PA6207, I found a brown paper bag along with another note:

Dear Gustavo,
      You have kept your end of the bargain and now I have kept mine. Here are all your cards plus a staple remover. I bet you are surprised. But all I wanted was a fair return for my effort. I gave up the stapler, staples, and staple remover as a bonus for your being so good. How about doing me a favor. Stick your big cock in this bag and jerk off and then leave it here for me. Think of me getting into your panties etc. I will keep in touch with you. When are you coming back?? Bye

Sandy

P.S. I am enclosing a book to help you get it up.

Everything was there, just as Sandy said. My cards were intact, in the same quirky order I had arranged them. Sandy's gift book was a magazine called *Exotique,* whose cover displayed a nasty-looking blonde woman wearing nothing but a black leather bustier and spike heels. The caption said, "Bianca—Mistress of Exquisite Pain."

Oh, the pleasures of exile. Oh, the pleasures and the exquisite pain of exile. Old Auerbach never had it this good.

Although I never heard from Sandy again, I thought about her often for several years. Who was Sandy, and what was she *really* trying to tell me? In my mind, the card heist demonstrated how out of place I was in Ann Arbor. As the descendant of Cuban *almacenistas,* I had no business living two thousand miles away from home or getting a Ph.D. in literature. I had no business choosing the life I had chosen. Rather than a petty thief or a sadistic prankster, Sandy may have been a ghost from my Cuban past encouraging me to drop out of graduate school and return to Miami. But I had gone too far in my academic career to be able to turn back.

When I told my adviser, Professor Ilie, how the cards had been retrieved, he suggested I write the whole thing up as a fictional story and send it to *The New Yorker.* "But not now," he added in that hollow voice of his. "Only after you've finished your dissertation."

Several years later, with Michigan and my dissertation far behind me, I'm a professor of Spanish at Duke and Gustavo Sr. is driving me to Miami International Airport, where I'm about to catch a plane to New York and the annual Modern Language Association Convention.

In a certain way, my relationship with my father boils down to a succession of car rides spread out over four decades and two countries. Practically the only time we have spent by ourselves during our lives is when we have been together in a car. As a child in Cuba, I rode with him to the *almacén* and to baseball games; when I was growing up in Miami, we would go to pick up my grandmother from her canasta games or to mass on Sunday evenings. Often he simply said to me, "Junior, want to go for a ride?" If I said yes (sometimes I declined his invitation), we would head for Downtown Miami or Miami Beach and spend an hour or two driving around, always at some point stopping at a sidewalk coffee stand for a cup of *café cubano.*

The trip to the airport is a short drive through Cuban neighborhoods, perhaps fifteen minutes in the light Sunday morning traffic. Going down Douglas Road, barely exceeding the 45-mile-per-hour speed limit, Gustavo chews on his fifty-cent cigar. A few months earlier, Mr. Evans, the owner of the car dealership where my father works, decreed that there would be no more cigar-smoking in company cars. In response, my father hung a tiny pine tree from the rearview mirror and now keeps a bottle of Lysol under the driver's seat. After each trip, he makes sure to empty the ashtray and spray a few puffs of deodorizer into the car. What Mr. Evans doesn't know won't hurt him, or my father.

A couple of minutes into the trip, Gustavo says, "Junior, sometimes people come to the lot and they ask me what you do, and I don't know what to say. I tell them you're a professor at Duke University, but I'm not sure what that means. Tell me, junior, what do you do?"

Oh-oh. What I like about these car rides is that I spend time with my father; what I hate is that he gets the chance to ask the two questions that always make me squirm. One is whether I would go back to Cuba; the other is what I do for a living. It's too early in the day for these vexing, unanswerable questions, which stir up all of my mixed feelings about my choice of profession. Given where and who I come from, I didn't figure to be the kind of gusano who would grow up into a bookworm. Although my mother is an avid reader, she wasn't very successful in imparting her passion to her children, or at least to Carlos, Mari, and me (Pepe is a different story), and as a kid I never read anything other than biographies of sports figures and textbooks (Nena always said that the Cuban textbooks contained everything one needed to know). Later, as an adolescent, I was too preoccupied with girls and athletics to pay much attention to books. It was not until my last year of college that I developed anything like a taste for reading.

And yet here I am now, more than twenty years after our departure from Cuba, making a living from books, those I write and those I read, and waiting anxiously for the green light at the corner of Calle Ocho and Douglas Road, where the lot's cars are gassed up. Mine is a scholarly career compacted in equal parts from vocation and equivocation. For years I have known that my choice of profession was a knee-jerk response aimed at my father's balls. As an undergraduate,

I majored in English partly because I liked to write, partly because I couldn't think of anything better, but mostly because I wanted nothing to do with my father's world. After I finished college and didn't get drafted (the only lottery I've ever won), the one concrete thing I could do with my English degree was go to graduate school, so I married someone who was headed in the same direction, and off we went. Then came Michigan, Duke, scholarly publications, promotion and self-promotion.

But the more I ascended the academic pecking order, the more I lost my way. Deep down, I always knew that my choice of career was a strange one, a reflex reaction rather than a true choice, but I was too busy to think about it very much. Sometimes my father would joke that when Castro fell and he and his associates took over (Gustavo is a cabinet member of one of several Cuban governments-in-exile), he would install me as chancellor of the University of Havana. Although this may have been his way of merging my life and his, I saw no future in it. In graduate school, every time someone I knew dropped out, I was secretly envious. But dropping out was never a serious option for me, even when the index cards were stolen. Just the opposite: the more unhappy and isolated I felt, the harder I worked. A monomaniac who rued his ruling passion, I imagined the professor I wanted to be, and I became him.

I went through graduate school at a time when the prevailing wisdom had it that language spawned reality. I was taught that novels were self-reflexive and that the meaning of a poem was always another poem. The favorite image of a professor of mine was the Mobius strip, always recoiling on itself. I read in lit-crit books that fatherhood was a discursively untenable position and that death was another name for a linguistic predicament (the man who wrote this is now buried in New Haven). This profoundly shallow view of literature shaped the way I saw the world. Living outside of the text, I thought that there was no life outside of the text. My *vita* became my life.

To judge by my academic accomplishments, I'm exceedingly industrious and erudite. My articles have appeared in the best journals, my books have been published by prestigious university presses, I have been the recipient of selective fellowships. But although I love literature, I'm no intellectual. What I am is vivo, the Cuban term for a survivor, someone who thrives by dint of his wit. Early on in graduate school, I figured out how the system worked, and I beat it.

Like my uncle Manolo, who wrote dirty plays under a pseudonym, I know the art of disguise. Like my uncle Pedro, who started a painting company never having held a brush in his life, I know how to improvise. And like my father, who does not suffer fools gladly, I know a *comemierda,* a shithead, when I see one, and American universities are chock full of them.

My academic career has been a picaresque tale, a rogue's progress. Every time I'm at a departmental meeting with my Ivy-poisoned colleagues, mostly worthless people with whom I'm pleased to have little in common, I realize that I have gotten away with murder. They went to Ivy League colleges and universities; I attended Miami-Dade Community College and the University of Miami, Suntan U. They speak English effortlessly, with formulaic articulateness; I prattle on in my rapid-fire Ricky Ricardo rant. The men among my colleagues sport wispy beards and grubby corduroy pants, while their female counterparts wear comfortable shoes and dispense with jewelry and makeup. I have a diamond stud in my earlobe, tasseled loafers on my feet, and I spend as much time at the mall as I do at the library.

Listening to my colleagues quarrel with each other over meaningless committee assignments or stupid curriculum reforms, I sometimes think to myself-you jargon-spouting, distinction-mongering, literature-hating, life-denying *comemierdas. ¿Qué carajo estoy haciendo yo aquí?* What the hell am I doing here with you?

In the car, Gustavo is still waiting for an answer. Think fast, Professor. This is no time to vent, this is time to invent. What do I say? What do I do? What do I say I do? My father's question hangs in the air, mixes with his cigar smoke, and makes a wreath that circles our heads—a chaplet of smoke and unanswered questions. I can't tell him I teach Spanish, which is the simplest reply, because that doesn't sound impressive enough. What's the big deal in teaching Spanish when you were born in Cuba? You don't need a Ph.D. for that. Dozens of times already I've had to deal with that reaction, and right now I need a more potent and definitive answer, one that will not only shut him up but that he can use later with his cronies and customers, most of whom would not know Joyce from juice or Tolstoy from toast.

"I teach *literatura comparada,*" I reply. This is half-true. The true half is that my Ph.D. is in comparative literature; the less-than true half is that Duke doesn't have a comparative literature program. But it sounds better than Spanish.

"And how do you say that in English?" he asks.

After I tell him, he repeats the words slowly, breaking them up into syllables the way one would in Spanish. Since he still doesn't know how *not* to pronounce final *e's,* he gets five syllables per word: com-pa-ra-ti-ve li-te-ra-tu-re. Trapped inside his mouth, the *t's* and r's roar like a racing engine. The cigar doesn't help his diction any, and I'm sure he has no idea what the rubric means anyway. Nor should he.

So he asks one more question. "What literatures do you compare?"

It's a logical follow-up, but another tough one to answer. Now I need to explain that comparative literature does not necessarily involve the comparison of literatures. I'm in a quandary again, and we're only up to Bertram Yachts, where Carlos Rego worked for a while, still blocks away from the airport. My discomfort is hurtling toward panic. If only my father were a book, then I could slam him shut. That's one thing about books; unlike people, they don't ask embarrassing questions. Books are predictable, they always stick to their script. At the beginning of *Anna Karenina,* "unhappy" always precedes "families" and "families" always precedes "all alike." No matter how many times I have read this sentence, it always offers me the same words in the same order. If I don't know a word in a book, I can go to a different book, find its meaning, and the word will be there waiting for me when I come back. And if I don't like what the book says, I close it and the book will leave me alone. But I can't do that to my father. What I'm really afraid of is that he'll read *me* like a book.

Since Gustavo Sr. thinks that I speak French and read German, I could go the language route and reply that I compare Spanish and French and German. But in truth I don't speak French fluently and my German became extinct years ago.

"That's just the name. What I do is teach literature."

"But you don't write novels."

Another zinger, and he doesn't even know it.

"No, I don't write novels; I teach students how to read novels."

As soon as I say this, I realize that I'm using reading the way that literary critics always use the word, as a synonym for interpretation. But for Gustavo, reading is what he does every night with the

Diario Las Américas. He doesn't understand how it is that college students need to be taught to read.

"What I do is discuss the structure of novels, what they mean, how they are put together, their themes and symbols. I try to make my students understand what makes novels works of art."

Even this is only partially true, for usually what goes on in my classes is far more pedestrian than I make it sound. Gustavo is listening intently, he's paying more attention even than my students, but what I'm saying still leaves him in a fog. Not because he isn't smart enough—he's smart enough, all right—but simply because lit-crit talk is totally foreign to his already foreign-enough life. Structure? Themes and symbols? These words probably strike him as vaguely religious. Works of art? That's my mother's department. The fact is that what I do is difficult to explain to anyone who doesn't do it. You don't have to cut diamonds to understand jewelers and you don't have to slaughter cows to appreciate butchers, but it helps to teach or take college literature courses in order to fathom literature professors. We don't write novels, we don't review novels, and we don't train students to write or review novels. In the good old days we used to write biographies and histories, but that's passé. What we are is literary critics—"So you're a literary critic, huh? Well, what do you criticize?"

This Sunday morning, riding with my father toward the airport, zipping past the *bodegas* and gas stations, stopping behind a bus with an ad for La Cubanísima radio station, looking up at billboards displaying olive-skinned models, the only thing I criticize is myself for ending up in a profession that I can't explain to my father. I'm a literary critic of myself. It's not enough that I know what I do if I can't explain it to him. It's not enough that I make a decent living at it or that my students like me if I can't explain it to him. I wish I did something that I could explain to him. Say to him, I sell shoes, or I bake loaves of bread, or I run an *almacén.*

Finally, we get there, Miami International Airport. Departing Flights, No Stopping or Standing. In the old days Gustavo used to park in the garage and wait with me until the plane boarded, but now he prefers to drop me off at the curb. I like it better this way also, because he has less time to get sentimental. It's only a three-day trip to New York, where he spent his honeymoon with my mother, where we vacationed when I was nine years old, where his sister still lives, but he acts as if I were taking off on a one-way journey to Mars. I feel that way a little bit too.

Pulling my bags from the trunk, he reminds me to phone my mother when I get to the hotel. I assure him that I will and kiss him on the cheek. He kisses me back, with tears in his eyes.

The convention is just about what I've come to expect—too many people wearing too many cheap suits trying too hard to read each other's name tags.

On the flight back to Miami, I'm relieved that it's over. As soon as I get off the plane, I phone my father, who has been expecting my call all evening. Picking me up at the airport is the main event of his day, and by the time I've gathered my bags, he's at the curb, standing with one foot out of the loaned Nissan, waving to me, the cigar still in his mouth. As I walk over, I realize that on the ride home I may have to explain what I did for three days at the MLA Convention in New York. If he asks, I'll tell him that I screwed around, that's all. That's as much of an explanation as I can manage. Although I make a living explaining things, when I'm facing my father, all my explanations don't help very much. Somehow, they always sound like apologies.

Because what can I say to him, really? I left for Ann Arbor, he stayed in Miami. I became a professor, he remained an *almacenista*. I regret my choices, but perhaps I wouldn't change them.

NINE
Love in a Foreign Language

On the fault line between Cuba and America, beginning in 1988

Last night Mary Anne said to me, "Just begin writing and worry about the ending later." That's what I want to do, begin writing, tell you a love story about a Cuban man and an American woman, about Mary Anne and me, and for the time being ignore that our story is still in the malting.

When Mary Anne and I fell in love in 1988, I felt I was entering a fascinating but, in some ways, fearsome new world. Not only was she the first *americana* I had been intimate with, she was the first nonCuban—male or female—that I had gotten to know in any depth. Having spent all of my adult life married to a Cuban woman whose family—like mine—lived in Miami, I found it disconcerting to have a relationship with someone who didn't speak my language, didn't understand my customs, and—most importantly—didn't share an exile's nostalgia. At the same time, however, our sharp differences ignited a passion that I had never felt before. Although I had lived contentedly with Rosa, my first wife, for many years, Mary Anne reached a side of me that had not expressed itself until then.

Initially, I thought that Mary Anne would give me the opportunity to live my adolescence over again, to make up for everything I had missed growing up as a Cuban exile. As a ponysized version of the *yeguas* of my high school days (her nickname was not "Mar" for nothing!), she was the *americanita* of my dreams—twenty years

161

later. When we first started going together, I used to tell her that she was not just a *tipa* but an *arquetipa,* not just a pair of legs but a paradigm. Hearing about her adolescence in Northvale, a New Jersey bedroom community, I was able to imagine myself an American teenager growing up in the suburbs. In truth, my own adolescence had not been all that different from what I imagined hers to be, but my fantasies had to do with exclusion rather than inclusion. What I truly wanted were teenage years unencumbered by exile.

When Mary Anne was still living with her husband and I had already separated from my wife, sometimes in the evening I would get into my car and spend an hour or two circling her block, hoping to catch a glimpse of her through the kitchen or the living room windows. Driving by her house in the dark, I played a Billy Joel tape that she had made for me. Before I met Mary Anne, I didn't even know who Billy Joel was. As I listened to songs such as "This Night" and "Innocent Man"—which to my Cuban ears sounded like a slow cha-cha—my Integra turned into a time machine, and Mary Anne was my passport to the past. I was no longer a Cuban exile and Mary Anne was no longer someone else's wife. We were both back in Northvale, and she was my date. We went to a dance. She let me hold her hand. We necked in the car (I had a car!). As in the Billy Joel song, the night lasted forever.

Of course, I soon came to understand that Mary Anne was far more real than an archetype, far more vital than a time-release teenage crush. Her adolescence—which I idealized beyond recognition—was neither as happy nor as uncomplicated as I made it out to be. I may have longed for Northvale, but she wanted no part of it. A bigger irony, however, was that by dreaming up a different adolescence for myself, I was indulging in the kind of wishful thinking for which I criticized my parents. Instead of settling in the present, as I wanted them to do, I replaced one nostalgia with another: if not "Next year in Cuba," then "Next year in Northvale." But the Northvale of Mary Anne's teenage years was no more accessible to me than the Cuba of my childhood was to my parents. At least my parents had once lived in Cuba, while all I knew about New Jersey was what Mary Anne told me.

The grain of truth embedded inside my fantasies was that the relationship with Mary Anne had cultural as well as personal consequences. If I divorced Rosa, the prominence of Cuba in my life would surely diminish. I would no longer be able to speak Spanish at home, raise Cuban-exile children, or live in Miami a part of each year. My life would come to resemble that of a middle-class American man, and I wasn't sure whether I could be happy living that way. Given how I had been raised, given my investment in the past and my expectations for the future, how could I stand to loosen my moorings in my native tongue and culture? And yet, I also thought that life with Mary Anne might give me the opportunity to advance beyond exile, to settle down once and for all. Even though Rosa and I owned a house in Chapel Hill, we had never made a real home here. Our marriage had been held together by the promise of *regreso*—not just to Cuba but, more pointedly, to Miami. Mary Anne seemed to offer a release from a promise that sometimes felt like an obligation.

For my family, and particularly for my mother, my turmoil and indecision were hard to take. Part of it was that Nena, like other women in her situation, tended to identify with the abandoned daughter-in-law rather than with the (in her eyes) derelict son. As she told me many times, Rosa was *la doliente,* the aggrieved one. More importantly, the breakup of my marriage imperiled the cohesion of a family that had already been precariously stressed by exile. By falling in love with Mary Anne, I was dismantling a structure that my mother had worked tirelessly to maintain. After all of the crises our family had already been through, she couldn't understand why I was willing to wreck our peace again. In her own life, the family's welfare had always taken precedence over her own happiness (she would argue that the family's welfare *was* her happiness), and she expected me to behave the same way. It was okay for my brothers Pepe and Carlos to act crazy, that was almost expected of them, but I was always the predictable one, the son she counted on for stability and support. "Your brother Carlos is a saint compared to you," she said to me at one point. "He may have had his troubles, but he never treated his wife like this. He was always a *caballero,* a gentleman."

Although my father didn't much care who my wife was (family relations have always been my mother's department), he also tried to dissuade me from leaving Rosa. A few months after the separation, when I was in Miami on vacation (staying in a motel because my mother had declared her house off-limits to me), he and my uncle Pedro took me out to dinner at a Cuban restaurant called Casa Paco. As soon as we sat down and ordered drinks, I realized that the purpose of the dinner was not social but educational. My father and my uncle were Cubans with a mission—to make me see that I was ruining my life and the lives of the people who loved me. Although they had always been reluctant to teach me the finer points of dominoes, they were quite willing to give me lessons in life. The problem with me, my father began, is that I had been a faithful husband for too long, and therefore was suffering from a bad case of *atraso,* the Cuban word for long-term or protracted horniness (the literal meaning of the word is "backwardness"). According to his old-country mores, it was one thing to have a fling—everybody had them—but it was very different to leave your wife for another woman. Cuban men sometimes cheat on their wives, Pedro said, but we do not abandon them. They didn't understand why, in order to cure my *atraso,* I had to turn the whole family upside down.

Hearing them talk this way, I wondered whether they would have changed their tune had Mary Anne been a Cuban exile like us. I don't think their problem was simply my impending divorce, but the fact that my relationship with Mary Anne threatened our integrity as an exile family. By leaving a Cuban woman for an American one, I was not only changing spouses, I was putting our family on a different track. In effect, I was behaving like an immigrant, not an exile. One of the dogmas of exile is that you marry your own kind—because that's what you would have done in your native country. It's true that my brother Pepe had also married an American woman, but since he hardly visited Miami and had no children, the impact of the intermarriage on the family was nearly imperceptible, whereas if Rosa, the kids, and I stopped going to Miami together, our family's life in exile would change. What could "Next year in Cuba" mean to someone like Mary Anne?

Like me, my parents and the rest of my family turned the dissolution of my marriage into a symbol, or more precisely, into an omen, and they did everything they could, in both gentle and not so gentle ways, to get me to reconcile with my wife. For several months hardly a week went by without my hearing from some relative in Miami—a cousin, an aunt or an uncle, one of my teenage nieces—who called to ask (or instruct) me to come to my senses. Although at the time I resented their meddling, now I realize that it was probably dictated less by pettiness than by fear. At bottom, they were terrified of Mary Anne, or rather (since they didn't actually know her) of what they thought she represented, and they reacted in a normal human way by circling the wagons and putting up their defenses. They hoped that if they put a high enough price on my relationship with her, I would not be willing to pay it.

For my part, I needed the security of an intact family almost as much as my mother did, and I certainly didn't get any joy from hurting Rosa or disrupting our lives. Above all, I found it very depressing not to live with my children. When I first moved out, Rosa would only allow David and Miriam to come to my apartment to visit for a couple of hours once or twice a week—as she put it, she didn't want them sleeping under the same roof with an adulterer. Because of my flexible teaching schedules, I had always spent a great deal of time at home, and it was heartbreaking to have to say goodnight to them on the phone every evening. Only after a protracted and difficult struggle with lawyers and child psychologists did I receive joint physical custody, and David and Miriam then began spending half of each week at my apartment.

I also agreed with my uncle and my father that a major factor in my attraction to Mary Anne was sexual passion. But unlike them, I did not regard making love merely as a mechanism for relieving *atraso* or retrieving a past I'd never had. Although they didn't seem to understand it, my desire for Mary Anne couldn't be reduced to middle-aged horniness. If atraso there was, it came from my soul as much as from my body. The catching up that I needed the most was spiritual and emotional, not physical. I hungered for Mary Anne with a desire that transcended lust.

When she and I made love, I felt I was embarking on a marvelous journey of exploration and discovery. For the first time, sex became for me a form of soul-searching. Going inside her, I was going inside myself. Getting to know her body, I was learning things about myself that I had ignored before. With my arms around her, I felt less conflicted, more whole, multiplied rather than divided. Sex was a way of intensely living in the present, as if both our pasts fell away once we wrapped ourselves around each other. Whatever my initial fantasies about Northvale, when Mary Anne and I were together, I did not want to be anywhere else, and I did not want to be anybody else. I felt I was settling, not sinking; I felt I was making a home in the here and now. Sometimes I joked with her that her body was my country, that I was a citizen of Mary Anne. Profound physical intimacy, I discovered, could also be a remedy for exile.

I suspect that my well-being arose primarily from the natural chemistry between us, and that this chemistry may have been present regardless of our nationalities. But I also know that the fact that she was American and I Cuban acted as a powerful catalyst in our romance. The complementarity of our bodies increased with the diversity of our cultures, as if Cuba and America were complementary too. Strangely perhaps, the more different we felt ourselves to be, the more intimacy we achieved. For us, the natural motions of love entailed not only the reduction but the recognition of differences. I loved Mary Anne for all of the ways—and they were countless—in which she did not remind me of Cuba or Miami. Against the backdrop of our disparity, the things we did have in common—and those, too, were numerous—became all the more visible and precious. Because in many ways we didn't speak the same language, it was remarkable that we communicated as well as we did.

And yet, no matter how close I got to Mary Anne, no matter how many new worlds I explored voyaging on her body, often I felt utterly alone and unaccompanied. Then I sensed an abyss between us that no amount of coupling could bridge. I loved being with her, but I couldn't stand to live apart from my children. I dreamed about cutting the umbilical cord of Mami and Miami, but I needed their sustenance. I wanted to be American, but I couldn't afford to give up Cuba. Because of my waffling, I did a lot of erratic things during those years, but one particular episode stands out in my mind as the most painful example of my hopelessly mixed feelings.

In the summer of 1989, I had been separated from Rosa for several months and family and work pressures were starting to get the best—and the worst—of me. Not only were my parents and other relatives giving me a hard time, but strained relations with my colleagues—among whom Rosa had friends and sympathizers—isolated me even more. Mary Anne and I decided to escape for a long weekend to Cedar Key, a tiny, backwater town on the west coast of Florida. We had found out about Cedar Key from the travel section of the *New York Times,* where it was touted as the Redneck Riviera. The Beachboys' "Kokomo" had been a hit that year, and we saw this cut-rate Key West on the Gulf Coast as our Kokomo hideaway. For the first time in my life, I got on I-95 and didn't head for Miami.

Since I had just turned forty, perhaps the time had come to declare my independence from the world of my parents.

In Cedar Key we stayed at the Paradise Inn, an old wooden hotel with a wrap-around porch. When we weren't in bed, we spent our time at a seafood place owned by a gay woman whom everybody called Fred. At night we went to the local hangout, the L&M, a bar on the ground floor of another old wooden building with peeling grey paint. The first night we were there, the street was lined with pickups. When we walked in around ten-thirty, the place was packed; it was like the redneck sea parting and letting us through to the bar. Gordon and the Red Clay Ramblers were playing what Mary Anne told me was rockabilly, which for some reason I liked. Before that night, I'd never really danced rock-and-roll, but it wasn't difficult to get into the swing.

Having a ball in the Redneck Riviera, I saw myself as a Cuban discovering America. Never mind that the deep South was almost as unfamiliar to Mary Anne as it was to me. I wasn't dancing with one woman, I was dancing with a whole country, and it felt great. I was so out of my element that somehow I fit right in. When Gordon and the boys covered "Betty Lou's Getting Out Tonight"—changing it to "Betty Lou's Going Down Tonight"—I became a Bob Seger fan on the spot.

The last night in Cedar Key, Mary Anne and I sat on the porch, drank Amaretto from plastic cups, watched people drift in and out of the L&M, and talked endlessly, mostly about sex. It was our usual way of not talking about anything else—our spouses, our children, our jobs, our murky future. Sex was our distinctive form of achievement, the one secure thing we had. For the past few months, she and I had been living through an unabating storm. The clouds gathered, the winds swirled, the tide kept rising. In the middle of this hurricane of our own making, our only anchor was the passion we felt for each other.

I remember gazing at Mary Anne, gently swaying next to me on the porch swing, and thinking that she looked both infinitely desirable and intolerably foreign. Although I loved her more than ever, I missed my past life. Rosa and the children were spending the summer in Miami, and I wanted to be with them, eating the food I grew up on, dancing to Cuban music, and speaking my native language. And yet here I was, three hundred miles away, in the Redneck Riviera, on a creaky porch with an American woman from Northvale who had married her high school sweetheart and already had grown-up children. Cedar Key? Bob Seger? Amaretto? Stepchildren? End-less lovemaking? None of this seemed to have anything to do with me. Rock-and-rolling the night away at the L&M was fun, but I couldn't make a life out of it.

A couple of days later, back in Chapel Hill, after telling Mary Anne that I couldn't bear any longer to be separated from my chil-dren and my family, I got on a plane and flew to Miami. I got in around noon, and my wife and my children were waiting for me at the gate. Coming back from the airport, I explained to David and Miriam that Mami and Papi had worked out their problems and that everything was going to be fine. I told them that our life would return to what it had been before, with the four of us living together.

But, as Professor Ilie at Michigan liked to remind me, I spoke too fast. What happened when I got to Miami is that nothing had happened. My old life was intact, preserved, like a mummy in a museum. At my parents' house the family had gathered for a late lunch of *ajiaco,* my mother's Cuban specialty; the mood was festive and and no one breathed a word about Mary Anne, as if she didn't exist and I had never been away. My mother, my father, my cousins and aunts and uncles were all delighted to welcome the stray sheep back into the fold. It was like coming back from the dead, or return-ing from exile, or getting out of rehab. I resented heir hypocritical casualness, but I didn't break the vow of silence either. After what I had done—to Rosa, to my children, to my mother, and now also to Mary Anne—who was I to criticize anybody? Let sleeping *ameri-canas* lie. What we don't acknowledge won't hurt us.

When I walked in through the door, my uncle Pedro hugged me and gave me a knowing wink. My father kissed me with tears in his eyes. Nena was beaming. The family was back together, the way it was meant to be. Another catastrophe of exile had been averted.

The next morning, the illusion of normalcy came crashing down. I opened my eyes to my old life and I couldn't stand it, couldn't stand the faces and the routines I loved. I lay there next to Rosa in the same sofa bed I had slept in for years. David and Miriam were asleep on the bunk bed in the tiny bedroom next door. The thick beige curtains with the plastic backing were drawn. The rickety old air conditioners were blasting away. I was surrounded by family pic-tures that went back thirty years and more. All the weddings, baptisms, and First Communions. All the birthdays and graduations. Many Nochebuenas. Across from the bed, a little above eye level, was a black-and white photograph of me and my brothers and sister on the steps of our Havana house, accompanied by cousins and childhood friends. The short pants with creases, the white socks and lace-up shoes, the hair stiff like bristles. All of us looking so clean and untouched.

As I waited for everyone else to wake up, I felt hemmed in, too big for the bed and the room and the house. I thought of Gulliver in Lilliput. I was Gulliver in Little Havana. Although I clung to the exile life, it wasn't my life anymore. The well-being I had felt with Mary Anne told me so. The exile life didn't fit my body or my soul, and I was terrified by the prospect of spending the next thirty years the way I had spent the last thirty, in a cozy, cramped Cuban cocoon. My routines had decayed into ruts, my grooves had twisted into coils that wound tightly around me. I felt an overwhelming urge to bolt from that room, from that house, from that town. I couldn't stand the thought of spending the rest of my life looking at thirty-year-old family pictures. I wanted a new deal, a different compact with history, a life after exile. Most of all, I wanted Mary Anne. I couldn't bear the thought of never again waking up beside her.

And so, later that same day, after a wrenching conversation with my family, I got on another plane and went back to Chapel Hill.

Over the two-year period between the time Mary Anne and I separated from our spouses and the day we finally got married, these scenes, with variations, replayed themselves more times than I like to remember. In retrospect, it seems that all I did during those years was leave and come back, caroming between my Cuban and my American lives, between the man I had been and the man I wanted to be, all the while making everybody miserable and running up a huge tab of guilt on my Catholic conscience. I left and I left until there was no more leaving left inside me.

To others, I may have looked like the bull inside the china shop. But the way I felt, I was both the bull and the china shop. The problems I'd had a few years earlier with Carlos were nothing compared to my current predicament. All Carlos did was use my name for a few months; but by falling in love with Mary Anne, I was turning my back on a lifetime of choices. I wasn't simply wavering between two companions—this is common enough—but between two cultures, two languages, and two countries. What my family tended to regard as a midlife crisis, I knew was something deeper and more disturbing—a mid-culture, mid-language, and mid-homeland crisis. My grandmother Constantina's words to me, that I was like a weathervane, never rang truer.

On February 1991, Mary Anne and I finally married.

What helped me to stop waffling and settle down, in addition to plain weariness, was the realization that, in order to be with her, I didn't have to choose between Cuba and America. By framing our relationship in this simpleminded way, I had left myself an insoluble dilemma, for evidently I couldn't sever my ties to Cuban culture any more than I could stop wanting a more permanent settlement in the United States.

What I should have known all along, but what took me literally years to find out (a Ph.D. in literature doesn't guarantee any of knowledge of life), is that by being with Mary Anne I wasn't giving up much that I hadn't already lost, and I wasn't gaining anything that I didn't already have. She could make me American no more than Rosa—or anybody else—could keep me Cuban. This is not to say that the details and routines of one's life are not affected by the person one lives with, for obviously they are, but rather that these details and routines sometimes bear an oblique relation to one's identity. I used to think that if you spent enough time in Siberia, you would become Siberian. But this isn't true—or true only if you are already a little bit Siberian to begin with. Beginning again with Mary Anne redefined my relations with my family, with my children, with my native country, and with the person I had been until then, but it did not cut me off from them.

Leaving my first wife was, for me, part of growing up. Some people grow up when they're twenty or twenty-five; others of us wait until we're forty and married with children. The longer we wait, the more disruptive our coming-of-age, and the bigger the upheaval when it finally happens. Still, growing up is a good thing to do, at whatever age, for the rewards normally outweigh the risks. Even my mother, who used to be a one-woman pressure group for Cuban-family values, has come to accept the reasons for my divorce and remarriage. She doesn't necessarily agree with my choices, and I suspect that secretly she wishes that things would go back to the way they used to be, but she tries to make the best of the new situation. Although she is still closer to my ex-wife than to me (Rosa, she says, is the only person in the world who understands her), she and I have found a way to get along peacefully. We're not as friendly as we once were, but at least she understands me a little better. Her old hostility toward Mary Anne has given way to warmth and hospitality.

The great, gratifying paradox of my marriage to Mary Anne is that, while it has made me feel more rooted in this country, it has not diminished my ties to Cuba. Living with an American spouse, dealing with American stepchildren, and speaking English at home, I am now much more aware of my nationality than I ever was before. When I was married to Rosa, the fact that we were Cuban exiles almost went without saying. First in Michigan and then in North Carolina, we knew we were different from the people around us, but since she and I were alike in being different, exile was not an issue between us. With Mary Anne and her family, the ground rules are very different, with the result that I spend a fair amount of time explaining—and yes, at times justifying—myself to them. Although there have been moments when I have wanted to get by without explanations, when I have wished that more things went without saying, talking to Mary Anne and her family about who I am and where I come from has also allowed me to understand more vividly the things about my heritage that I cannot do without. Because my hold on Cuba is now more precarious, I grasp my island more firmly.

During my first marriage, Rosa and I used to switch back and forth in conversation between Spanish and English without giving it a thought. A lot of the time I wasn't even aware of which of the two languages we were speaking. Now when I want or need to use a Spanish phrase at home, I have to substitute an English equivalent, or I have to explain what the words mean. Every time English words fail me—or every time we fail each other—I realize how much I need the Spanish language, the extent to which I rely on Cuban or Hispanic channels of thought and communication in my everyday dealings with the world. Even if I don't speak it very much except when I am teaching, Spanish is always with me. If I didn't have Spanish, I couldn't identify many of the things I see or the emotions I feel. Sons of bitches—*hijos de puta*—would leave me speechless; and happiness—*felicidad*—would not have a name.

Something similar has happened with Miami. One of my biggest fears when my first wife and I split up was that I would lose Miami, that I would not feel connected to the Cuban enclave if I had an American spouse. But I love going to Miami now more than ever, for it still feels like *regreso,* but no longer like regression. Because I'm more self-possessed than I used to be, I enjoy my old haunts more completely, and I am more willing to try new things. Over the last few years, I have remapped the city, as it were, drawn a mental picture in which the house where I spent my adolescence is no longer at the center. This, too, is part of growing up.

In the company of Mary Anne, my trips to Miami have become not just a retreat but an adventure. Seeing the city through her eyes, I have seen it as if for the first time. We eat at restaurants I have patronized for twenty years and instead of routinely ordering from the menu, as I always did, we talk about it. When we go dancing, I repay her rock-and-roll lessons with salsa moves (as it turns out, my *americana* has Cuban hips). When we visit my parents, I take out old family albums and fill her in on people and places. Together, we explore the city, investigate Cuba-related subjects in the libraries, and hunt for memorabilia to bring back with us to Chapel Hill. Taking long walks in Coral Gables, which we love to do, we daydream about living a part of each year in one of those lushly landscaped houses with the arched doorways and inner courtyards.

By now, Mary Anne and I have been to Miami often enough to make the city our own. We usually stay in the same apartment on the outskirts of Little Havana, and we have our favorite restaurants, bookstores, bakeries, malls, and movie theaters. At first Mary Anne was a little intimidated by the fast-talking, expressive Cuban merchants and waitresses, and whenever we went into an establishment run by Cubans, I did the talking for the two of us. But over time she has grown enough of a thick skin and picked up enough Spanish so that she can fend for herself in bakeries and bodegas. Undaunted by the Cuban *ambiente* which—I admit—is sometimes as sticky as burnt sugar, she roams free among the butchers, beauticians, sales ladies, cashiers, and street vendors. When she needs something, she asks for it—in Spanish: the sweetest, softest Spanish I have ever heard. She has found that most Cubans appreciate her efforts to communicate in their language. It's not often that the ugly American turns out to be a pretty *americana*. Sometimes I think that my American wife would enjoy living among Cubans even more than I would.

It makes me happy—*feliz*—and proud to be in Miami with Mary Anne, who has come to think of herself as Cuban by marriage. (Her wedding vow, she says, was also a naturalization oath.) Although I understand my attraction to America much better than her interest in Cuba, I accept gratefully her gestures of approximation. Our fondness—indeed, our fascination—for each other's otherness enhances our sense of ourselves and nourishes our romance. The Argentinian novelist Eduardo Galeano once remarked that nostalgia is good but hope is better. In its best moments, my marriage to Mary Anne, who is truly the *americanita* of my dreams, has been the perfect blend of nostalgia and hope, of good and better. Once, not so long ago, I could not conceive of living with her; now, I cannot imagine a fuller life than the one we have made.

TEN

Ricky Ricardo with a Ph.D.

Duke University, is the last fifteen years

At the start of every semester, in September or in January, I walk into my classes and I fall in love again. Most of the time, I am loved back. I enjoy it, I encourage it, I thrive on it. Teaching is romance. I'm a successful teacher to the extent that I can get my students to fall for me. There's no learning without love, no knowledge without passion, and for students to feel passionately about the material, they need to feel passionately about me. In a deep sense, I *am* the material. Whether we are reading *Don Quijote* or nineteenth-century Spanish fiction or modern Spanish-American poetry, I am still the conduit for the emotions and ideas and attitudes of the authors and texts under discussion. My job is to make Cervantes or Galdós or Neruda speak to my class. I give them a face and a voice. I am medium and ventriloquist.

Years later, when my students remember the novels and poems they studied as undergraduates, they won't be able to separate them from the man in whose classroom they first read them. They will remember *Don Quijote* as the joint work of both Cervantes and Pérez Firmat. I'll be as much a part of the book as the author himself. I know this because the same thing has happened to me. I cannot pick up *Emma* and not think of Professor Newman, in whose undergraduate class at the University of Miami I first read Jane Austen. The green paperback cover, the words on the page, the characters in the story—all of them depend on him, as if the novel could

175

not exist without his intercession. I still read this and other books in Professor Newman's shadow, under his supervision. It's not anything that I can reduce to a set of propositions about the particular work or author, and there's nothing monitory or censorious about his presence. He doesn't make me feel self-conscious, doesn't make me look over my shoulder, doesn't control the meanings I extract from the work. Although he's invisible to all eyes but mine, he's right there on every page, like another character, or perhaps like an eager host who welcomes me into his house. When I open the book and turn to the first page, he always greets me.

Like other love affairs, teaching has its own pace and moods, its good and bad days, its coded language, its rewarding or bitter conclusion. Sometimes you walk into a class and it's love at first sight. From the first day, something clicks. You go through the door, introduce yourself, make a couple of cracks to break the ice, have them write their names on index cards, make some more remarks, use the Cuban angle, and already you've got them. Nobody plays hard to get because everybody's eager to please; you want to be liked by them as much as they want to be liked by you. By the end of the first session, you have them believing that yours is the best course they will ever take at Duke. And maybe you even believe it yourself. When you walk out of the classroom after that first day, once all the students have left (you're always the last to leave, like the captain of a sinking ship-except this ship's sailing, not sinking), all's right with the world. You're not thinking about exile. You're not thinking about Castro or the *almacén*. You're thinking that maybe it wasn't such a bad idea to become a professor after all, for a warehouse full of rice is not nearly as appetizing as a classroom full of bright young faces. You're thinking of all the clever words and bright ideas with which you will romance them over the next four months. You're thinking of the familiarity, even the intimacy, that you will achieve with each other. You're thinking this: teaching is not exile, it is a cure for exile. The classroom is home, not asylum; *terra firma,* not *terra incognita* (indeed, *terra* Firmat!). Tenure doesn't even begin to explain the kind of *bienestar,* or security, you feel when you are teaching students you love.

But the danger with love at first sight is that a passion that's so quickly ignited may fizzle out just as quickly. I'm wary of instant chemistry because I have learned that if they love you on the first day, they're likely to become bored with you by the end of the semester. Years ago I was sometimes baffled that a class that had started so well had ended so poorly. But even professors sometimes learn from experience, and by now I know what to expect. When a class loves me too much too quickly, I know that I must not overplay my hand, must not count too much on affection that was so easily tendered. So I try to temper and pace my students' *embullo* by controlling my own. Playing hard to get, I refuse to surrender to their affection. I pretend not to notice how much they like me. I try to like them less than I really do. As I teach, I tease. But even in the best of circumstances it's difficult to alter the course of love. The fact that they loved you from the first day will shape the dynamics of the rest of the semester, and sometimes you have no choice but to accept that the romance is through by October. Then you and the class are like a couple caught in a loveless marriage. You stay together because you have to, because you have obligations to meet, because it would be irresponsible to part so soon. The books on the reading list are your children and you can't abandon them now. So you muddle on from week to week, doing the best you can, every once in a while briefly relighting the old spark, but after the last class you can't get out of there soon enough. It wasn't meant to be.

The best classes are those in which the romance develops gradually. At first, there's nothing, only a tingle of interest on your part and theirs. But little by little, as the semester progresses, you can see and feel the class becoming more drawn to you and you to them. They see it and feel it too. I don't know how to describe this attraction in any terms other than erotic. You are falling, have fallen, in love. On the day of the class—Monday, Wednesday, or Friday—you wake up in the morning looking forward to seeing them. In between classes, you miss them. Once in class, if the discussion is going well, you're in heaven. It's like doing the rumba with a good partner: you lead well, they follow easily. Anticipating each other's moves, sensing when to turn and when to twirl, you glide across the floor. The classroom turns into your ballroom, and you use every inch of it. You scribble on the blackboard, lean on the lectern, stand by the windows, stroll up and down the aisles. And they're with you every step of the way. You also know, however, that whatever rhythm and intimacy you achieved during one particular hour will not necessarily carry over to the next. You have to start over each day, let the material set you in motion, ask them to dance all over again. But that's the challenge: to lead them on from session to session, to fuel their interest, to make them love you until they can't live without you. When the semester ends, you want them to be heartbroken. The way you will be.

I need to be honest: what I feel when I'm teaching is not only love for the class as a whole but an attachment to individual students. Collective and personal crushes feed off each other. It may be scandalous to admit this—I'm sure my colleagues will deny it happens to them—but I fall in love with some of my students every single semester. I do it almost on purpose, to get myself ready for the class. Because I teach language and literature, most of my students are female. Throughout the years, although they have not known it (although some may have sensed it), I have been in love with dozens of them. I'm at my best as a teacher when romancing a class, which usually means when romancing certain students in the class. My most successful classes, those where I have given the most of myself as teacher and where the students have been most receptive to what I have offered, are the ones with women I love. Being in love makes me smarter, jogs my memory, puts words in my mouth. I take one look at Suzanne, and I get ideas. I sneak a peek at Karen, and she loosens my tongue. Robin speaks, and I listen. Yes, romance even improves my hearing. When I'm teaching students I don't love, I tend to listen only to myself. Any good professor likes to hear himself or herself talk, likes the sound of his or her own voice, the way he or she articulates syllables and words; but it's dangerous to like your voice so much that you stop hearing other voices. For me, this happens when I'm indifferent to the students before me. In a loveless classroom, I may give the same lectures and say the same things that I would when I'm in love, but I do it in a detached, mechanical way. My brain may be engaged, but my heart's not in it. If I'm not in love, I can't concentrate. Like the poets of old, I need Muses to inspire me; but once inspired, I can do great things. There are few things more joyful than talking about literature with a group of women whom you love. Like dancing, which I also have been known to do in the classroom, it is sex by other means—the safest, least entangling kind of sex.

Of course, the romance comes to nothing. Its outward displays are confined to a hug or a handshake on the last day of class, maybe a peck on the cheek. What you feel toward them is a mixture of adolescent crush and paternal affection, a blend of puppy and *papi* love. Although you care for them as students, you understand that if you weren't physically attracted to them, you wouldn't care half as much. You know this and you do not shrink from this knowledge. Instead, you take advantage of it. If you require a teenage Muse in order to say inspiring things about *Don Quijote,* then go get one. If falling in love every semester makes you a good teacher, then by all means fall in love. (Love? Infatuation? Romance? I keep using the word "love" and wondering whether it's right for what I'm talking about. All I know is that it feels like love. I experience a lover's emotions—the excitement, the curiosity, the ups and downs. As I do with other people I love, I make a point of memorizing poses, gestures, mannerisms, what they say, what they wear, how they sit, where they come from. Every detail is a revelation. Every detail brings me closer to them. The beloved students inhabit my life until they become a part of it. Is this love? What else could you call it?)

As the semester enters its last weeks, our romance goes into overdrive. Class discussions acquire a new urgency. Like star-crossed lovers seeing each other for the last time, we try to squeeze as much as we can into the final meetings. The last week of class is always the most intense, as much climax as catastrophe. By then the romance has ripened. We're like a couple who has advanced past the early, tentative groping. We know each other. We trust our love. We're familiar with each other's likes and dislikes, what works and what doesn't; we have developed a private language, a repertoire of jokes and phrases understood only by us. We call each other by our first names, something we have done since the first day of class, but now it feels like a token of intimacy. You have become a professor who doesn't have to finish his sentences. They have become students who aren't afraid to complete theirs. But wonderful as all this is, you and they know that the affair is coming to an end. You hate it, you try not to notice, but you know that it must happen. Sometimes you protract the end a little with a party or makeup classes. But by the time final exam week arrives, you have taken to strolling aimlessly through the campus hoping to see a familiar face, longing for one last glance and a couple of minutes of conversation with your beloved. Sometimes the students may take another class with you and then the romance could continue for another semester, or it may fizzle out, since the dynamics of the new class will be different. But sooner or later, they leave you. You love them and they leave you.

I brag to *cubano* friends that I've never been dumped by a woman, but of course it's not true: they have dumped me dozens and dozens of times. Not only this: if I have done my job really well, if I have loved them to exhaustion, I will have taught them to dump me. A good teacher makes himself obsolete. The best teachers end up as useless professors.

Spring-semester crushes are for me the hardest to get over. Fall classes have an autumnal quality that matches the end of the affair to the mood of the season. I try to schedule fall classes in the afternoon, the better to suit the atmosphere. Autumn is for dusky, dying things, like our doomed love affair. The leaves fall, the days grow dark, the semester ends, the students go away. And then comes Christmas in Miami, which jolts me out of my melancholy, or replaces one type of melancholy with another. Not so with the spring semester, which begins in the dead of winter but ends with the azaleas in bloom. Teaching or living, spring is always harder to deal with. At first, the arrival of warm weather energizes the class, provided that you have material vibrant enough to compete with the dazzling dogwoods. But after a few weeks of shorts and sandals, when the end of the semester approaches, it becomes difficult to wind the affair down to a satisfactory conclusion. Who wants to mourn in May? Who wants to grieve when the legendary Duke gardens are bursting with color? Tempo and temperature don't match, the rhythm of romance is out of sync with the season.

After spring classes I often think that the semester concluded too soon, or not soon enough. End it in February, please, the abortive month, the month of premature conclusions. Or keep it going until summer has sapped my energies and I'm spent, incapable of more love play. The way it works now, spring semesters lack closure, even if they mark the termination of the school year. Come the first of May, I always feel that a door that needs shutting in my life has been left open. I see my students go off to the beach or return home to Long Island, and I stay behind, wanting more, but with nothing to look forward to except a couple of lonely months of writing and reading in the empty library. Books can't do for me what my students do. All those assistant registrars in short-sleeved shirts and paisley ties who concoct the academic calendar don't know a thing about romance. They don't know what it is to fall in love with your students; they don't know the happiness of walking into class and having them smile at you; they don't know the frustration of having your *cogito* interrupted. How can they put my Muses on such a heartless schedule?

As I get older, I'm neither more nor less prone to fall in love with students. I have been teaching full-time for fifteen years, and I get crushes today with the same regularity and intensity that I did when I was a twenty-three-year-old teaching assistant. The difference is that after all these years I understand the process a little better, and I'm no longer frightened or worried by my chronic lovesickness. When I was younger, I felt guilty and fretted that I would never get over it. Now I know better. There will always be another Marjorie and another Heidi and another Suzanne. I may never forget them, but I will replace them, for I'm just as fickle as they are. As my grandmother Constantina used to say, I'm like one of those cocks on the weather vanes. Since by now I'm old enough to be these girls' father, it's actually easier to fall in love these days, for my age relieves the ambiguity. Whatever my private fantasies, there's little chance that I'll end up in bed with any of my classroom paramours. The students realize this too, and they're less self-conscious with me now than when I was younger. The older I get, the more we can love each other, and when I get old enough to be their grandfather, then I will finally be able to love them without reserve. Like my own father, I'll slip effortlessly into the part of wise old Tech, randy but safe, erudite but raucous. A lusty *gusano*, I'll worm my way into their hearts. A canescent Cuban Cupid, I'll smite all of those bright and lovely young women with guava-dipped barbs. My pearls of wisdom will be aphrodisiac. My nuggets of knowledge will go down with a smile. I'll wear my heart on my sleeve, and I won't be sued for it!

There are many things that this useless professor doesn't know, but I do know this: the day I no longer fall in love with my students, it will be time to stop teaching.

In the meantime, a female student writes on her course evaluation form: "I understand how trying to reconcile all that is in society about being macho and what you truly are is difficult—I understand and respect you for saying all this—especially in a class that is very *feminista*. I also know the others feel pretty nearly as I. People ask who's my teacher and I say you and they say I heard he's *machista* and I say yeah, but it's cool."

The comment occurs at the end of a class I have been teaching on the literature and culture of U.S. Hispanics. We have spent fourteen weeks reading novels and poems, watching films and TV programs, and listening to records by or about Hispanic Americans. Of all the courses I teach, this is my favorite one because it's the most personal. I even bring to class some of my own poems and we spend a couple of sessions analyzing them. I do it not only to show off a little but to make the point that writing poems is something done by a real human being in response to concrete, often banal, circumstances. For inspiration, a head cold is sometimes just as good as the Trojan War.

As we move through the material, what comes across to the students is how unlike we "Latinos" are. Cubans, Mexicans, Puerto Ricans, Colombians, Dominicans—all of us have some things in common, but we don't have everything in common. We can't be squeezed into the same box on the census forms. The high point of the class, for me and for them, is the section on *I Love Lucy,* which I save for the end. Since these kids are so young that a few of them have never seen reruns, we watch several of my favorite episodes: the one where Ricky tells little Ricky the story of Little Red Riding Hood in Spanish; the one where the tutor Lucy hired to improve Ricky's English ends up singing "Babalú" with a Cuban accent; and my favorite of all, where Lucy tries to cure Ricky's homesickness by dressing up as his mother. Her idea of the Cuban Mrs. Ricardo is Carmen Miranda, dressed in a *baiana* outfit and wearing a fruit hat, singing a lullaby in Portuguese!

Some of our discussion revolves around Hollywood's stereotyping of Hispanic culture—what does Brazilian Carmen Miranda have to do with Cuba?—but what I really want to talk about is Ricky Ricardo, the "I" in *I Love Lucy.* A Cuban-American student in the class says that he learned how to behave like a Cuban man by watching *I Love Lucy* reruns from his home in Hialeah. He means to be funny, but his confession moves me, and as we delve deeper into the series, I find myself more and more drawn to Ricky. Like him, I'm married to an American woman; like him, I'm sometimes befuddled by what goes on in my own house; like him, I lose my temper too often; and like him, I married who I did partly to get away from my mother tongue and my mother country, to advance beyond exile. The poet Derek Walcott says somewhere that to change your language you must change your life. My version is more pedestrian: to change your language you must change your wife. This may sound overly flip, but since marrying a woman is like embracing a culture, one of the most efficient ways to embrace America is to embrace an *americana*.

Ricky knows what I mean. When he falls into Lucy's arms, he loses and he finds himself. What he loses is his primitive identity as his mother's son; but what he gains is a renewed self compacted from his Cuban past and his American present. It's difficult to watch *I Love Lucy* without noticing that one of the not-so-hidden themes of the show is Ricky's fascination with the "glorious hunks of stuff" that he talks about. More than a theater of domestic war, *I Love Lucy* *is* a mellow drama that plays out Ricky's romance with otherness, his love for various sorts of Americana, and his refusal of *regreso*. When Lucy confronts him with her cockeyed Carmen Miranda imitation, Ricky responds: "Lucy, honey, if I wanted things Cuban I would have stayed in Havana. That's the reason I married you, because you are so different from anyone I ever met before." I could say much the same thing to Mary Anne.

And yet, it's not as if Ricky wants to assimilate. That would wreck his marriage, for if he loves Lucy because she's American, Lucy loves him because he's not. As she says, he's her Cuban dreamboat, an exotic import from a fantasy island. Beyond all the jokes and jibes, Ricky's "dunts" and "wunts" are music to her ears. Every time he says "Ay, ay, ay" or launches into one of his rapid-fire Spanish-language tirades, Lucy relishes it. His accent spices her life. If Ricky were a banker from Minneapolis, Lucy wouldn't love him half as much. I'm sure that when they have sex, she asks him to whisper into her ear in Spanish. No, Ricky can't run to Lucy to escape his past, for she is constantly reminding him of it. The paradox is that you are never so entirely yourself as when you fall in love with someone who is unlike you. Want to feel American? Marry a Cuban.

As I share these ideas with my students, who agree with some of them and reject others, they begin to see me as a professorial version of the show's Cuban protagonist: Ricky Ricardo with a Ph.D. I've been trading on stereotypes, yet showing them that stereotypes can also be portraits. Ricky becomes for us a symbol of what it means to be Cuban in America. I love Ricky because he loves Lucy, and I'm thrilled that the class seems to love him too.

We play back scenes and listen carefully to Ricky's Spanish out-
bursts, where he makes remarks that he would never allow himself
in English. One time he says that if she fucks him over again, he is
going to leave her. Fucks him over, *me jode,* that's what he says. The
class concludes that bilingual households are overrated; it's a good
thing that Lucy doesn't understand a word of Spanish.

Our discussion of Ricky's character opens out into an argument
about Latin men and American mores, about gender roles and
machismo. We bandy this word about, machismo, but without saying
exactly what it means. All semester long, Hispanic machismo, mine
included, has been a recurring topic of discussion. I ask what macho
means to them, and they reply that it refers to boorish, sexist males.
With a couple of exceptions, none of the girls in the class wants a
boyfriend who's macho. Even many of the guys proudly proclaim
that they're not macho, that it wouldn't occur to them to want to be
macho. I counter that for me machismo is a doctrine of responses and
responsibilities. To illustrate, I quote my grandfather's words when
my brother was born about having another *machito* for the *almacén.*

Then I explain, "When Abuelo Pepe said this, he was thinking
about my brother becoming a man like himself, who began working
when he was twelve or thirteen and never stopped, who founded a
family, who provided for his children and grandchildren. And if he
had a fling or two along the way, well, maybe he earned it."

The class reacts with smirks and skepticism.

Karen, a beautiful girl with long brown hair who sits in the front
row, says to me, "But then you aren't really macho; that's not what
we mean by machismo, really."

"In Spanish macho is usually coupled with *hombre,*" I reply. "An
hombre macho is a manly man, but the two words are complementary rather than redundant, since hormone-driven machismo is not the
same thing as conscience-driven *hombría. Hombría* teaches somber
truths, umbrous truths, hard dark truths that the heat-seeking macho
ignores at his peril. These truths have to do with limits, with consequences. Machismo says the world is your oyster and *hombría*
responds that every oyster has a price tag; machismo says take what
you want and *hombría* responds that some of your wants are impos-
sible to take. When the macho settles, he sinks; *hombría* teaches him
to settle without sinking. Abuelo Pepe, he was an *hombre macho.*"

Since I have given this speech before, it all comes out in precise, sonorous Spanish, like Ricky singing. My father should hear me now. In a different setting, I would have added, "Machismo says no one has a bigger prick than yours, and *hombría* responds that all that makes you is a big prick." But in class I water down the Caribbean sauciness in my speech, especially the informality that often runs into profanity. Still, Karen is not totally convinced.

"The true *machista* doesn't care about those things your grandfather believed in. What you are is a sensitive macho."

Yes, Karen, that's me—I'm a sensitive macho, all right. I'm somewhere between the cavemen and Iron John, somewhere between the Stone Age and the New Age. By confessing my machismo and explaining it as I have, I have bracketed it, enclosed it in quotations—Gustavo is only "macho"—and thus removed some of the threat. I'm glad this happens, even if a part of me wishes I could live outside quotation marks. But if I were a plain unquotable macho like my grandfather, I wouldn't be standing up in front of a class of twenty-year-olds explaining myself. The *hombre macho,* at least the Cuban garden variety, is voluble but not talkative. He may brag, he may bluster, but he doesn't talk. Just as he doesn't believe in sex without courtship, he doesn't believe in conquest without propaganda. And yet nothing that he says is deliberately selfdisclosing. Remember the game of dominoes? It was invented by a mute.

For my part, I talk way too much to be macho and I can't help it, since a professor is someone who opens his mouth for a living. So my machismo will always be enclosed in quotation marks, sequestered inside my loose tongue like a dildo wrapped in fancy paper. I'm too sensitive to be macho, but too macho to be really sensitive. I'm the one-and-a-halfer of gender politics. My class is a celebration of difference, a fiesta of diversity. I am a multiculturalist's worst nightmare.

After all is said and we are done with *I Love Lucy,* I haven't made any converts to machismo, but my openness has made the students more open. They may continue to reject the macho ethic in their own lives, but at least they have acquired a better understanding of this code of conduct. This is as much as I expect. On the last day of class, I give each student in the class a valentine—an autographed *I Love Lucy* trading card, autographed by me of course, the

Ricky Ricardo of Duke. I can see them melting in my hands; I have already melted in theirs.

A week later, when we meet for the final examination, Karen attaches a rhymed postscript to her paper.

There once was a Cuban Gustavo
who taught at the U to make *chavos*.
He dealt with the spies and the feminist chicks
even though they all thought him a *pavo*.

Chavos is money; *pavo* is slang for someone who's a pushover or a soft touch. I reply to Karen:

There once was a feminist chick
who wrote her professor a limerick.
He was so impressed
with her verve and her verse
that he gave her an A for her schtick.

Yes, teaching is not exile, but a cure for exile. Even if I never spend next year in Cuba, I can still spend next semester with my students. Every time I enter a classroom, I think of Ricky's familiar greeting as he walks through the door of his New York apartment, simple yet memorable words that every exile longs to utter: "Lucy, I'm home."

ELEVEN

Earth to Papi, Earth to Papi

Chapel Hill, 1993

Today is Father's Day. My son is at a basketball camp and my daughter is spending the day with her mother. A few days ago David turned twelve, which makes him older than I was when I arrived in the United States. A couple of weeks before that, Miriam turned nine. Since the custodial arrangement with David and Miriam's mother, who still lives in Chapel Hill, is that I will celebrate their even-numbered birthdays, this year my son's birthday party was held at my house, while my daughter's took place at hers. If this pattern holds, Miriam will celebrate *los quince,* the traditional coming-out party for fifteen-year-old girls, with her Cuban mother, and her Sweet Sixteen with me and her American stepmother.

In the lives of exiles, as in the lives of the children of exiles, the personal and the cultural make a dense tangle. Almost all of the crucial decisions in my life—decisions about career, marriage, divorce, place of residence—have had cultural implications. When I decided to become an undergraduate English major, I embarked on a career that separated me from my native language. When I left Miami in order to attend graduate school in Ann Arbor, I exiled myself from Little Havana. When my first wife and I divorced and I later married Mary Anne, I took my distance from certain Cuban rituals and family traditions.

In my children's lives, too, the personal and the cultural intertwine, and not always by choice. If I lived in Miami, they would be

187

growing up Cuban. If I were still married to their mother, they would be speaking Spanish at home, would see their Cuban relatives more often, and would have more Hispanic friends. For them, split parental custody has entailed split cultural custody. Although David and Miriam started on the road to assimilation long before I married Mary Anne, during the half of every week that they live with me, they're American in a way that they never were before.

Every American-born child of exiles or immigrants begins his or her life in the womb of a foreign country; it doesn't matter whether or not the baby comes into the world in the most American hospital of the most American city—at the moment of birth he's no different than he would have been had he been born in the old country. I know that David and Miriam were at their most Cuban when they were smallest. Even afterward, during the early months of infancy, they remained swaddled in Cuban culture. The voices they heard, the faces they saw, the way they were coddled and cooed to—all of them spoke of Cuba. Yet even then David and Miriam had started a journey that would take them away from the culture of my birth.

I used to find it very hard to accept that my children would grow up and away from my homeland. For years after David and Miriam were born, the Cuban in me longed for the Cuban in them. I desperately needed them to be like me, to see the forests through my *árbol*-seeing eyes, to hear my *clave* rhythm in their souls. I even convinced myself that after having children I'd be more firmly linked to my past than ever before. I expected David and Miriam to secure my own, somewhat tenuous ties to my homeland. Once I had kids, I tried to make doubly sure that I remained faithful to old-country ways. I decided to speak Spanish in their presence, talk to them about our homeland, transmit Cuban attitudes and traditions. Never mind that I lived in Chapel Hill, a town with an insignificant Hispanic population, or that very early in their lives David and Miriam started addressing me sometimes as "Pop" rather than always as "Papi," or that their mother and I often caught ourselves speaking English to each other. And never mind, also, that from the moment they turned on the TV or stepped into a preschool class, what they heard was English. Since I was an exile, they had to be exiles too. Instead of seeing my children as a bridge to the future, I saw them as a tether to the past.

This way of thinking may sound crazy, but I wasn't all that unusual among my countrymen. For Cubans in this country, exile has been as much a spiritual legacy as a political status. Exile is our inheritance, like wealth or good looks. You're not born in exile, you're born into exile. By now, at least three generations of Cubans have regarded themselves in this way. One-and-a-halfers like me straddle the generational fence; in some ways we're exiles, while in others we're the children of exiles. But strictly speaking, the same person cannot be both an exile and the child of exiles. Just as the American-born daughter of immigrants is no longer an immigrant but an American, so it is with the children of exiles. The abbreviation for second-generation Cubans, ABCs (American-born Cubans), exposes the paradox. How can anyone truly be an American-born anything? If you're born in America, then you're American, whether your parents were Haitian, Bosnian, or Vietnamese. And yet there are many young Cubans who were born in Miami, who speak English more fluently than Spanish, who live according to American mores, who socialize with American friends, and who still look upon themselves as exiles.

Some time ago a Duke student that I had never had in a class came to my campus office. Wearing a baseball cap, a Polo shirt, and brand-new sneakers, he looked like many Duke undergraduates. After identifying himself as José Luis Costa, he proceeded to tell me in broken Spanish that he was a Cuban exile like me. But, unlike me, José Luis was born and raised in Miami, which made him an expatriate from a land he had never seen. His American birth didn't prevent him from asserting that, once Castro fell, he was planning to "return" to Cuba.

When my children were younger, I wanted them to be American-born Cubans like Joe (the name José Luis goes by among his friends). But since my kids lived in Chapel Hill rather than Coral Gables, in order to raise them Cuban I had to try to enclose them inside a time capsule; I had to create my own version of Old Havana. And so I undertook to do in my home in Chapel Hill what Cubans had done in a larger way in Little Havana. I believed that even if I "resided" in North Carolina, I could actually "live" in Miami. That's where my soul and my family were. That's where my food and my music came from. That's where my kids and I really belonged.

Had you walked inside my house during those years, the first thing you would have seen was a row of posters with Cuban motifs. The first and largest was a photograph of the interior of an old Cuban mansion, with its traditional *mediopuntos* or stained-glass arches, over the doorways, giving visitors the feeling that they were walking into the living room in the picture rather than into my own. Another poster was a picture of *tinajones,* large terra-cotta planters typical of the Cuban province of Camagüey. Another was a picture of a cobble-stoned street in Old Havana. And yet another showed an eighteenth-century map of the island. Of course, old maps and stained-glass arches and four-foot-tall planters had nothing to do with the house I actually lived in, a ranch-style home with cedar siding and hardwood floors. If you looked out my window, what you saw was gravel, not cobblestones; and instead of *tinajones* stuffed with hibiscus, the flower beds in the yard had rhododendron and azalea bushes. These incongruities tortured but did not deter me. My home was a piece of Cuba relocated in Chapel Hill; my home was a humidor full of Cuban-seed children and cigars. My home was truly a Little Havana.

What applied to the decor applied also to the way of life. The stereo constantly played Cuban music, usually younger Miami artists like Gloria Estefan and Willie Chirino. The pantry was always stocked with bottles of *mojo* seasoning and cans of Goya products and packages of Café Bustelo. The bar was stocked with Bacardi and Anís del Mono. Every night after dinner, I sat in my favorite chair and smoked a Padrón or Partagás cigar. During my visits to Miami, I recorded many hours of Cuban radio programming, which I listened to while I drove around in Chapel Hill. For the first three or four years of their lives, David and Miriam spoke and heard only Spanish. When we were at home, their mother and I used Spanish all the time, some-thing we had not done before they were born. When we weren't at home, we found Hispanic or Spanish-speaking baby-sitters. As a result, David and Miriam's first words were the same as mine— *mami, papi, agua, galletica, abuela.* I even taught David the all-pur-pose Cuban expletive *coño,* roughly equivalent to dammit. Picture a restless two-year-old running up and down the house shouting, "*Coño, coño, coño.*" Although Rosa wasn't thrilled with her son's for-eign language skills, my Cuban heart swelled with pride.

We had moved into this enchanted cottage in June 1981, right after David was born. The last thing I did before clearing out of the apartment where we had lived for the past several years was remove my name tag from the front door. When I did so, I found the follow-ing sentence scribbled on the back of the name tag: "Go Home

Spic." This injunction may well have been there for a long time, although I had no way of knowing. When I first read it, I thought, "What do you mean, go home? *Coño*, this is my home." But then I realized that my unfriendly neighbor was right: this may have been my apartment, but it wasn't my home. Although I resented the slur, I endorsed the sentiment. Even now, I realized, when I had just bought a house, home wasn't here. How could someone named Gustavo Pérez Firmat, who had just had a son named David Pérez, possibly be home in Chapel Hill, North Carolina? The names belied the residence. The people did not fit the place. The Spanish on one side didn't match the English on the other. How I felt then—out of sync, lost—must be a familiar experience for immigrants, particularly those in the transitional generations. Part of me wanted nothing better than to do as my neighbor suggested—head for home, or at least for Miami, my home away from my homeland. But another part of me knew my only home was in Chapel Hill.

For many years after I left Miami in 1973, I suffered from unexplained dizzy spells, ranging from a fuzzy feeling of disorientation that sometimes lasted for weeks to sudden bouts of vertigo where I would lose my balance and the room would spin. This condition began when I was in graduate school and lasted through my early years at Duke (my first scholarly books and articles were all written in a fog—and they're probably the better for it!). I underwent all kinds of tests, which showed that something was amiss in my inner ear but failed to pinpoint the cause. Each specialist I saw had a different diagnosis: the neurologist thought it might be a brain tumor; the ear, nose, and throat person diagnosed Ménière's disease; the allergist theorized about foods and ragweed. My Miami physician, Dr. López Gómez, said that although I didn't seem to have anything, what I didn't have couldn't be cured.

The ultimate diagnosis for my dizzy spells was "bilateral positional vertigo of undetermined etiology." That is, they couldn't figure out what was wrong with me. I now think that my dizziness arose from a cultural rather than a medical pathology. My own diagnosis is that I suffered from cultural vertigo, a feeling of disorientation rooted in the experience of unfamiliar surroundings. After all, exile too is a kind of motion sickness. When I used to get dizzy, I felt that the earth wasn't solid under me, that I was walking on shifting ground. Sometimes when I looked at myself in the mirror, my image shimmered, as if I were seeing my reflection in water. Perhaps what made me feel this way was too much displacement. To avert the vertigo, I kept still. As long as I remained totally motionless, I didn't feel dizzy. Immobility worked even better than drugs.

Although I didn't realize it at the time, the problem may not have been the labyrinth inside my ear, but my perception of the United States as a labyrinth. Like other immigrants, I had grown up in the sheltered environment of an ethnic enclave, and I wasn't quite ready for life outside Little Havana. When I left Miami to go to graduate school, I felt I was entering an unstable and threatening world, a space of danger rather than possibility. I had only the foggiest notions about North American geography; ask me what states I had to fly over to go from Miami to Ann Arbor, and I couldn't have told you. The way I felt, I could have been in the middle of darkest Africa. That's why I wanted to stand still, to end displacement, to efface exile. As a victim of cultural vertigo, I longed for stasis, I craved stillness. For me, this quiescent state could be found only in the Nirvana of Little Havana. There I got my bearings, and my dizziness subsided. In Miami I came to rest.

In the mid-seventies and early to mid-eighties, Rosa and I—and eventually Rosa, Miriam, David, and I—traveled to and from Miami so often my mother used to complain that all she ever said to us was either hello or good-bye. In 1986 I wrote in my journal: "For almost fifteen years now, we have been coming back to Miami two, three, or four times a year. I wouldn't describe our trips as vacations, though they normally occur during the spaces allotted for vacation: Christmas, Easter week, summer months. We come to Miami like a starving man lunges for food, or like a pilgrim goes to Mecca. A vacation, literally, is an emptying; but we come here to be filled, and fulfilled. When we're in Chapel Hill, that's when I feel depleted, that's when I'm away. When we get to Miami, I'm back."

In Miami we stayed with my parents or, if we were going to stay for more than a few days, in the upstairs apartment where my grandmother Constantina had lived. Although by the time, my children were born she had been dead for a couple of years (I wonder what she would have thought of our two little Carolina Cubans), many of her things remained in the apartment. The portable range where she fried my eggs in water, the stove full of clean dishes, the refrigerator on whose top she put the white enamel pot with the *escabeche*. The moment I got to Miami and settled into my grandmother's folding rocking chair, I was home. The familiar creaking was like the sound of her voice. Sitting next to the window the way she used to do and listening to the Spanish sounds coming from the street, I kept thinking of the word *bienestar,* which doesn't quite translate as well-being, because it has to do as much with location as with existence. *Bienestar* designates the emotion that arises from the match of person and place. This is how I felt in Miami—well placed, especially during long summer vacations, when I could pretend that we were actually living there. I didn't feel dizzy because I knew exactly where I was. For the weeks or months that we spent in Miami, the distended family contracted again. With the grandparents downstairs, the cousins and uncles a few blocks away, the Spanish daily on the doorstep, and the *bodega* on the corner, everything was in its place. I no longer had to rely on posters of Old Havana and maps of Cuba to feel at home.

For the kids, the best parts of our Miami summers were the *cumpleaños*, or birthday parties, which we usually celebrated jointly. For David and Miriam, *cumpleaños* were as big a deal as Nochebuena was for me. If in our family Nochebuena was the nocturnal, adult winter celebration, *cumpleaños* were the diurnal, kid-oriented vernal equivalent. Like Nochebuena, *cumpleaños* are communal feasts, tribal pursuits of happiness. American birthday parties tend to be brief affairs for children only. With my children's friends, birthday celebrations barely produce a ripple in the family's routine. The birthday child invites four or five friends who spend a couple of hours at the pool or the skating rink, eat some cake, and go home. But Cuban birthday parties, the kind I grew up with and the kind we replicated in Miami, are prolonged affairs for the entire family. Although the focus is on the children with their piñata and birthday cake and games, the adults have their *pastelitos* and *cangrejitos,* their drinks and their music. While the children run around outside, the men play dominoes or watch a baseball game on TV. The party may begin at two or three in the afternoon and go until ten or eleven that night.

The idea behind the *cumpleaños* is that a child's birthday is a cause for rejoicing not just for the child but for parents, relatives, and friends. By limiting the celebration, the way Americans tend to, one asserts the child's separateness, his or her independence from a larger whole. This is why there is no Spanish expression analogous to "birthday child," which singles out one member from the rest of the family. The truth is that the birthday of every member of the family changes the whole family. Like deaths and weddings, birthdays are family events, causes for communal mourning or rejoicing. I was brought up to congratulate parents and grandparents on children's birthdays, to congratulate children on Mother's and Father's Day, and to buy presents not just for the birthday girl but for her brothers and sisters as well. When my kids were younger, and I was less assimilated, I used to congratulate the parents of David's or Miriam's friends in Chapel Hill on their child's birthday. Every time I did so, I was met with a quizzical stare. Eventually, it sank in that Americans don't expect to be congratulated for birthdays that are not their own.

The centerpiece of our Miami *cumpleaños* was the piñata, a cardboard box decorated to look like a particular animate or inanimate object. When I was a child, houses (for girls) and ships (for boys) were the staples, but nowadays, depending on what cartoon or movie character happens to be popular, the designs run the gamut from dinosaurs to Madonna. But the key to a Cuban piñata is not the papier-mache Tyrannosaurus rex, but the colored ribbons dangling from the belly of the beast. The piñata is hung from á tree or a clothesline, and the children stand under it and pull on the ribbons, making the candies and party favors tumble down. Suspended above the children's heads like a heavenly womb, this box full of bounties brings the family together. In our parties, when the time came to break the piñata and kids and grownups gathered in the yard, I always felt the family coalesce, as if the colored ribbons were the ties that bound us.

During that period when I escaped to Miami at every opportunity, I often felt that living in Chapel Hill was like holding my breath; I went to Miami to breathe, to inhale Cuban oxygen, to let off steam. Miami nourished my nostalgia and healed my loneliness. Miami was like a gigantic bottomless piñata. At the Versailles or at Dadeland I met other refugees from *el norte* who, suffering from the same asphyxia, also came down for air. My father's friend Julito used to say that he visited Miami once a month for a shot of *cubanicilina*, "cubanicillin." A week or two enveloped in the sounds and sights and smells of Little Havana gave you a few months' immunity from the American culture. After the immunity wore off, you had to return once more to Miami for another Nochebuena, another *cumpleaños*, and more booster shots of *picadillo* and salsa music.

But in spite of all the *coño* lessons, in spite of all the maps and posters, in spite of all the *cumpleaños* and Nochebuenas, in spite of all the shots of salsa and *picadillo,* I didn't succeed in making my children Cuban.

As David and Miriam got older, the language we used at home began to change. Gradually, almost imperceptibly at first, I found myself using more and more English with them. Once they began to spend most of each day at school, I could no longer assume that whatever they saw and felt they saw and felt in Spanish, and it seemed unfair to ask them to repeat in one language events and thoughts that had occurred in another. The choice was either to let them speak in English or limit the range of things they could talk about; having to pick between language and communication, I picked communication. I also became apprehensive that our Spanish-only household was creating too stark a contrast between our domestic and our public selves. In Miami, Spanish *is* a public language, but not in Chapel Hill, where if you say *qué hubo* the guy next to you thinks you're muttering in Chinese. I worried about the effect on my children of hearing their parents speaking one language and the rest of the world speaking another. I knew that until the day I died my first impulse on greeting someone would be to say *qué hubo* the way Cubans do, but I didn't want my kids to feel the same way. One side of me expected David and Miriam to be *cubanitos;* but another side of me cringed at the prospect of having a son and a daughter who, like me, didn't feel at home in their home.

What happened with language happened also with culture. As the years went by, the visits to Miami became less frequent or less prolonged, cousins were replaced by friends, *cumpleaños* were replaced by American sleep-overs, and the *boleros* on the stereo began to alternate with rock or rap. Although I didn't promote these changes, I didn't resist them either. I allowed myself to be carried along, half knowing that by so doing I was changing my own life. Finally, the day came when I realized that I had more or less given up on my project of re-creating Cuba in Chapel Hill. My campaign to raise *cubanitos* had slowed to a standstill. By the time David and Miriam were seven or eight years old, they spoke only English and felt mostly American. When I left their Cuban mother and married an American woman, my house became even less of a tiny Havana.

There are still times when I wish that I had tried harder to make my children preserve more of their Cuban heritage. Sometimes when their grandparents call from Miami and David or Miriam, after saying hello in Spanish, switch immediately to English, I feel like a traitor. At times like these I make up my mind to begin speaking in Spanish to them once again, but I never carry through. As the one-and-a-halfer, I'm supposed to be good at bridging generations, and yet instead of building a bridge between my parents and my children, I've dug a moat between them.

No, I didn't make my kids Cuban, and I'm sure that up there in Cuban heaven my uncles Pepe, Octavio, and Manolo are giving me the evil eye even now. But something else happened that I did not expect: David and Miriam helped to make me American. Before they were born, I thought I had little stake in the United States. I didn't read local newspapers, I paid little attention to current events, I never thought about voting. I saw myself as a transient, not a settler, as just a man passing through. My present was my future, my future was my past, and my past was Cuba.

After becoming a father, and especially after living with my children by myself for a couple of years when I was between marriages, I realized, first, that it's not good for children to be raised as exiles, and second, that it's also not good for children to have parents determined to remain exiles all their lives. Fortunately, children can help push even the most recalcitrant parents beyond themselves. David and Miriam have had no choice but to follow their father in his journey from language to language, from culture to culture, from wife to wife. But they have themselves, without knowing it, helped me along the way, made the trip worth the trouble.

Being American is for me a reverse inheritance, one that flows from the younger to the older generations, from children to parents. I gave Cuba to my kids, and they have reciprocated by giving me America. Partly by design and partly by accident, we have reached a middle ground between assimilation and exile. As they grew up, so did I. I didn't grow away from Cuba, for I'm as Cuban now as I ever was. I'd rather say that I grew out of Cuba, that I learned to treat exile as something other than a disability. I haven't raised my kids—we have raised each other. The ABC child is the father of the Cuban-American man. I'm as much their creation as they are mine, for sometimes children mold their parents in ways that they never realize. Although they don't know it, David and Miriam have given me the opportunity and the incentive to reach this place that I call "after-exile." It does not follow that once an exile, always only an exile. If exiles can mire their children in nostalgia, the children of exiles can bring their parents into a new world. When and if I reach this new world, I know that David and Miriam will be the main reason I got there at all.

My children have helped me become American not only in spirit but in many practical, down-to-earth ways. Because of them, I know a lot more about the land I live in than I used to—an informal education that I'm sure many other exiles and immigrants have also received. My friend Isabel, who was born in Cuba but lives in Massachusetts, says that she learned early American history only after volunteering to talk about the Pilgrims in her son's second-grade class. I picked up American geography and the names of the state capitals by helping David and Miriam prepare for tests. With David and Miriam in school, I had the opportunity—indeed, the obligation—to fill in the gaps in my knowledge of America. When they began elementary school, in a way I went right along with them.

Contrary to what I used to think years ago, I don't need my children to be Cuban; I don't need them to see the forest through my *árbol*-seeing eyes or hear the *clave* rhythm in their souls. It's enough that they understand and value my Cuban ways, enough that the place where I come from is for them an everyday presence, like a familiar aroma or a melody always at the edge of sound. David and Miriam are not ABCs, but CBAs, Cuban-bred Americans. Even if they cannot trill their r's or swing their hips, they have grown up around people who do. I'd find it maddening if my children were deaf to my music or if they disdained icons or customs that to me are indispensable. But for them, Cuba is a normal feature in the landscape of their lives. When one of David's or Miriam's friends walks into our house and hears the loud Latin beat coming from the stereo, the reaction is inevitably, "What's *that*?"—as if the rhythm of claves and bongos were a clamor from another planet. I would feel diminished if David and Miriam reacted the same way, but their reaction, instead, is to give a simple, straightforward answer to their friend's question: "Oh, that's Willie Chirino, he's a Cuban singer."

In fact, the older they get, the more interested in Cuba David and Miriam become. Now on the brink of adolescence, David likes to dis-

tinguish himself from his friends, and Cuba gives him a way to do
that. When he shows up at junior-high dances wearing a silk shirt
rather than a T-shirt, he'll brag that it's his "Cuban style." At school
he does projects on the evils of the Castro Revolution, to the dismay
of his liberal social studies teachers. For a long time one of David's
favorite songs was "Macho Pérez," whose lyrics he memorized without fully understanding that it's a put-down of machismo (Macho
Pérez—no relation—is an *abusador* who mistreats his wife). Last
Father's Day he bought me a card that said, "Here's a real MACHO
Father's Day greeting." Inside, it had the picture of a gorilla and the
signature "Macho Pérez the Second." Whether he's displaying his
143 José Canseco cards or showing off his knowledge of Spanish
cuss words (the *coño* lessons stuck!), David intuits that, since his
father and his father's father are Cuban, without Cuba he would be an
incomplete man. Thus, he calls himself *machito* and tries to strut. And
by building part of his sense of self from me, he endorses who I am.

David's cultivation of his Cuban heritage has brought him closer not only to me but also to my father. When he was eight or nine,
David went through a poetry-writing phase. Although most of his
poems were in English, he composed a few in Spanglish, a mixture
of Spanish and English. My favorite was "Me y Abuelo," a bilingual
poem whose subject is generational and cultural continuity. Since
part of the poem is in Spanish, you may need help with a few
words—*la silla café*, the brown chair; *una silla negra*, a black chair;
estamos, we are; *pan cubano*, Cuban bread; *jamón*, ham; *yo estoy*, I
am—but the meaning isn't hard to get.

Me y abuelo are watching TV.
Abuelo en la silla café y yo en una silla negra.
Yo y abuelo estamos eating pan cubano y jamón.
For dessert
estamos eating fudge
then mi abuelo está zzzzzz.
Yo estoy eating pan cubano y josé canseco is up to bat
ready to hit his home run
and abuelo está zzzzzz.

I know the scene David is describing, for I have witnessed it
many times. It's a Saturday afternoon, we're in Miami on vacation,

and David and his grandfather are sitting side by side in front of the TV set in the Florida room. In front of them Abuela has placed a folding tray table with their lunch of Cuban bread and ham. Partly because of the language barrier and partly because Abuelo is a little hard of hearing, grandfather and grandson don't say much to each other, but every once in a while Abuelo will ask David about the game—"How we doin', pardner?" David replies with the score, which he'll have to repeat in a louder voice because Abuelo doesn't hear it the first time.

Even as the poem catalogs the things that bind David to his Cuban grandfather—Cuban bread, baseball, the Spanish language itself—it also shows the different worlds that the two of them inhabit. When Abuelo dozes off at the critical moment in the game, he retreats from the present, from the American here and now, and maybe into dreams of Cuba. When David lapses into English in the poem to describe this moment, he is himself withdrawing into a world of his own, where Abuelo cannot accompany him. Riddled with anglicisms and misspellings, the Spanish of the poem is far from perfect—but that's also the point. If Abuelo falls out of touch by dozing off, David does the same when he slips into English. The connection between grandfather and grandson is authentic and strong, but also intermittent. Like dancers in a minuet, David and Gustavo touch and move away, touch and move away.

Unlike her brother, Miriam doesn't need to flaunt her search for roots in order to find out who she is. In this she resembles her grandmother. Like Nena, Miriam travels through cultures rather than inhabiting them, or having them inhabit her. She knows the difference between the practical and the possible and leads her life in the realm of the practical. Although she realizes full well that Papi and Mami are Cuban, this fact has primarily to do with them, not her. One reason for this is her matter-of-fact, down-to-earth personality, which she certainly didn't inherit from me or from her grandfather. Hard-core Cuban exiles aren't down-to-earth because the earth isn't good enough for us—unless it's that floating fantasy island in the Caribbean. We're *desterrados,* the other Spanish term for exile, which refers to someone who has been separated from the earth, or *tierra*. But there's nothing unearthly about Miriam. Like any nine-year-old, she playacts and daydreams, but her head has yet to touch a cloud. More inquisitive than her brother, she'll ask questions about my or her mother's childhood in Havana, and sometimes she'll volunteer a few words in Spanish. But her curiosity flows from her interest in others rather than from her involvement with herself. Miriam doesn't need Cuba, but she realizes that others of us do.

Picture this: One evening I'm on the living room sofa with my legs twined into a pretzel writing in my journal. Miriam sits next to me reading another Baby-Sitters Club novel. All of a sudden she says, "Papi, don't cross your legs that way, it's not macho."

After I recover from the shock of her comment, I manage a feeble reply. "But if I cross my legs this way, I have somewhere to rest my notebook."

"I don't care, Papi, it's not macho."

"Who says, Miriam?"

"I say," Miriam says.

End of discussion. She is right, of course. In the world I grew up in, men didn't twine their legs as if they had something to hide; rather, they crossed their legs by resting one ankle on the opposite knee, in effect flaunting their crotch, perhaps without realizing it. I remember my surprise when, sometime in the sixties, I noticed more and more men crossing their legs in the manner I thought characteristic of women. To this day, when I catch myself sitting the "wrong" way, I change positions.

Although Miriam doesn't know any of this, she understands that I try to live by a code of conduct that contemporary American society stigmatizes as outdated and *machista*. She may not agree with what she understands machismo to mean, but she does perceive that the code is important to my own sense of self—what's bad for the gander may actually be good for the Gustavo. While David sometimes shows his love for me by exaggerated imitation, strutting around like a young rooster on steroids, Miriam expresses it by encouraging behavior that's foreign or irrelevant to her. Her tolerance of my machismo is as crucial as David's espousal of it. Miriam doesn't need to share my views or my prejudices. But I do need her to understand and accept who I am, even if my *yo cubano* runs afoul of attitudes promulgated by her peers and teachers. To her, macho may not mean mucho, but to her father, it's something to live by.

One afternoon recently she came home from school talking about the geographical terms she had learned that day in Spanish class: *continente, istmo, península, isla*. I asked her: "Let me see how well you know these words. Tell me, Miriam, *¿Cuál es la isla más hermosa del mundo?*" "What's the most beautiful island in the world?" She smiled, and without missing a beat replied, in her best Spanish accent, "Coo-bah." That's what she said—not Cuba but Coo-bah, and she pronounced it that way for my benefit. My macho melted in a moment. Right then I could have been a scoop of mango ice cream puddling in the harsh Havana sun. To me, one Coo-bah from Miriam is worth a thousand American words. The smile on her face as she fed me the answer I wanted to hear in the language I wanted to hear it, said to me, "I know you, Papi. I know you have all these crazy ideas and that you get moody and angry and sometimes you think that you don't belong here. But you do belong, Papi, you belong right here in this house and Cuba belongs here too. See, I even know how to say it the way you do—Coo-bah. There it is, Papi, my gift to you—Coo-bah."

Miriam, in some ways, is wiser than all of us put together. When we're sitting around the dinner table and I'm off in space somewhere, pining for piñata or mooning over Miami, Miriam will bring me back in a flash by saying, "Earth to Papi, Earth to Papi." Her words do me more good than all the *pan cubano* in Miami, for a cloud-sitting, water-walking, domino-playing *desterrado* like me needs now and then to be brought down to earth. As young as she is, Miriam grounds me, makes me land. A sign at the gym where I work out counsels, "BE HERE NOW!" Miriam's gentle mocking reminds me that the best thing I can do for her and her brother is precisely that—be here now. I cannot get back my Cuban life, and I cannot get back all of those years that my parents and my brothers and sister spent in Miami waiting, just waiting, but I *can* make sure that I don't do the same with my children. I don't want them to have to wait too. Sometimes when I become irritated at American customs, which I do more often than I'd like, when I get ready to pack it up and turn it in the way my father has done, when I've just about had it with the United States, I hear Miriam's sweet small voice whispering in my inner ear, "Earth to Papi, Earth to Papi." And then I come back from exile.

Miriam and David, Chris and Jen, me and Mary Anne—ours is what is called a blended family. We blend diverse cultures, generations, and personal histories. Sometimes I wonder whether we're truly blended or merely mixed-up.

Chris and Jen, Mary Anne's children from her first marriage, are now twenty and twenty-four years old. Since Jen lives in D.C. and Chris goes to college, they have not lived with us for more than a few weeks at a time, yet through the years we have gotten to know each other fairly well. My relationship with them is guarded but intense. Given that I'm the man for whom their mother left their father *(¡dominé!)*, they have reason to be wary. I'm the Cuban interloper, the Latin lover who swept Mary Anne off her feet and broke up their happy home (which wasn't all that happy). They can't quite figure me out, and I can't quite figure them out. Ultimately, we're ciphers to each other, though perhaps not more than I am to my own wife, or she is to me. I like their slim, healthy, clean looks and their casual, laid-back manner. Neither one is given to grand gestures; neither one of them struts or wears much jewelry. Jen gets her clothes at The Gap or Casual Corner, while Chris's tastes run to oversized T-shirts and baggy jeans that he buys for a dollar at the PTA thrift shop. Jen likes Jimmy Buffett and the Counting Crows; Chris is a Deadhead.

When their parents divorced, Jen and Chris took it in stride. They were always polite and civil. No hysterical middle-of-the-night calls, no accusations of abandonment, no threats of suicide. Unlike my mother, neither one lit a candle to Saint Jude, the patron saint of hopeless causes (but then again, my stepchildren wouldn't know about Saint Jude). Raised in the wake of the sixties, they were taught not to be judgmental. When Mary Anne and I finally got married, after years of storms and stresses, they gladly came to our wedding and acted as witnesses.

Not that Jen and Chris aren't mystified, and sometimes even a little miffed, by my values and habits. One of them once remarked to Mary Anne that I seemed always to be either working or dancing. I argue with Jen about politics, and I argue with Chris about women. Alas, my machismo seems to hold no more truck with him than it does with Miriam. Since by the time I crashed into their lives Jen and Chris were already grown, I'm not sure how much intimacy we will achieve. I suspect that in their eyes I'll always be their mother's husband rather than their stepfather, and that in mine they'll always be Mary Anne's kids rather than my stepchildren. Still, we try in unstated ways to reach out to one another. Chris likes tequila, so sometimes we get tipsy together. Jen likes to dance, so sometimes we party. Chris took up Spanish in college and won the school's Spanish award; Jen and her fiancé signed up for rumba lessons. Every once in a while, searching for common ground, they'll talk about some Cuban-related person or thing that they have come across. Jen will call to say that Jimmy Buffett has a song called "Everybody Has a Cousin in Miami" (now Jen has cousins in Miami too). Chris tells us about his Spanish friend Jaime and brings his girlfriends home to meet his mother's Cuban husband, who's always talking about sex. He calls me G-man, I call him C.

It surprises me to realize that they and the rest of Mary Anne's family are the first Americans that I have gotten to know really well. More than three decades in the United States, and up to the time I remarried, most of what I knew about Americans I had learned from going to the movies, looking out my window, or watching TV. For us Cubans, insularity is not a geographical fact, but a way of life, part of the Cuban condition. Sometimes when our kids and stepkids get together, I fancy that our rather zany lives are the stuff from which sitcoms are made, an *I Love Lucy* for the nineties. Imagine that before Lucy married Ricky she already had grown children from a previous marriage. Imagine that Ricky himself had been married in Cuba and had children by his Cuban wife. In the place of Fred and Ethel put Mary Anne's hippie sister and her live-in boyfriend, who teaches graphic design and has a ponytail down to his waist. In the place of an apartment in New York, put a suburban home in the New South. For Ricky's nightclub, substitute Duke University. I'm Ricky Ricardo with a Ph.D. and Mary Anne is a Lucy who would rather stay home but can't afford to.

On one such evening, I'm already sitting at the table, waiting for dinner to get organized, when David comes down from his room, wearing a baseball cap pointing backward and Umbros, and mumbling something to himself that sounds like, "Come on, baby, drive me crazy, come on, baby, drive me crazy." Miriam, with her hair in a neat ponytail, has put on her pink and black dress. Although she looks as sweet as guava paste, I know she's got the bite of bitter lemon. Chris, who believes that he has dressed up for the occasion, wears rolled-up Bermuda shorts and a T-shirt with Jerry Garcia's mournful face on it; his girlfriend, Kim, sports an extra-large flannel shirt over sagging jeans precariously held up by a thick black leather belt. Jen and her fiancé, Jeff, look preppy but unhappy; for the hundredth time they've given up smoking, and the lack of nicotine makes them irritable. Of the women, only Mary Anne, who is forty-five, and Miriam, who is nine, are not wearing a bra. Of the men, I bet you I'm the only one not wearing boxers.

The *lingua franca* at the table is English, or some contemporary dialect of it—"word up, dude"—but I'm likely to force some Spanish in, either because I want to assert my heritage or because I can't remember how you say *mantel* in English (Mary Anne gently reminds me that the word is tablecloth). But whatever language we speak, we're all eating Cuban food. This evening Mary Anne decided to prepare *quimbombó*, rice with ham and okra, the recipe for which she found in one of her seven Cuban cookbooks. I haven't eaten *quimbombo* in thirty years. Not everybody likes the taste, but they all think the name is "rad." As the serving plate goes around the table, our children begin chanting: *quimbombó, quimbombó.* They repeat the word as if making an oblation to the Afro-Cuban deity of blended families. *Quimbombó, quimbombó.* As they chant, the word undergoes a strange mutation; it begins to assimilate, to lose its accent, to become American. By the time they're through, *quimbombó* has metamorphosed into "King Bobo." And according to Miriam, that lovely little princess of put-down, I am he. I am King Bobo. "King Bobo the First," she adds, "King of Coo-bah." Does Miriam realize that *bobo* is Spanish for dummy? Probably.

But since I've already had a couple of tall, cool *mojitos* (mint juleps with rum instead of bourbon), I don't care what names Miriam calls me. King Bobo suits me just fine. Tonight there will be no expressions or explosions of Cuban-American angst. My distemper is at half-mast, I'm no more than residually *empingado*. King Bobo is chilling tonight. The swizzle stick is my scepter, and my edict is *felicidad bienestar para todos,* happiness for all. This house is our place—mine and Mary Anne's and our children's. Everyone who is here belongs here, and everyone who belongs here is here. I must remember to stay in our place; I must remember to be here now.

When I was born in a Havana hospital forty-some years ago, there were a lot of things that no one could have told my father. One of them is that his eldest son would end up married to an American woman who had grown children not by him and who spends her evenings scouring Cuban cookbooks in search of recipes for *quimbombó* Another is that his own grandchildren would grow up eight hundred miles away (Cuba is about four hundred miles from tip to tip), and that when he talked to them on the phone his grandson would exclaim, "Dang, Abuelo, wasn't Canseco awesome last night?"

After dinner is over, we all go our separate ways. David and Miriam head for the TV set, Chris and Kim disappear into the night, Jen and Jeff go upstairs to finish the fight they had begun that afternoon, and Mary Anne and I sit on the porch quietly scalping the last of the *mojitos*.

If I stick to the traditional Cuban idea of family, I'm not sure that my far-flung, osterized clan would count. For better and for worse, family has to be fierce, has to be love and hate and stickiness. This mellow blend of mine, it doesn't seem fiery enough. Most of the time we don't even attend each other's *cumpleaños*. Much like the clouds of smoke from my cigars, we come together for a little while and then we disperse. All the children at my table have another table, and tomorrow all four of them will be having dinner with other parents and stepparents. I find this disorienting, as I'm sure our children must. Sometimes when we're all together I have the impression that this is happening to somebody else; other times I have the impression that this could only happen to me. Is this what is meant by after-exile? Is mine a family or an after-family? Am I Gustavo or post-Gustavo?

As I sit on the porch with the fireflies flickering in the trees, I wonder how much of an impact I'll have on my stepchildren, or they on me. Given their age and our limited contact, we're not likely to change each other substantially, but if my marriage to Mary Anne has made David and Miriam and me more American, perhaps it will make Jen and Chris a little bit Latin. I kid them that in order to become honorary Cubans all they need to do is eat *quimbombó* and scream *qué rico* when they have sex. But Jen and Chris are not ABCs or CBAs but ABAs—American-born Americans. Why should I want these kids to be something other than what they are? For my loneliness I have my gallery of Cuban ghosts, who keep me company and sit on my shoulder at dinnertime. The truth is that when I'm with my American family, I enjoy the play of differences as much as the pleasure of recognition. It's crazy to expect to look at them and see myself; I'd rather look at them and see them.

And David and Miriam? How Cuban will they grow up to be? I'm not really sure, but I plan to do my darnedest so that we continue to understand and accompany each other. Like most parents, I recall vividly my children's first day in school. I remember seeing

David get out of the car and walk up the ramp, a tiny desolate-looking figure in shorts and a T-shirt, carrying a Thundercats lunch box in one hand. I remember saying to myself, "This is it, I've lost him. Now he's going to be taken over by *los americanos.*" When Miriam began school, I had the same sinking feeling, that she was going over to the enemy camp and leaving me for good. Both times my mind wandered to the boy on the dock, the Cuban boy that I was on the dock that morning in 1960, who had seen me board the ferry and leave. As Miriam walked away timidly, the way little kids do on the first day of school, it occurred to me that some sort of cycle was closing that day. The journey that began one October morning in Havana was ending on another morning, many years later, in Chapel Hill. So be it—sooner or later, everybody leaves on their journey. But what I want to believe, what I need to believe, what I cannot find peace without believing, is that when David and Miriam went up that ramp, they took me with them. I don't intend to stay behind again.

EPILOGUE
This Must Be the Place

How Cuban is my life now? I write maybe three letters a week in Spanish, not much else. Unless I'm teaching, I speak Spanish mostly on the telephone with friends or with my parents, two or three hours tops in a typical week, if that. Every once in a while, I'll try a phrase or two on my wife or my kids, to which they will reply in English. I read more in English than Spanish, and I listen to American music almost as much as I do to Cuban music. I may fret about losing my native language, but I don't seem to do much about it. As I have worked on this book, many times English has seemed insufficient, like a dictionary with letters missing, and yet I suspect that I couldn't have written this in Spanish, perhaps less for linguistic than for cultural reasons. At least in its outward details, my life is much like that of many other middle-aged, middle-class, twice-married American men.

But it's not as if someone who came to my house couldn't tell that I was Cuban. Beginning with the license plate that says QUE RICO and the welcome mat with the palm tree and the Spanish greeting—*¡Bienvenidos!*—my home is full of Cuban memorabilia. On top of the kitchen cabinets, a queue of *santería* candles ends in an effigy of my favorite Afro-Cuban deity, Eleguá, the god who opens and closes doors. (If I were to go by the hoodoo book, however, I would place Him behind the front door instead of on top of a cupboard.) As in my other Chapel Hill house, the one I lived in with my first wife, the walls of the living and dining rooms are lined with Cuban posters and paintings—art by painters like Humberto Calzada and Arturo Cuenca, posters of the Miami Sound Machine and Willie Chirino,

207

drawings of Cuban landmarks, a Desi Arnaz autograph, a menu from a Miami restaurant, the 1951 issue of the Cuban magazine *Bohemia* that had my baby picture on the cover (it cost my parents a pretty penny). In my study the lion's share of the shelves is taken up by Spanish-language books, and propped up in a corner I keep a nightstick that used to belong to one of Fulgencio Batista's bodyguards. Every time I go to Miami, which I still do two or three times a year, I return to Chapel Hill with more reminders of my homeland.

Are these scattered mementos enough to make mine a Cuban household? A Cuban-American household? I certainly don't regard this house the way I did my last one, as a little piece of Havana in Chapel Hill. Perched on a little promontory, with rows and rows of windows, my home is too exposed to be an asylum. At night, with all the lights blazing, it looks like a houseboat, or better, like a gleaming ark resting on the crest of a hill after the Flood. Designed for us to look out and for others to look in, this house wouldn't do as a shelter for shut-ins or a sanctuary for the persecuted. Everywhere you turn in this house you face curtainless windows, and beyond them the pine trees and the cedars and the dogwoods. More an aviary than a nest, more a stronghold than a sanctuary, this house is definitely not a Cuban refugee center. My house says, "Be here now." My house says, "You can look back all you want, you can look in all you want, but you cannot look away. You cannot shut your eyes."

And yet sometimes I think that if I lived in a whitewashed stucco house on a Spanish-named street in the middle of Coral Gables, or better, if I lived in a fifties mansion in the Reparto Kohly in Havana, I wouldn't feel any more or less Cuban than I do now, in my study, looking out at the lawn that needs mowing, at the woods where every once in a while I see a deer, and at the hundred-year-old log cabin just beyond. Maybe in Havana or Coral Gables I would feel more in sync with my surroundings, but I wouldn't feel any more Cuban. I'd feel less alone perhaps, but I wouldn't feel more like myself. Even if places brand people, one cannot reduce a person to his place. Although sometimes I have been unwilling to admit this, I can stop being Cuban no more than I can get out of my own skin. In this way at least, I'm very much my father's son. Trying to make sense of my past and my present has taught me that, unlike what I once thought, being Cuban doesn't depend on the pictures on your wall or the woman in your bed or the food on your plate or the trees beyond your window. Because Cuba is my past, Cuba is my present and my future. I will never not be Cuban. Whether a burden or a blessing, being Cuban in America is for me inescapable.

But the paradox about one-and-a-halfers is that everything that I've just said about Cuba applies also to America, my second skin. I could rewrite the previous paragraphs and list all the tokens of Americana in my home—from the Confederate flag on my desk to the voter's registration card in my wallet. A one-and-a-halfer is too *cubano* to ever become American, but too American to ever become anything else. For people like me, the truth always comes gift-wrapped infancy paradox: that our exile has already ended, and that our exile will never end; that no exile is forever, and that there is no after-exile. Sometimes I revel in this doubleness, sometimes I revile it, but the doubleness is me: I am *yo* and you and *tú* and two.

Many times throughout the last twenty years I have thought that I was a different person in Chapel Hill or Miami, inside or outside the classroom, writing English or speaking Spanish. I thought of myself as a Cuban chameleon, taking on the shadings of the world around me. There was Pérez and there was "Prez"—two syllables or one, with or without the accent, but always with the stress. I was the man who goes to the TCBY in Chapel Hill to have a low-fat yogurt and also the one who drives to the Versailles restaurant on Calle Ocho to munch pastelitos, sip Cuban coffee, and puff on a cigar. Those two people don't seem like the same man, but they are, but I am.

Living in exile fosters the human tendency to circle the wagons (a Cuban might say, circle the *guaguas*). I know Cuban-American men and women of my generation who have never strayed from home, who lead happy and healthy lives in the warm shadows of Little Havana. As someone who lived that way for years, and as someone who at times still longs to live that way, I'm envious of those people, though I sense that their choice may not have worked for me. Even though I love Miami more than any other place I know, even though Miami remains home and haven, I can't conceive of not having left. If I still lived in Little Havana, I'm afraid I would be trapped by memory, the way my father is. Every time I'm in Miami and run into someone I knew in high school or college, I'm struck by how "Cuban" they look, dress, and sound. Take them out of Miami and they will wither as fast as hibiscus in a desert. Although I may appear as Cuban to them as they do to me, I know that inside I have changed, and I wonder whether inside they have changed also. As an exile from Little Havana, I say to myself that it's better to live up to change than to try to live it down.

And yet. And yet. I don't necessarily think that leaving home is always better than staying put. How could I, given all that exile has done to my family? Exile can be a dead end or it can be an access ramp, but I doubt that it's ever a road that circles back to its beginning. In December 1993 the Miami papers carried a brief item about a man named Paul Hernández, a veteran of the Bay of Pigs invasion who had just passed away. Thirty-two years earlier, during the landing at the beach, Hernández had been wounded in the head. Since then he had been having brain seizures, one of which finally killed him, three decades after the original wound. Some wounds don't heal, do they? Is there really an after-exile?

Let the Spanish language come to my rescue one last time. In Spanish the word for country is *país*, while the word for fatherland is *patria*. For one-and-a-halfers like me, Cuba remains our *patria* but the United States has become our *país*. *Patria* is itself an odd word, since it combines a masculine root (pater, father) with a feminine ending, as if the fatherland were a she-male. The idea must be that one's homeland is both he and she, both father and mother. When I assert that Cuba is my *patria*, I'm telling you where I come from, I'm naming the father and mother who engendered me. The other word, *país*, doesn't have to do with lineage but with location, for it comes from *pagus*, Latin for a district or a town. Thus, if *patria* sends you back to the past, *país* plants you in the present. For the exile, and particularly for the long-term or chronic exile, *patria* and *país* don't coincide. Cuba is my *patria*, the United States is my *pais*. Cuba is where I come from, the United States is where I have become who I am. When I pledge allegiance, I have to do it to two flags at once.

I love Cuba with the involuntary, unshakable love that one feels for a parent. I love the United States with the no-less-intense but elective affection one feels toward a spouse. I cannot choose not to love Cuba; perhaps I could choose not to love the United States, as I could choose not to love Mary Anne, but I don't want to. Even if originally a marriage of convenience, a relation of such long standing creates ties that aren't easily broken. Although my marriage to the United States hasn't always been peaceful, it has given me many of the richest and happiest moments of my life.

I became an American citizen in the summer of 1977, more than fifteen years after arriving in the United States. Ten years later, sometime in the mid-1980s, I registered to vote. I was in the mall one Saturday afternoon during a voter registration drive, and partly to spite my then wife and partly as a lark (what Cubans call *parejería*), I registered as a Republican. But I did so without planning to vote. Voting was something Americans did, and I wasn't American.

Over the last several years, as I have tried to stake out a claim in this country, I have thought about voting often. Although I know that my ballot won't alter the course of American civilization one *jota,* voting has become for me a crucial symbol of placement. If I'm as American as I say I am, I must vote; if I want to bet on the future rather than the past, I must vote; if I'm to set an example for my children, I must vote. When I was in Mrs. Myers's civics class, she drilled into us that good Americans always exercise the right to vote.

During the 1992 presidential elections, I thought my time had come. After many hours of stormy discussions with Mary Anne (a lifelong Democrat), we decided to go to the polling place at Mount Carmel Church and vote together, in this way sealing personal and political rifts. But when the first Tuesday in November came around, my day got complicated, other commitments intervened, and neither one of us made it to the voting booth. Although I didn't say so at the time, my problem was not logistics, but loyalties. I simply couldn't bring myself to vote for an American president.

The voting question came up again not long ago, apropos of local school-board elections. My children attend public schools and, like many other parents, I'm angry and dismayed about some of the things that they are taught and not taught in school these days. More than ever I felt that it was my American fatherly duty to vote. I had already lied to David and Miriam about voting in the presidential elections because I was embarrassed to say I hadn't done it, and I didn't want to lie to them again. The way I looked at it, I couldn't be a good father, a dad, and not do what was in my power to ensure that they got proper schooling. I convinced myself that it was okay to vote in local elections so long as I refrained from participating in national contests. Chapel Hill is my *pagus,* my town. If I do right by my *pagus,* I'm doing right by my *país,* and I avoid betraying my *patria.*

But that morning, as Mary Anne and I were getting ready to go off to the polling place together, I cracked. We had talked about the election over and over, had our candidates picked out (all the same ones!), and still I cracked. I just couldn't do it. First I got angry, and then I began to cry. I heard myself saying, "I can't do this to my father. I'm not American, I'm Cuban." I heard myself saying, "What does Chapel Hill have to do with me? This isn't my country and it will never be my country." Incredibly, I heard myself saying, "I want to go back to Cuba."

A couple of months earlier, during our summer vacation in Miami, I had spent two weeks glued to the television set watching heartbreaking pictures of Cubans leaving the island on rafts and inner tubes. That morning in Chapel Hill I felt like one of those rafters, drifting at sea between two countries. Having departed my homeland thirty-four years ago, I still hadn't reached American shores. In fact, what I wanted at that moment was to turn back to the place I had left three decades earlier.

In the course of this book, I have referred to myself alternatively as Cuban, as American, and as Cuban-American. Depending on mood and occasion, all three labels fit me. There have been periods in my life when I refused to put on the stereo anything but Cuban music; there have been other times when I found Cuban music unbearable and instead played Bob Seger or Beach Boys tapes endlessly. These contradictions—if that's what they are—don't ever leave me. I will always harbor split loyalties and divided allegiances. I could spend the rest of my life listening to "Surfin' U.S.A." and it would not make me one whit more American than I am now. Conversely, I could wall myself up in a real Little Havana or in a Miami of the mind, and still I would respond to Americana. The truth is that I will never not feel torn between my father's and my children's worlds. Rather than merging Cuba and America, I oscillate ceaselessly, sometimes wildly, between the two. My life is less a synthesis than a seesaw.

Seeing my anguish, Mary Anne went off by herself to Mount Carmel Church, but before leaving she announced to me that she was going to vote on behalf of the entire Pérez family—myself included. After she had gone, I got up from the sofa, scrubbed my face, and went into my study to write. Sitting at the desk staring at the red and ocher leaves beyond my window, I imagined myself walking into the voting booth with her, closing the curtain behind me, and pulling the levers. Although I realized that I would probably never come any closer than this to voting, I also knew that I would never again allow myself to withdraw into exile, to turn my back on the life around me. I have lived that way long enough.

Before the next election, Mary Anne and I will again discuss the issues and select our candidates. Then she will cast the family vote. Inside the voting booth, two hands will pull the levers, hers and mine.